D1639689

Shakespeare's Visual Regime

Shakespeare's Visual Regime

Tragedy, Psychoanalysis and the Gaze

Philip Armstrong
Lecturer
Department of English
University of Canterbury

First published 2000 by
PALGRAVE
Houndmills, Basingstoke, Hampshire RG21 6XS and
175 Fifth Avenue, New York, N. Y. 10010
Companies and representatives throughout the world

PALGRAVE is the new global academic imprint of
St. Martin's Press LLC Scholarly and Reference Division and
Palgrave Publishers Ltd (formerly Macmillan Press Ltd).

ISBN 0–333–77935–5

This book is printed on paper suitable for recycling and
made from fully managed and sustained forest sources.

A catalogue record for this book is available
from the British Library.

Library of Congress Cataloging-in-Publication Data
Armstrong, Philip, 1967–
   Shakespeare's visual regime : tragedy, psychoanalysis, and the gaze /
Philip Armstrong
      p. cm.
   Includes bibliographical references and index.
   ISBN 0-333-77935-5
   1. Shakespeare, William, 1564–1616—Tragedies. 2. Psychoanalysis and
literature—England—History—16th century. 3. Psychoanalysis and
literature—England—History—17th century. 4. Shakespeare, William,
1564–1616—Knowledge—Psychology. 5. Visual perception in literature.
6. Drama—Psychological aspects. 7. Psychology in literature. 8. Gaze in
literature. 9. Tragedy. I. Title.
   PR2983 .A75 2000
         822.3′3—dc21
                                                              00–033324

For Annie,
and for Ian and Doff

Contents

List of Figures

Acknowledgements

Most of the work for this book was carried out at the Centre for Critical and Cultural Theory at the University of Wales College of Cardiff. I am very grateful to the British Council for funding my stay in Britain; I also owe a general debt of gratitude to all the staff and students who, during my time at the Centre, helped to create an atmosphere that I found both stimulating and highly motivating. In particular I want to thank Professor Terence Hawkes and Professor Catherine Belsey, whose critical interventions in the field of Renaissance cultural history have fundamentally influenced what follows. I owe a more personal debt to each of them as well: to Kate, for her energetic teaching and her lucid exposition of critical theory; and to Terry, for his scrupulous editorial and stylistic advice, as well as for the generous support he has given to this project over many years, and without which this book certainly could never have materialised.

I also acknowledge, with sadness, my gratitude to Victor Neo, for his warm friendship from the time that I first met him until his untimely death in 1994. I wish I could thank him in person.

Other friends whose company and help were crucial to me throughout my time in Wales include Mary Bratton, Marie Sloane, Alison Munro, Andrew Molloy, Anna Maria Cimitile and Anna Hirsbrunner; as well as my non-human companions, Joan and Doris G.

Further vital contributions to this project came from people at home in Aotearoa. Professor Michael Neill of the University of Auckland advised me on an early draft of Chapter 5, which was inspired in the first place by his own work on Shakespeare and Empire. I am indebted to the Department of English at the University of Canterbury for providing research funds to help me to finish the book; to Jim Acheson for taking an interest in my efforts to publish it; and to Sarah Mayo for her meticulous assistance in updating the text for publication.

Finally, I thank the three people to whom this volume is dedicated: my parents, Ian and Dorothy-May Armstrong, for their unwavering support and love, without which this study would not have been attempted, let alone completed; and Annie Potts, my partner, for her love and best-friendship, her sense of fun and her down-to-earth feeling for politics – in other words, for helping me keep in touch with the things that academic work finds it easiest to ignore.

Versions of three of the following chapters have already been published. A form of Chapter 1 appeared under the title 'Watching *Hamlet* Watching: Lacan, Shakespeare, and the Mirror/Stage', in the volume *Alternative Shakespeares 2,* edited by Terence Hawkes (New York and London: Routledge, 1997): 216–37. A version of Chapter 2, entitled 'Uncanny Spectacles: Psychoanalysis and the Texts of *King Lear'*, featured in *Textual Practice* 8.3 (Winter 1994), ed. Terence Hawkes (London: Routledge): 414–34. Chapter 5 was first published under the title 'Spheres of Influence: Cartography and the Gaze in Shakespearean Tragedy and History', in *Shakespeare Studies* 23 (1995), ed. J. Leeds Barroll (Washington D.C.: Fairleigh Dickinson University Press): 39–70; it was then reprinted in abridged form as 'Spheres of Influence: Cartography and the Gaze in Shakespeare's Roman Plays', in the collection *New Casebooks: Shakespeare's Tragedies,* edited by Susan Zimmerman (Basingstoke: Macmillan, 1998): 64–83. I am grateful to Routledge, Fairleigh Dickinson University Press and Macmillan for permission to republished this material.

Introduction

It is, of course, not possible to 'introduce' Shakespeare or psychoanalysis as though neither had been encountered before; nor to
'introduce' Shakespeare *to* psychoanalysis, as if the two had never
met, or were no longer on speaking terms, or were not already in
dialogue from the outset. Instead, since '*intro-ducere*' means 'to lead
into', it might only be possible to introduce these names, or texts,
by attempting to direct inwards a reading which pursues the internal workings of both Shakespearean theatre and the psychoanalytic
text, to in-duce or con-duct a flow of meaning back and forth between the two, rendering the intervening spaces ductile, and tracing
the always circuitous leads connecting them.[1]

In the attempt to do so, each of the following chapters makes its
way into the plays through an encompassing and pervading cultural mechanism, consisting of contemporary theatrical pamphlets
and political treatises; scientific, mathematical and cartographical
tracts; and of the reactions of editors, audiences and critics encountering the plays at various times. All these influence my
argument, as of course do certain recent psychoanalytic texts. There
are at least two assumptions motivating this approach, and being
tested in its application.

The first is that access to Shakespearean texts cannot be gained
apart from, or outside of, the historically, culturally and politically
determined currents to which they constitute a response, and which
in turn respond to them. Such a position demands, wherever possible,
an attentiveness to the contemporary context and the reception of
the plays in their first performances, while at the same time recog-
nising that any reading of this material is in turn inevitably refracted
through the mediations of historians, editors, and commentators.

1

The second factor motivating my critical trajectory is thus the belief that psychoanalytic theory provides opportunities to trace some of the less well-established links between early modern theatre and its surrounding culture. Psychoanalysis – certainly in that form most usually associated with the name of Jacques Lacan – shares with Shakespearean tragedy a fascination with vision, attributing to it various almost occult effects. This book aims to explore that vision in all its manifestations – as theme, metaphor, structure, dramaturgy – and to explore its contribution to the construction of the subject as it appears (and disappears) in early modern English culture, as well as in postmodern European theory.

For, if the psychoanalytic exploration of subjectivity participates in something called 'postmodernity', it should not be surprising that it discovers much in common with the texts of Shakespeare's time. In so far as the late sixteenth and early seventeenth centuries have come to look less like a 'Renaissance' and more like an 'Early Modern' – that is, a culture viewed not so much as the resurrection of something prior to it, as the precursor of the 'modern' or 'postmodern' – recent critical approaches have found this period increasingly conducive to the identification of various elements lost, repressed or neutralised by the subsequent history of the Enlightenment.

Consequently, the relationship between late twentieth-century theory and the culture of the 1500s and 1600s can be conceived in terms of Lacan's understanding of the Freudian notion of *Nachträglichkeit*, or deferred action. For Lacan, this means not that the past eerily and inevitably determines the future, but something more like the opposite: that symbolic value is only conferred upon history retroactively. The return of the repressed, for Lacan, 'doesn't come from the past, but from the future':

> what we see in the return of the repressed is the effaced signal of something which only takes on its value in the future, through its symbolic realisation, its integration into the history of the subject. Literally, it will only ever be a thing which, at the moment of its occurrence, *will have been*. (Lacan 1988a, 158–9)

Pursuing the compatibilities between Lacanian psychoanalysis and the early modern stage, the aims of this study will therefore always have been double-ended, and its trajectory reversible. On one hand, the various identifications described by psychoanalysis provide opportunities for rethinking the transactions taking place between the early modern spectator and the stage, within the former and upon the latter. But I am also concerned with re-examining the role played by theatrical and visual structures in the Lacanian account of subjectivity. Ultimately, these are simply two different directions to be followed on the same path between psychoanalytic theory and Shakespearean tragedy.

In seeking to reveal and to remain aware of this voracious and infectious relation between analysis and early modern text, a consideration of the history of their association becomes both inescapable and problematic. For this reason the later chapters aim to relocate the components of a certain visual regime, which will have become characteristic of the modern subject, within a context of classical and medieval optical theory, as well as in early modern perspective painting, cartography and dramaturgy. Out of the emergence and coalescence of this array of visual technologies there arose that fantasy which Enlightenment Europe would came to call 'Man', that is, the Western humanist subject. Within the field of vision, this subjectivity featured – still features, often enough – as the privileged locus of spectatorship within a geometrically ordered space, the one place from which emanates 'true sight' – objective, empirical, distanced.

Shakespeare's plays offer a peculiarly dense nexus within which to locate the major co-ordinates of this incipient modern subjectivity, in so far as they have occupied – at least in the English-speaking world – an increasingly privileged place throughout the period in which this version of the human subject has come to be thought as such. Moreover, the theatre of Shakespeare's time, as that cultural medium which was most thoroughly populist and yet at the same time intimately related to the power of the State, offers a critical site for the playing out of this reorganisation of visual space. Shakespeare's plays occur at the point of transition between the multiple viewpoints offered by the late medieval 'theatre in the round', and the singular, monocentric, sovereign gaze exemplified by the court masque. For this reason, they typify the conflicted and emergent nature of the geometrical visual order and of the subjectivity associated with it. Thus, in these plays we can read not only the constituents of the modern visual regime, but also that prior plurality of unsettling perspectives which would need to be excluded in order to achieve it. This study attempts to identify in the plays both the emergence of the new scopic order, and its repression of various eccentric and anamorphic alternatives. This historical repression corresponds, I will argue, to that which Lacan calls the gaze, and psychoanalysis the unconscious: that necessary space of the unseen upon which the sovereign ego depends for its existence. The genealogy of these competing visions thus remains always reversible, and can be read back into the psychoanalytic texts of, among others, Sigmund Freud, Joan Riviere and Jacques Lacan.

My discussion begins with an image of visual identification shared by Shakespearean tragedy, early modern theatrical pamphlets, and Lacanian psychoanalytic theory: the looking glass. Following the logic of the Lacanian mirror stage, the various transactions between spectator and spectacle appear to be characterised by an aggressive rivalry, according to which the threat from a reflected double emerges in the conflict between the eye's visual mastery and an uncanny alternative perspective. The return of vision from the mirror, and from the early modern stage, comes at times to exemplify the gaze of the Other.

The capital 'O' here, and wherever it occurs in the following chapters, designates the Lacanian concept of the 'Other', as distinct from an 'other' who may be any person, object or point from which a different perspective derives. These 'other' viewpoints may unsettle the central position from which the subject sees: in so far as they do so, however, they merely stand in for the gaze of the Other. Associated by Lacan with both the unconscious and the symbolic, the gaze cast by this Other represents that to which the subject is subject. 'Finding itself' repeatedly in the eyes of this Other, the subject seeks to display, and thereby to produce, its identity within a given milieu: as a gendered being, perhaps, or as belonging to a particular nation or social class. If 'identity' is a stage, and all the men and women merely players, then the Other constitutes their ultimate Audience. Theatre therefore becomes most unsettling when the spectators experience the gaze of this Other Audience turned towards them.

For the most part, subjection to this Other look would remain itself unconscious, repressed by the ego's imaginary mastery of the visual field. At certain moments, however, the split between the illusory sovereignty of the eye and the gaze of the Other may emerge, and the contingency and vulnerability of the subject's viewpoint becomes evident. The following chapters concentrate upon those instances – in the texts of Shakespearean tragedy and its performances, in the surrounding culture and in psychoanalytic theory as well – where this rift between eye and gaze proves incommensurable. Anamorphosis, as the disruption of the monocentric eye composing the perspective painting, provides one recurrent example. Mimicry also proves important, as a representative figure of the subject's adaptation to a gaze always deriving from elsewhere. Guilt offers a third instance of this surveillance by an Other, in whose eyes the subject stands already accused and condemned. In the scopic economy perpetrated by tragedy, both actor and spectator feature repeatedly as what Hamlet would call 'guilty creatures' – that is, beings created by guilt, in so far as their reaction to the spectacle institutes and maintains a subject position defined by a display of deference to the Other.

By the end of the following chapters, therefore, a figure like Macbeth will have come to exemplify this split between the eye and the look. For in the violence of his reaction to the accusing glare of Banquo's ghost, my reading will identify the betrayal, not only of Macbeth's crimes, but of his subjection to a mastering gaze. It is this gesture – the subject's guilty start – which returns the last chapter to the anecdote with which the first can now begin:

1

Hamlet: The Stage Mirror

A strange accident happening at a play

The scene: a town in Norfolk, late sixteenth century. A theatrical company is performing the *History of Friar Francis*, in which a woman, besotted with a younger man, murders her husband. Subsequently, the dead man's ghost continues to appear to her in private. Now, however, as the spectre comes on stage, a certain woman in the audience, a respected local widow, cries out in distress: 'Oh my husband, my husband! I see the ghost of my husband fiercely threatning and menacing me.' Distracted from the play, the other spectators turn to stare as she claims to see before her eyes the menacing ghost of her own dead husband. She requires no further prompting to confess that seven years earlier, she too had been infatuated with a young man, and had poisoned her husband. To her, the ghost on stage represents his exact likeness. Following this incident, an investigation by the local justices results in this woman's conviction for murder and, presumably, her execution.

In his *Apology for Actors* (1612) Thomas Heywood recounts what he calls this 'strange accident happening at a play' as evidence of the power of drama to improve the moral and social responsibility of its audience (Heywood 1978, sig. G1v–G2r). But Heywood's anecdote also suggests an intriguing moment of interaction between audience and stage. Not only does the woman's outbreak cut into the performance, it actually inverts the conventional trajectory of the theatrical gaze. Everybody, actor as well as spectator, turns from staring at the play to focus on this other drama taking place among the audience. Instead of theatre reflecting 'real life', the reverse occurs: a spectator repeats exactly the scene of accusation and guilt she has just witnessed on stage.

Nobody writing in Heywood's time seemed to doubt the capacity of theatrical representation to produce such effects in its behold-ers. Whether these might be for good or ill, however, remained a vexed question. For the Puritan anti-theatrical pamphleteers, the power of theatre to mould its spectators into copies of the charac-ters seen on stage was altogether pernicious.[1] Stephen Gosson, in *Plays Confuted in Five Actions* (1582), considers that players are 'vnworthy of the Credit of honest Citizens', since their professional hypocrisy, their assumption of fraudulent appearance and demean-our, loosens the socially (and theologically) necessary bond between seeming and being (Gosson 1974, 174). Therefore, according to his co-religionist Phillip Stubbes, 'if you will learn falshood' – along with slaughter, robbery, rebellion, greed, idleness, bawdiness, ven-ery and a half-page list of other sins – ' . . . you need to goe to no other schoole, for all these good Examples may you see painted before your eyes in enterludes and playes . . .' (1877, 1: 144–5).

Like Heywood, the Puritan pamphleteers ultimately seek to prove their point by turning from the examples shown on stage to the responses of the playgoers. Stubbes fixes his critical gaze obsessively upon the spectators:

> but marke the flocking and running to Theaters & curtens, daylie and hourely, night and daye, tyme and tyde, to see Playes and Enterludes; where such wanton gestures, such bawdie speaches, such laughing and fleering, such kissing and bussing, such clip-ping and culling, Suche winckinge and glancinge of wanton eyes, and the like, is vsed, as is wonderfull to behold. Then, these goodly pageants being done, euery mate sorts to his mate, euery one brings another homeward of their way verye freendly, and in their secret conclaues (couertly) they play the *Sodomits*, or worse. (Stubbes 1877, 1: 144)

Stubbes urges his readers to 'marke' the spectators, whose acts are 'wonderfull to behold', as they reproduce what the theatre has shown them, taking part in a 'play' of their own. Again and again, con-temporary critics of the theatre will turn from their scrutiny of the play to concentrate upon the farcical performance enacted by the audience. Stephen Gosson remarks, not of the players but of the playgoers, 'when the sportes [that is, the plays] are ended, that it is a right Comedie, to marke behauiour, to watch their conceites' (1974, 92). For these writers, the play – whether a 'Comedie' or any other genre – is not simply something that occurs on stage. It is also constituted by, and it constitutes, what happens among the audience.

The glass of fashion

> I have heard that guilty creatures sitting at a play
> Have by the very cunning of the scene
> Been struck so to the soul that presently
> They have proclaimed their malefactions;
> For murder, though it have no tongue, will speak
> With most miraculous organ. I'll have these players
> Play something like the murder of my father
> Before mine uncle. I'll observe his looks...
>
> (Hamlet II.ii.591–8)[2]

Hamlet seems familiar with the kind of incident documented by Heywood, in which the stage, like the ghost of a murder victim, casts its accusing gaze upon the audience. And like the Puritan pamphleteers quoted above, Hamlet identifies with this reverse gaze returning from the stage upon its spectators: he intends to 'observe' the king's 'looks', to watch the king watching the performance.

In his stage-managing of this play within the play – as he selects the plot, revises the script and coaches the actors – Hamlet offers various insights into the contemporary understanding of the transaction between audience and stage. He extols above all the concept of *imitatio*, according to which 'the purpose of playing... both at the first and now, was and is to hold as 'twere the mirror up to nature, to show virtue her own feature, scorn her own image, and the very age and body of the time his form and pressure' (III.ii. 20–4). The metaphor of the stage as a mirror appears ubiquitous in the Renaissance.[3] The writers cited so far, however, suggest that the stage, if it is a 'mirror', must be double-sided, for the trajectory of theatrical imitation proves consistently liable to inversion, so that spectators appear to emulate what they see in the playhouse. This provokes anxiety among contemporary writers, for if drama does not passively imitate real life, but actually participates in its formation, the power of theatrical representation becomes frighteningly versatile.

Hamlet's comments imply just such a double view of the theatre.

First, the stage displays the reflected image of the culture, showing to 'the very age and body of the time his form and pressure'. Drama works not only like a mirror, but like a mould, keeping the impression or imprint left upon it by contemporary society. But any 'reflection', by definition, implies a movement of return from the mirror. So when Hamlet also describes an audience 'struck' by the 'very cunning of the scene', he imagines the stage turning upon them with a violent reflex action, showing something quite different from the passive or receptive face normally associated with the mirror. Moreover, the word 'strike' connotes the operation of a mould, the inscription of a mark, the minting of a coin, or the printing of a text, as well as the impression of a sensation or image in the mind.[4] An audience, then, also offers a receptive surface upon which the scene leaves its mark. Similarly, Stephen Gosson remarks that by means of the theatrical transaction 'impressions of mind are secretly conueyed ouer to the gazers, which the players do counterfeit on stage' (1974, 192–3). Stubbes also spells out the visual, even typographical, mechanics of this process: 'For such is our grosse & dull nature, that what thing we see opposite before our eyes, do pearce further and printe deeper in our harts and minds, than that thing which is heard onely with the eares . . .' (1877, 1: x). As in a printing press, the visual images from the stage pierce the heart and mind of the spectator, inscribing or copying themselves there.

Many contemporary references repeat this ambivalence between the mirror as a passive reproduction of the image, and its more active role in constituting the beholder. Hamlet himself, for example, will be described as 'The glass of fashion and the mould of form, / Th'observed of all observers . . .' (III.ii.156–7). In *2 Henry IV*, Hotspur is remembered as the 'mark and glass, copy and book, / That fashioned others' (II.iii.31–2). Both phrases repeat the ambiguity already observed, according to which the mirror replicates the twofold functions performed by a mould, or a printer's template: that of recording impressions, and that of stamping these upon another receptive medium. The mirror 'speculates' the image of the observer, in the economic as well as the visual sense: it invests the image with a value which returns to the gazer redoubled and augmented.

Theatrical representation appears ambiguous, then, because of its unpredictable and uncontrollable 'reflective' capacity, its tendency to reverse and turn upon the beholder, forming, informing and reforming identity and behaviour. Does the spectator of *Richard II*, for example, identify with Richard or with Bolingbroke, with the inadequate monarch or the energetic usurper? The supporters of the Earl of Essex had a version of this play performed before their abortive rebellion against Elizabeth I, whose famous remark to Lambarde on a later occasion suggested an acute awareness of the potential for revolutionary identifications offered by historical figures: 'I am Richard II,' she said, 'Know ye not that?' (Ure 1956, lix). Essex's attempted insurrection may well lie behind the reference to a 'late innovation' which in *Hamlet* exiles the players from the city and brings them to Elsinore (II.ii.334; Jenkins 1982, 255). The Prince's stagecraft, and his discussions of audience identification, are therefore most likely provoked by an actual Elizabethan crisis arising from precisely these concerns.

In such a context, questions relating to the transactions taking place between audience and stage assume a certain degree of urgency. A more thorough consideration of the different kinds of identification occurring between spectator and actor is needed to elucidate the issues involved.

Enter the imaginary and symbolic

The psychoanalyst Jacques Lacan defines 'identification' as 'the transformation that takes place in the subject when he [*sic*] assumes an image' (1977b, 2). Like the theorists of early modern theatre, moreover, Lacan invokes the mirror as a paradigm for this adoption, appropriation or putting on of the 'image' of the viewer's own body. He describes the formation of the ego as a series of such 'assumptions', and envisages this process in explicitly theatrical terms: 'the ego is like the superimposition of various coats borrowed from what I would call the bric-à-brac of its props department' (Lacan 1988b, 155).

Insisting, however, that 'the word identification, without differentiation, is unusable', he qualifies it by drawing a distinction between 'projection' and 'introjection' (1988a, 125). Projection, for Lacan, describes the spectator's perception of itself according to the apparently complete and masterful image seen in the mirror. An infant, held up to the glass, reaches out towards its reflection, which appears co-ordinated and erect, unlike its actual body. This illusion of an equivalence between the child and its image, along with the false sense of mastery it excites, provides the defining paradigm for what Lacan calls the 'imaginary'.

The concept of introjection, by contrast, describes subsequent attempts to incorporate the mirrored image, by assimilating it 'within' the archive of identifications that compose the 'self'. However, in its very reliance upon successive recognitions of displaced and alien images, this 'self' remains constitutionally 'other'. The moment of identification threatens always to replace the ego with its own image or representation. Thus introjection, in contrast to projection, engages predominantly with what Lacan designates as the 'symbolic' register – the domain of language – which functions through this unending substitution of signifiers. In exchanging image for image, representation for representation, the symbolic renders the 'original' point of reference – the body or the 'self' – inaccessible.

Lacan's double version of identification recalls the oscillation observed so far in relation to the theatrical stage, between an image left *in* the mirror and an image left *by* the mirror: 'The projection of the image is invariably succeeded by that of desire. Correlatively, there is a reintrojection of the image and a reintrojection of desire. Swing of the see-saw, a play of mirrors' (1988a, 179). In assimilating its image from the mirror, the subject adapts itself to an imagined gaze from outside. The 'imaginary' relation, a fascinated absorption with its own reflection, is interrupted by the spectator's awareness of how it 'looks', its subjection to a perspective directed back upon itself, just as the theatrical gaze might swing round to survey the performance of the spectator. By means of this dialectic of projection and introjection, then, the spectator enters the imaginary and symbolic registers. Alternatively, it might be said that these registers enter the spectator, through the imprinting of both image and language upon the psyche.

This construction of identity according to the impressions left by images can also be compared with the conventional understanding of memory in the Renaissance, where the mind was frequently imagined as a book, canvas or table upon which memories were inscribed. Mnemonic systems were devised whereby data was collected in a so-called 'theatre of memory', within which images could subsequently be prompted to reappear. Robert Fludd's *History of the Two Worlds* (1619) describes how 'all actions of words, of sentences, of parts of speech or subjects, are demonstrated as in a public theatre, where comedies and tragedies are acted'.[5] So Hamlet, in response to his dead father's injunction to 'Remember me', responds 'Ay, thou poor ghost, while memory holds a seat / In this distracted globe' (I.v.91–7). Hamlet's memory will rehearse its store of images and words within the 'globe' of his head, just as the spectator identifies with the characters on stage in the Globe theatre, in which the performance of this play might well be taking place.

For psychoanalysis, of course, with its constant emphasis on the unpredictability and waywardness of the unconscious, the kind of intellectual and rational mastery which the theatre of memory claims to grant the mind over its images would have to be considered an illusion. While the desire for such masterful consciousness is characteristic of an emergent Renaissance humanism, Hamlet's description hints that the actual public theatre of Shakespeare's time still represents something other than a fully 'conscious' mode of thought. His 'distracted globe' implies that the identifications between the image and the (mind's) eye remain radically dialogic and communal, rather than focused on a central and integrated ego – just as the Elizabethan theatre plays to a dispersed semi-circle of gazes, rather than to an audience which, ranged along a 'fourth wall', approximates a singular point of view.

Recalling Stubbes's and Gosson's vivid evocations of the dramatic spectacle 'imprinting' or 'impressing' itself upon the spectator, Hamlet's description of both mirror and stage receiving the 'form and pressure' of the contemporary social body can once again be juxtaposed with its reverse, the impression left upon the beholder by the theatrical image:

> Yea, from the table of my memory
> I'll wipe away all trivial fond records,
> All saws of books, all forms, all pressures past,
> That youth and observation copied there,
> And thy commandment all alone shall live
> Within the book and volume of my brain
> Unmixed with baser matter

> (I.v.98–104)

The traces of any former identification left upon the 'table' of Hamlet's memory will now be overwritten by the figure of his father's ghost, and by his words.[6]

The mirror/stage

Like the apparition confronting Hamlet at this point, the ghost of patriarchy haunts both the Renaissance stage and modern psychoanalysis. Along with the woman menaced by the figure of her dead husband in the anecdote with which I began, Hamlet typifies the theatre-goer confronted by the spectacle of her or his own subjection to an accusing and masculinist gaze. For Lacan, patriarchal power will be prefigured at first by the position of the 'actual' father within the family unit, but thereafter manifested in what he calls the symbolic, the operation of language, through which the subject comes into being as such and upon which she or he remains dependent. Lacan nicknames this patriarchal linguistic order the *nom-du-père*, with a pun on *non-du-père*: the name (word), or 'no' (prohibition), of the father (1977b, 67, 199, 217; 1988b, 259–60). Once it has been assimilated into the psyche, he applies to this embodiment of the Law the psychoanalytic term 'super-ego' (1988a, 83). The word 'introjection', then, refers specifically to this process, 'when something like a reversal takes place – what was the outside becomes the inside, what was the father becomes the super-ego' (1988a, 169). Or, in Hamlet's case, what was the father reappears . . . where?

> HAMLET. My father – methinks I see my father.
> HORATIO. Where, my lord?
> HAMLET. In my mind's eye, Horatio.
>
> (I.i.183–4)

All these models of cognition – the eye of the mind, mirror of the intellect, mind as inner arena – have been identified by Richard Rorty as emerging in the Renaissance and deriving from Greek and particularly Platonic philosophy (1980, 38–69). Moreover, Rorty relates such metaphors to the capacity of the Cartesian subject to 'reflect' and to 'speculate', thereby emphasising the close affinity, in the Western philosophical tradition, between the process of conceptual thought and the function of vision; even more specifically, between the perception of the self and the function of the mirror.[7]

It would seem that the psychological and perceptual spaces represented by both mirror and stage have been influential not just in early modern theatre, but also in the subsequent development of both philosophy and psychoanalysis.[8] Lacan, in fact, entitles his initial paradigm for the child's entry into relation with its surroundings 'The Mirror Stage', *'Le stade du miroir'*. The word *'stade'*, like its English translation, signifies both a developmental phase and a stadium, an arena for the repeated performance or playing out of identity: 'The *mirror stage* is a drama . . .' (Lacan 1977b, 4).

In the mirror stage, the child constructs its fantasy ego according to the upright and co-ordinated figure in the glass. This always and only offers what Lacan calls a *méconnaissance*, a misleading recognition, because the masterful image apprehended in the mirror does not correspond to the actual degree of muscular co-ordination attained by the infant. The imaginary identification thereby produces a frustrated aggressivity, for the spectator desires to assimilate this image of the body as a totality, but remains at odds with it, experiencing its own body only partially and in fragments. The ego then desires the destruction of the ideal other but, dependent upon it for its own identification, remains locked in a disabling impasse, like the master and slave of Hegel's dialectic (Lacan 1988a, 170; Hegel 1977, 111–19).

In his seminar on 'Desire and the Interpretation of Desire in *Hamlet*', Lacan takes Hamlet's relation to Laertes as a model for this imaginary fascination. He quotes the Prince's description of Laertes to Osric – 'his semblable is his mirror and who else would trace him his umbrage, nothing more'[9] – commenting that 'The image of the other . . . is presented here as completely absorbing the beholder' (1977a, 31). In this struggle only one outcome is possible: the destruction of both parties. In eventually fighting his ego ideal, therefore, Hamlet effects his own death.

> The playwright situates the basis of aggressivity in this paroxysm of absorption in the imaginary register, formally expressed as a mirror relationship, a mirrored reaction. The one you fight is the one you admire the most. The ego ideal is also, according to Hegel's formula which says that coexistence is impossible, the one you have to kill. (Lacan 1977a, 31)

Characters other than Laertes also function as mirror images in this play. Most interestingly, from the point of view of the theatrical transaction between audience and actor, Hamlet identifies himself with the player who delivers the speech about Pyrrhus, especially at the moment where he describes how the avenger's sword, raised over the head of Priam,

> seemed i th' air to stick.
> So, as a painted tyrant, Pyrrhus stood,
> And like a neutral to his will and matter,
> Did nothing.

> (II.ii.482–5)

Acting out, as well as speaking these lines, the player vividly foreshadows the moment at which Hamlet, a few scenes later, will stand
with his sword poised above his uncle's head, embodying once again
the inert aggressivity produced by an imaginary identification with
the 'painted tyrant' before him.

Hamlet makes his identification with this minidrama even clearer:

> Is it not monstrous that this player here,
> But in a fiction, in a dream of passion,
> Could force his soul so to his whole conceit
> That from her working all his visage wanned,
> Tears in his eyes, distraction in 's aspect,
> A broken voice, and his whole function suiting
> With forms to his conceit? And all for nothing!
> . . . .
>   Yet I,
> A dull and muddy-mettled rascal, peak
> Like John-a-dreams, unpregnant of my cause,
> And can say nothing . . .
>
>   (II.ii.553–71)

Despite the arguments of the contemporary theatrical pamphleteers, the acting out of Pyrrhus's 'dream of passion' before Hamlet's
eyes suggests that an imaginary identification with the dramatic
'fiction' produces in its spectator only a disabling fantasy, a speechless
fascination. It fails to prompt him to any kind of imitative action
whatsoever.

However, Hamlet does now recognise the formative power of
another type of identificatory dynamic between stage and audience,
which, following Lacan, I would designate as symbolic. He conceives of the play within the play, recalling instances in which the
stage, by its 'very cunning', has provoked the participation of its
guilty beholders, confronting them with a sight so striking 'that
presently / They have proclaimed their malefactions' (II.ii.593–4).

The consciousness of the king

Within the visual field, the symbolic order materialises as a look
directed at the subject from that which Lacan calls the 'Other', a
gaze that disturbs the imaginary correspondence established between
the ego and the mirror image. The story of the woman at the

performance of *Friar Francis* vividly displays the reaction of a spectator when subjected to this intrusive gaze. Various characters in Shakespeare's play repeat this response when confronted with the figure of the dead king: Hamlet, Gertrude and, most critically, Claudius.

Claudius reveals his unease before the accusing gaze with which Hamlet associates himself: 'the king becomes unsettled and visibly reveals his own guilt, incapable of viewing the dramatisation of his own crime' (Lacan 1977a, 17). A famous critical struggle over this scene can be said to circle around the type of audience identification involved.[10] Why does Claudius ignore the dumb-show, and react only to the second, spoken representation of his crime? Both his reactions – ignorance and anxiety – involve a disruption of the spectatorial gaze. He displays a blind ignorance in front of the dumb-show – so that more than one critic has even argued that he simply does not see it[11] – and then responds to the second version with a distress also patently characterised by a failure to see: 'Give me some light' (III.ii.257).

The difference between these two moments can be seen as a movement from the imaginary to the symbolic register. Initially, Claudius makes an imaginary identification with the drama, rendering him paralysed by a fascinated rivalry with his masterful specular image: he projects himself into the dumb-show as the King, not the poisoner. He remains captivated by the resurrected image of Old Hamlet, his elder brother and rival: 'The ego ideal is . . . the one you have to kill' (Lacan 1977a, 31). Such an identification suits the dumb-show, from which speech, the paradigmatic form of the Lacanian symbolic, remains absent. For his exemplary mirror relation, Lacan specifically posits a child not yet capable of speech, 'at the *infans* stage' (1977b, 2). Similarly, transfixed by a disabling inertia, Claudius cannot even protest. The dumb-show leaves him dumb. Hamlet gives his reconstruction of the crime an apt name – 'The Mousetrap' – for it provides, as Lacan has said of the function of perspective painting, 'a trap for the gaze' of its primary spectator (Lacan 1979, 89).

So it is only when the gaze returns upon Claudius from the second, spoken version of the play that he becomes caught up in the action himself, and begins to perform in turn. Moving from projection to introjection, 'The King rises' as soon as – but not until – the player-king, queen and murderer have spoken their lines (III.ii.253). Lacan describes this gaze returning upon the spectator as 'an *x*, the object when faced with which the subject becomes object' (1988a, 220). Becoming aware of himself as the object of an accusing vision, rather than a spectator, Claudius loses his illusory mastery over the visual field. He can no longer see, and can only stumble from the stage, calling for light.

Interrupting the duality of imaginary identification, awareness of the gaze of the Other radically challenges the identity of the subject and the security of its location within the optical field. Hamlet signals his identification with this other gaze directed at Claudius by interpolating a speech into the play, and by providing a constant tendentious 'chorus' designed to disconcert his audience (III.ii.233). The imaginary fantasy of the dumb-show gives way to the intrusion of a third gaze, whereby Claudius, as spectator, finds the spectacle looking back at him: 'There is never a simple duplicity of terms. It is not only that I see the other, I see him seeing me, which implicates the third term, namely that he knows that I see him' (Lacan 1988a, 218).

We have met this uncanny look before, in the gaze of Hamlet's father's ghost, fixed upon its beholder 'Most constantly' (I.ii.231–2). The ghost assumes the 'questionable shape' which excites Hamlet's own fascinated attention; it commands him before anything else to 'Mark me', and later to 'Remember me' (I.v.2, 91). Its appearance not only draws out and holds the eye of the observer – threatening to 'Make thy two eyes like stars start from their spheres' (I.v.17) – but, as discussed earlier, also imprints, or 'marks', itself upon his mind. Hamlet himself then reproduces this uncanny gaze, in the accusing stare that he directs at the King during the play within the play: 'I'll observe his looks, / I'll tent him to the quick. If a but blench, / I know my course' (II.ii.598–600). The Arden editor remarks that 'a *tent* was an instrument for examining or cleansing a wound', and that the word 'blench' here 'is related to *blink* ...' (Jenkins 1982, 273). This revealing and excessive gaze penetrates its object like a blade, disrupting and blinding the imaginary vision of the observing subject.

Drama would therefore seem to provide an inherently unstable medium, always possessing the potential to invert the hegemonic play of the gaze, so that the audience finds itself, repeatedly, unfounded. The subject positions occupied by the play's spectators are discomfited, and the complacent relation between the individual and the social undermined. In fact, producing such agitation in the audience seems to be a sufficiently familiar feature of theatrical practice for Hamlet to ask whether the reaction he has provoked in Claudius 'Would not . . . get me a fellowship in a cry of players?' (III.ii.263–6).

The symbolic identification between spectator and spectacle therefore entails certain risks. According to psychoanalysis, the subject's participation in this visual regime inevitably involves repetition. Freud associates the 'compulsion to repeat' with the operation of the unconscious, and Lacan with the subject's domination by the gaze of the Other, the symbolic order (Freud 1986a, 229; Lacan 1972, 39). Reading Poe's 'Purloined Letter', for example, Lacan identifies three positions in the triangular structure of the gaze, which each of the characters will occupy in turn:

> The first is a glance that sees nothing . . . . The second, a glance which sees that the first sees nothing and deludes itself as to the secrecy of what it hides . . . . The third sees that the first two glances leave what should be hidden exposed to whomever would seize it . . . (1972, 44)

Lacan makes analysis, and agency, dependent upon occupation of the third position in the symbolic structure, that of the glance which sees what remains hidden from the two others locked in their imaginary embrace. Drama operates as a means whereby these positions are continually negotiated, transgressed and exchanged. For in order to see and act, the spectator must risk – Lacan speaks repeatedly in both seminars of 'stakes' – exposure to another gaze. The spectator cannot avoid entry into the game. *Hamlet* dramatises this necessity of taking a position, and foregrounds also the risk of failure. At those moments in which the audience (or critic, or analyst) will be forced by the drama to see itself seeing, the gaze of the Other emerges, looking back at the spectators, who are not just observers but participants, caught in the act, taking (a) part in the plot. Theatre thereby perpetually contaminates the position of pure spectatorship, precipitating its audience into (the) action. These are the stakes in the psychoanalysis of drama, the drama of psychoanalysis: there is no pure interpretive exteriority, and participation always carries the risk of blind repetition, of being written into the script being read.

So, in the final scene of the play, Hamlet repeats the fate of his father, assuming the position of blindness in an imaginary rivalry with Laertes which will betray him to his death, once again by means of poisoning. The audience, Laertes and Claudius all see that the tip of the foil and the wine will prove lethal, but Hamlet does not: 'The foils are blunted only in his deluded vision' (Lacan 1977a, 32).

Hamlet's dying words address both the on-stage and off-stage observers as 'You . . . / That are but mutes or audience to this act . . .' (V.ii.286–7). 'Mutes', as the term for actors with non-speaking parts, suggests 'non-participants' (Jenkins 1982, 414). But the audience, like Claudius during the dumb-show, only remain mute as long as they are caught in an imaginary identification with the drama. However, the remaining moments of the play show the observers finding their voices, playing their parts and beginning to repeat. Fortinbras enters to occupy the spectatorial position: 'Where is this sight?' (V.ii.315). But then, at Horatio's prompting, he directs the final scenes of the play, in explicitly theatrical terms: 'give order that these bodies / High on a stage be placèd to the view . . .' (V.ii.331–2). With Fortinbras preparing to 'call the noblest to the audience', and to 'embrace my fortune', the spectator enters the game and the play begins again, ready for another repetition, a new performance (340–1). Horatio, finally, observes this recapitulation without even noticing: 'let this same be presently performed . . .' (347).

A thing of nothing

I have so far omitted any discussion of Lacan's third category, which he calls the 'real'. This is appropriate, for the 'real' functions more than anything else as what must be excluded from the imaginary and the symbolic, and therefore as that which might unsettle the interpretations produced by concentrating on those registers.

Lacan's deployment of the term 'real' becomes increasingly removed from any suggestion of an unmediated point of reference, or an accessible presence. In fact, the 'real' features in direct contrast to the perceptual or social 'reality' inhabited by the subject, which is by definition always constructed within the imaginary and symbolic registers, and therefore phantasmal. Lacan's real, on the other hand, stands for what must be excluded in order to found this imaginary and symbolic universe, and yet which persists as the traumatic condition of both. It is manifest only as a symptom, a recalcitrant element within the subject's discourse which analysis tries to identify but cannot grasp, experiencing it only as 'an essential encounter – an appointment to which we are always called with a real that eludes us' (Lacan 1979, 53). Therefore the 'real' may be located only negatively, by means of reference to the compulsive attempts made to represent it within the signifying network.

Within the optical field of drama, the 'real' enables the identification of yet another type of gaze. An imaginary vision founds and maintains itself according to the exclusive duality and illusory mastery of the mirror relation. The symbolic gaze of the Other disturbs this imaginary sovereignty of the optical field, by introducing that perspective from which the subject is surveyed as an object. Finally, the gaze as 'real' would suggest an impossible vision which the subject desires but can never attain, for it would dissolve the subject/object split, which founds and orders the symbolic and imaginary optical fields. This 'real' gaze indicates the failure of the other two regimes, as it escapes the representational strictures imposed upon visual perception:

> In our relation to things, in so far as this relation is constituted by the way of vision, and ordered in the figures of representation, something slips, passes, is transmitted, from stage to stage, and is always to some degree eluded in it – that is what we call the gaze. (Lacan 1979, 73)

In *Hamlet*, there are a number of places in which this effect may be located. The play repeatedly gestures towards 'nothing', a recurrent lacuna central to the 'round O' of the Elizabethan theatre. Hamlet locates this lack between Ophelia's legs, precisely in the position from which he will observe Claudius' response to the play:

> HAMLET. (*to Ophelia*) Lady, shall I lie in your lap?
> OPHELIA. No, my lord.
> HAMLET. I mean my head upon your lap?
> OPHELIA. Ay, my lord.
> HAMLET. Do you think I meant country matters?
> OPHELIA. I think nothing, my lord.
> HAMLET. That's a fair thought to lie between maids' legs.
> OPHELIA. What is, my lord?
> HAMLET. No thing.
>
> (III.ii.107–15)

To the Elizabethan audience, this exchange involves a series of sexual puns ('lie', 'head', 'country', 'no thing'), according to which, just as in the Freudian psychoanalytic account, gender difference resolves into the absence or presence of the penis. The unease surrounding this component lacking from the visual field displays all the characteristics of the Lacanian 'real'.

Lacan's own text also returns repeatedly to this same 'nothing'. He quotes Hamlet's exchange with Guildenstern –

> HAMLET. The body is with the King, but the King is not with the body. The King is a thing –
> GUILDENSTERN. A thing, my lord?
> HAMLET. Of nothing.

(IV.ii.26–9)

– and interprets the lines in terms of the phantom appearance and disappearance of the phallus: 'the body is bound up in this matter of the phallus – and how – but the phallus, on the contrary, is bound to nothing: it always slips through your fingers' (1977a, 52). For psychoanalytic purposes, of course – and this is the point of the joke – the phallus should not be equated with the anatomical organ. 'In Freudian doctrine, the phallus is not . . . the organ, penis or clitoris, which it symbolizes.' Rather, 'the phallus is a signifier' (Lacan 1982, 79). For Freud, sexual differentiation provides the prerequisite for the establishment of a 'normal' (that is, a socially recognisable) human identity (Freud 1979, 380, 397). But Lacan raises the stakes even higher: the phallus, as the 'privileged signifier' of sexual difference, provides the basis and paradigm for the entire network of substitutions and differences upon which the symbolic order and the unconscious, language and patriarchal law, are founded (1982, 82).[12] This 'nothing' of sexual difference, therefore, appears in Lacanian psychoanalysis to be everything. Towards the end of the seminar on *Hamlet*, Lacan remarks that 'Claudius' real phallus is always somewhere in the picture . . . . that fatal, fateful object, here real indeed, around which the play revolves' (1977a, 50).

Psychoanalytic theory returns recurrently to this no/thing, manifesting a perpetual unease around, and attraction towards, the issue of sexual difference. For Freud, of course, sexual formation inevitably turns upon the primal scene between the male and female child, that moment of visual apprehension in which anatomical difference, the perception of the absence or presence of the penis, remains always 'somewhere in the picture'.[13] In so far as he depends upon Freud, Lacan therefore cannot avoid, at important moments in his argument, relating the phallus as signifier to its visible, anatomical correlative. He obscures the nature of this relation by presenting many of his most critical assertions on gender in the form of provocative jokes: for example, his assertion that the phallus achieves its place as the pre-eminent signifier within the symbolic because it is 'what stands out as most easily seized upon in the real of sexual copulation' (1982, 82). In spite of his other claims, it would seem that for Lacan the phallus recurrently appears precisely as that which does not slip 'through your fingers'.[14]

The texts of both psychoanalysis and Shakespearean tragedy will therefore recurrently approach and retreat from this fundamental representational abyss constituted by the 'real' of the body, and specifically the anatomical asymmetry between male and female. Furthermore, the trauma raised by this question will always be projected onto the supposed 'lack' in the female body, upon which the masculinist visual regime focuses all its anxieties about the visible signifiers of sexual difference.

Identifying the representation of the woman's body as a location for the disruptive real has obvious implications for Elizabethan drama in general. On the Shakespearean stage, where all female roles were played by male actors, the 'female character' becomes symptomatic of the gap in representation surrounding sexual difference, for she cannot appear in the theatre except in so far as her body is replaced by an elaborate masquerade.

Hamlet will take this theatrical disguise of womanliness as the paradigm for femininity itself, which he persistently characterises as false and duplicitous: 'I have heard of your paintings, too, well enough. God hath given you one face, and you make yourselves another' (III.i.145–7). Using cosmetics to make 'another' face, the woman/actor makes her/himself *into* 'another': another gender, another identity. The mask threatens to turn the person who uses it into someone else: the actor becomes the role, the man the woman. For the Puritan anti-theatrical pamphleteers, moreover, the masquerade of femininity also exemplifies the hypocrisy of the theatre itself, which thereby undermines gender differentiation as one of the main foundations of social and individual identity (Gosson 1974, 175–6; Stubbes 1877, 1, 64–7).

The 'real' of femininity radically disrupts the play once more in Hamlet's exchange with the young actor who plays the female roles in the company visiting Elsinore. He comments that, as the boy grows up, he hopes his voice will 'be not cracked within the ring'

(II.ii.431). Again, bringing together a reference to the female body (the ring and the figure O were both common slang for the female sexual organs) with the evidence of the impossibility of its representation – displaying a male impersonating a female 'within the ring' of the Elizabethan playhouse – this line betrays the wilful blindness on the part of the audience upon which the actors depend for their depiction of Ophelia and Gertrude. Such a moment manifests the traumatic effect occasioned by the real within the symbolic and imaginary registers. As the boy's mock-female voice 'cracks', and masculinity breaks into the feminine, it threatens to split apart the 'wooden O' of theatrical illusion, the necessary fantasy of the 'female part'.

In terms of a wider Elizabethan politics, the same unease attaches to the body of the Queen herself. By the time the first performances of *Hamlet* took place, the English Queen's barren and ageing body itself featured as a symptom of the anxieties about the succession and the stability of the Tudor state. Increasingly, therefore, the monarchy relied upon a divorce between the iconography of Elizabeth and her actual body, giving rise to the cult of the Virgin Queen, Astraea, Gloriana. Identification of this recurrent trauma gives a new twist to the words 'frailty, thy name is woman' (I.ii.146), so that 'woman' becomes the name of the frailty of both political and theatrical representation in late Tudor England.

The representation of 'woman' also betrays the frailty of modern psychoanalysis, and of gender differentiation itself. Following Joan, Riviere (1986), Lacan also conceives of feminine sexuality in terms of masquerade (Lacan 1977b, 291; 1979, 193). But as in *Hamlet*, this concentration upon the visible signifiers of sexual difference (clothing, facial traits, body shape, genitals) plunges psychoanalysis into a profound uncertainty about the 'deeper' marks of gender, both male and female, making it impossible to define with any degree of conviction an essential psychic distinction between masculinity and femininity.[15] In the ever-more provocative assertions of Lacan's late seminars, this effect becomes increasingly manifest: 'A woman is a symptom', '*the* woman does not exist', 'there is no sexual relation' (1982, 167, 168, 170). In so far as '*a* woman' here indicates a subject representing herself according to the conventional 'masquerade' of femininity, she provides a symptom of the impossibility of essential gender: '*the* woman does not exist'. So by implication (although Lacan stops short of suggesting this) masculinity also fades into indeterminacy, inasmuch as it defines itself against its opposite through the male/female 'sexual relation', which cannot therefore 'exist' either.

Consequently, for psychoanalysis, ego-identification within the visual regime itself always betrays the anxious imposition of a gender hierarchy. In Lacan's description of the mirror stage, the idealised reflection seen in the glass already appears to bear visual traits conventionally associated with the male body. Erect, masterful and self-contained, the image in the mirror conforms to the privileged term of a binary gender distinction which portrays the other, the female body, as soft, vulnerable and incontinent. Nevertheless the mirror image also constitutes a masquerade, compared by Lacan to 'the armour of an alienating identity' (Lacan 1977b, 4; 1988b, 155).

In fact, all the mirror images I have considered so far have been masculine: even the female spectator with whom this essay began was prompted to confess by the persecuting ghost of the dead husband. Introjection of this sort always involves the assimilation of a patriarchal figure, as it does in Lacanian theory: 'what was the father becomes the super-ego' (1988a, 169). Similarly, when Hamlet confronts his mother, he claims he will 'set you up a glass / Where you may see the inmost part of you' (III.iv.19–20). But what he actually shows her are the portraits of her two husbands – 'the counterfeit presentment of two brothers' (III.iv.53) – demanding her disidentification with the image of Claudius and her re-introjection of the image of Hamlet's father. Once again, the 'glass' gives back to the woman not herself, but the super-egoic patriarchal figure, the assimilation of which implies her guilty submission to the gaze:

> Thou turn'st mine eyes into my very soul,
> And there I see such black and grainèd spots
> As will not leave their tinct
>
> (III.iv.79–81).

Woman has no mirror image on the early modern stage, a double alienation which Gertrude expresses by telling Hamlet 'thou hast cleft my heart in twain!' (III.iv.147).

Luce Irigaray criticises the ubiquity of this masculine optical and specular economy within the Western metaphysical tradition. The rational male subject of philosophical 'reflection' or 'speculation' stands always in relation to the mirror, a position of illusory empiricism. 'Does the subject derive his power from the appropriation of this non-place of the mirror? And from speculation?' (Irigaray 1985, 205). It comes as no surprise, then, that Lacan gives as an example of the introjected gaze of the Other 'the satisfaction of a woman who knows that she is being looked at' (Lacan 1979, 75). Here the subject appears as female, 'objectified' by the gaze which she invites – presumably through sexual masquerade – thereby implying a masculine gaze with which both Lacan and the reader identify, as analyst or voyeur. Again, as Irigaray suggests, 'Woman has no gaze, no discourse for her specific specularization that would allow her to identify with herself (as same) – to return into the self – or break free of the natural specular process that now holds her – to get out of the self' (1985, 224). Female identification with the Other always involves an excursion into 'masculine' territory.

What I wish to suggest, then, is that an identification with the traumatic place of the real within early modern theatre and psychoanalysis will provide, if not a 'feminine' gaze, then at least a critique of its absence. The non-existent real of the sexual relation indicates the frailty of the optical field, demanding a constant reassessment of the relation between gender and vision involved in every 'stage' of both early modern theatre and psychoanalysis.

Distracted globes

Any consideration of the conflicting identifications taking place in the theatre therefore invites the formulation of a number of questions which, although they cannot be 'applied' flatly to reading a play, nevertheless point towards the articulation of a relationship between Lacanian psychoanalysis and early modern drama.

Attention to the imaginary, as Lacan conceives it, reveals what fantasies of mastery are evoked in the play, and how the spectacle captivates its audience. In what ways does it offer a trap for the gaze? And – in so far as the composition of any scene institutes a certain position from which it should be observed, and constructs a certain audience appropriate to that viewpoint – to whom is the drama giving itself to be seen?

Along with this, an exploration of the symbolic relationships at stake seeks to identify how the stage reciprocates the spectator's gaze, or how it disconcerts her or his location within the visual regime. This involves looking for what Lacan calls the 'gaze behind' (1979, 113), a look 'on the part of' another: for example

Claudius, seeing Hamlet's gaze behind the play, and the ghost's accusing glare behind that. On whose behalf is the audience being invited to look? Emphasis on the symbolic register also involves examining what images, concepts, words or effects might be introjected during the play. In what ways, and by which hegemonic or super-egoic figures, is the audience being commanded to respond?

Finally, the problem of the real emerges as a recurrent complication at every stage of the analysis. Where are the disturbances that might betray the locus of a trauma around which the symbolic circles? And where does the imaginary identification falter?

These are questions that criticism of early modern drama needs to confront, not least because they envisage drama as a series of superimposed visions, conflicting gazes and multiple identifications between spectator and spectacle. After all, this best approximates the actual situation in the 'distracted globe' of the Shakespearean public theatre, where the drama does not play to a singular eye, but instead offers a whole array of perspectives to an audience surrounding the stage, whose innumerable lines of sight collide and intersect as the drama unfolds.

In the attempt to reconfigure the spectatorial diversity of the Shakespearean stage, different dynamics, identifications and elisions emerge simultaneously. Consequently, meaning becomes impossible to identify definitively, and can be glimpsed only as an ephemeral by-product of a particular set of transactions occurring and recurring between audience and stage. Realising this, Shakespeare critics have often tried to theorise the different kinds of identification that may take place in theatrical space, from Bethell's 'principle of multi-consciousness' (1944), to Weimann's distinction between *locus* and *platea* (1978), to Leah Marcus's emphasis on reading within the context of a local audience (1988), and so on.

The question of the local recurs, of course, because so many of the identifications taking place between the Shakespearean stage and the audience will inevitably be with figures of national significance: 'what English blood seeing the person of any bold English man presented and doth not hugge his fame, and hunnye at his valor ...' (Heywood 1978, sig. B4r). Shakespeare's histories, for example, as their titles suggest, provide serialised biographies of the English nation which the spectators are invited to reproduce as autobiography by assimilating the images of the various monarchs portrayed. Later chapters will argue that, through these nationalistic identifications, Shakespearean tragedy participates in a visual regime which colludes in the simultaneous centralisation of a nation and a mode of subjectivity.

The constitution of this imaginary nationality can be compared with Lacan's description of the ego, which coalesces out of all the fragmented and illusory identifications made by the subject. Lacanian psychoanalysis engages in a protracted critique and redefinition of the Cartesian and Enlightenment ego, which it characterises according to the illusion of a coherent, autonomous and consistent self which thinks, perceives and acts. Lacan, on the contrary, diagnoses an ego fundamentally alienated from its own illusory fantasy of mastery, its image in the mirror. The concept of the nation in Shakespeare's plays can be approached in the same way, as a loose bundle of desires, constructed and maintained through contradictory identifications of an illusory dominance.[16]

Recent developments in postcolonial theory also contribute to this decomposition of nationality. In relation to Shakespeare, the postcolonial perspective emphatically situates the plays within the context of an accelerating European (and British) imperialism. In relation to Lacan, it should be observed that the Cartesian ego also emerged at a time when Europe was constructing itself as the ego-centre of a world which, with the recently discovered Americas and the yet-to-be discovered Australasia, was proving to be both larger and yet more accessible than had been previously imagined.

The representation of the globe as an object of exploration and acquisition therefore colludes with the inception of an individualistic subjectivity also conceived as 'global' in form: as a centripetal, self-contained, self-enclosed interiority. Hamlet's reference to his memory as holding a seat in the 'distracted globe' of his head prefigures this development, although the punning reference to the interactive and communal space of the public theatre suggests a subjectivity still somewhat dispersed, in contrast to the absolute individualistic centrality it will later attain.

As Lacan points out, the appearance of the modern subject occurs in collaboration with the establishment of a geometrically based economy of vision, dependent on the technique of central projection, and thereby installing a singular, privileged locus of spectatorship. For this reason, psychoanalysis interests itself in Renaissance experiments with perspective, 'whose relation with the institution of the Cartesian subject, which is itself a sort of geometrical point, a point of perspective, we cannot fail to see' (Lacan 1979, 86). Later chapters will therefore consider the visual regime of the map, the

globe, the perspective painting and the dramaturgy of Shakespearean tragedy, in so far as each of these cultural texts participates
in the eventual installation of the Cartesian subject as the source
and focus of the radiating lines of geometry, navigation, and surveying which will come to anatomise and orientate the colonial
world.[17]

This study will therefore seek to identify the role of the visual in
the ego-identifications which constitute the history of the subject.
In doing so, a variety of anamorphic perspectives or unsettling gazes
will emerge from unexpected locations. *Hamlet*, for example, disconcerts the imaginary identification between audience and stage
once more when the gravedigger asserts that if the Prince remains
mad in England "Twill not be seen in him there. There the men
are as mad as he' (V.i.150–1). Imagining a perception of the English
nation from the 'outside', this moment disturbs the spectatorial
gaze by inviting its identification with an anamorphic perspective.
The imitation Danes on stage stare back at the English audience,
making them 'look mad', demanding that they perceive themselves
in a way divided from themselves.

The performance of identity always involves this paradoxical gaze
according to which the ego splits off from itself to look back at
itself: Lacan calls this the illusion of consciousness '*seeing itself seeing
itself*' (1979, 82). Theatre is the professional application of this illusion:
drama comes into being between the actor's and the spectator's
imagined gaze from the other. As such the theatrical ego exists in
its alienation from itself, its fundamental dis-ease: 'At the heart
of the subject, [the ego] is only a privileged symptom, the human
symptom *par excellence*, the mental illness of man' (Lacan 1988a,
16). It might be for this reason that Hamlet proclaims himself
'mad in craft' (III.iv.172): both he and the spectator of Shakespearean tragedy are both made/mad in that gap between representation and a reality which always slips away, constituted in
the split between the eye watching the stage and the gaze looking
back at them.

The following chapters will provide a series of studies of such
gaps and divisions, and of the appearance and disappearance of
the illusion of subjectivity between the intersecting co-ordinates
that construct the conflicted visual field of Shakespearean theatre.
Chapter 2 deals with *King Lear*, a play which, pre-eminently, reflects
back to its spectators their own self-exile, their exile from themselves; Chapter 3 explores the ways in which both gender and race

trouble the smooth functioning of the optical symbolic; Chapter 4 is concerned with that mode of aggressivity which constructs and undoes the relation between the ego and its ideal mirror image; Chapter 5 charts the tensions and conflicts implied by the reorganisation of the optical field as these impact on an emergent British nationalism and imperialism; and Chapter 6 examines the institution of an incipient mode of visual unconscious, in the form of mimicry.

2
King Lear: Uncanny Spectacles

Dividing the kingdom(s)

Discussions of *'King Lear'* always begin again. For the text in question is irreconcilably double: there are two plays, a Folio and a Quarto, and each has an equal claim to 'authenticity'. The Oxford *Complete Works* offers the two versions under different titles, *The History of King Lear* and *The Tragedy of King Lear*.[1] In spite of Wells and Taylor's deployment of a validating authorial presence behind each version – 'the 1608 quarto represents the play as Shakespeare originally wrote it, and the 1623 Folio as he substantially revised it' (Wells and Taylor 1988, 909) – the two texts could equally be said to represent the transcription of conflicting accounts of actors, shareholders, audiences, compositors.... whose mediations act as an intervening stage between 'Shakespeare' and *'King Lear'*, functioning as a glass to refract the (always lacking) 'original' text into an uncanny duplicity. This prohibits any recourse to a unique and authentic work, or to the invocation of a unified authorial intention.[2] Jacques Derrida describes this theatrical evocation of 'a double that doubles no simple, a double that nothing anticipates, nothing at least that is not itself already double' (1981, 206). He calls this movement 'dissemination', which 'can never become originary, central, or ultimate signified, the place proper to truth. On the contrary, dissemination represents the affirmation of this nonorigin' (268, n. 67).

King Lear – but here again, quotation marks are called for, to illustrate the distance between that title and any hypostatised or unified work which it may be thought to name – *'King Lear'* opens with just such a disseminatory division:

KENT: I thought the King had more affected the Duke of Albany than Cornwall.

GLOUCESTER: It did always seem so to us, but now in the division of the kingdoms it appears not which of the Dukes he values most; for equalities are so weighed that curiosity in neither can make choice of either's moiety. (Q 1.1–7)

These opening lines address the partition of 'Britain' between Albany and Goneril, Cornwall and Regan. This double realm continues to subdivide and multiply as the action unfolds, with the threat of a further conflict between Albany and Cornwall mentioned by Curan (F II.i.11) and Kent (F III.i.10–12), the estrangement of Albany from Goneril (F IV.ii), and of course a growing rivalry between the two sisters which eventually results in both of their deaths (F V.iii). Furthermore, the Quarto and Folio versions no sooner begin than they differ from each other. Where the former has 'the division of the kingdoms', the latter reads 'the division of the kingdom' (F I.i.4). The earlier text, then, posits a division prior to the action, while the later paradoxically reinstates a unity to be divided during the course of the play.

This excision of the letter 's', the repression of a plurality that precedes the opening, the deferral of a unitary point of origin, heralds the profusion of 'letters' (missives, characters) that will emerge throughout the play. Take the character Oswald, who is himself always a messenger; Kent addresses him as 'Thou whoreson Z, thou unnecessary letter' (F. II.ii.63). 'Zed' becomes unnecessary in Shakespearean English, because most of its functions are 'taken over by "s"' (Hunter 1972, 226). Kent also calls Oswald 'a base, proud, shallow, beggarly, three-suited, hundred-pound, filthy worsted-stocking knave; a lily livered, action-taking, whoreson, glass-gazing, super-serviceable, finical rogue', and 'one whom I will beat into clamorous whining if thou deniest the least syllable of thy addition' (F. II.ii. 13–22). Accusing Oswald of adopting the manner and dress of a gentlemen, Kent forces upon him instead a proliferating list of supplementary titles, unnecessary letters, additions. Oswald has overtaken Kent as a messenger, just as he takes over Kent's place in the social hierarchy. Stephen Gosson warns against this danger when he criticises the servants of players for assuming the garments and manners of gentlemen: 'Ouerlashing in apparel is so common a fault, that the very hyerlings of some of our Players … iet vnder Gentlemens noses in sutes of silke, exercising themselues too prating on the stage, &

common scoffing when they come abrode . . .' (1974, 96). Theatrical apparel constitutes a signifier out of control, an overflowing pride, an excessive 'character'.

Tracing the trajectories and detours of the many letters, and replies, and supplementary messages, that traverse the stage of *'King Lear'* brings home this disseminatory, 'postal' aspect of the theatrical space. Both the 'Lear' plot and the 'Gloucester' plot – the narrative also has a double structure – begin with purloined letters, messages sent astray. Like the map of Lear's Britain in scene i, drawn and re-drawn with new boundaries, parcelled up and distributed to various recipients, the kingdom(s) continue to disintegrate into a network of competing narratives and messages which cross and double-cross between the protagonists: Edmond's invented letter from Edgar, (ostensibly) diverted to Gloucester (F I.ii); the race between Lear's message (via Kent) and Goneril's (via Oswald) to Regan, and the conflict between these two messengers (F II.ii); the letter received by Kent from Cordelia, and the reply he sends with the Gentleman (II.ii); the letter received by Gloucester from the French (F III.iii), diverted by Edmond to Cornwall and Regan, and then reredirected from Cornwall to Albany to inform him of the French landing (F III.vii); the messenger who brings Goneril and Albany news of the death of Cornwall and of Gloucester's blinding (F IV.ii); Kent's discussion with his messenger of Cordelia's reaction to his letters (Q 17); Goneril's letter to Edmond, which Regan attempts to delay and confiscate (F IV.iv); the verbal 'note' she sends to Edmond in competition with Goneril's (F IV.iv); Edgar's interception of the first of these messages after he kills Oswald, and his redirection of it to Albany (F V.i); and, of course, the writ given by Edmond to the Captain instructing Cordelia and Lear's execution, which he sends Albany, slightly too late, to cancel (F V.iii).

'Beginning with an exchange of letters avoids the problem of finding the right beginning since, in effect, it is "not to begin at all",' writes Sarah Kofman, quoting E.T.A. Hoffmann's story 'The Sandman', which opens with a similar (though far less complex) digression of letters (Kofman 1991, 137; Hoffmann 1969, 149). On the other hand, the circulation of letters and writings generates an instability within the structure of the narrative, breaking down the limits – dramatic, fictional, generic and textual – which would de-fine it. In *'King Lear'*, the division of the kingdom(s) in the first scene of the play stages a duplication which sends disseminatory repercussions both forward and backward. First, the division precedes the ritual (since the Quarto's 'kingdoms' (l. 4) refers back to a plurality 'anterior' to Lear's staged dissection), and also precedes the play 'itself' (since its text(s) is(are) itself(themselves) never single). Second, this dissemination haunts the action of the play throughout, not only in the multiplicity of conflicting messages (mis)directed across the stage, but also in the doubling and division of plot, action, and character. Finally, certain effects of division can be shown to exceed the play and structure the reactions of audiences, readers, critics and editors.

Instances of this phenomenon can be discovered even in the most stolidly 'realist' of Shakespeare critics. A. C. Bradley comments that

> I tend to consider [*Lear*] from two rather different points of view. When I regard it strictly as a drama, it appears to me, though in certain parts overwhelming, decidedly inferior as a whole to *Hamlet*, *Othello* and *Macbeth*. When I am feeling that it is greater than any of these, and the fullest revelation of Shakespeare's power, I find I am not regarding it simply as a drama . . . .
>
> The stage is the test of strictly dramatic quality, and *King Lear* is too huge for the stage. (1991, 225–6)

Bradley here articulates a division between '*Lear*' as a stage play and that which exceeds this genre. This redoubling of dramatic effect causes the critic's own response to bifurcate into 'two rather different points of view', structured by two different gazes or ways of 'regarding' the play: as drama, but also as something 'greater'. What can it possibly mean for a play to be 'too huge for the stage' except that there must be in the play something more than the play, which returns upon the spectator? Other critics also encounter in '*Lear*' a supplementary excess that overflows generic boundaries. G. Wilson Knight documents the same effect in slightly different terms:

> The peculiar dualism at the root of this play which wrenches and splits the mind by a sight of incongruities displays in turn realities absurd, hideous, pitiful. This incongruity is Lear's madness; it is also the demonic laughter that echoes in the *Lear* universe . . . . in *King Lear* there is a dualism continually crying in vain to be resolved either by tragedy or comedy. (1949, 161)

According to this passage, a 'dualism at the root' of the play provokes a dualism in the mind of the beholder, a state characterised by the 'hideous' and the 'demonic', which crosses the boundaries of tragedy and comedy.

Such reactions suggest to the psychoanalytic reader the appearance of the 'uncanny', as discussed by Freud in relation to Hoffmann, which results from the apparition of the 'double', divided from the ego, and returning to it as a precursor of death:

> the 'double' was originally an insurance against the destruction of the ego, an 'energetic denial of the power of death', as Rank says, and probably the 'immortal soul' was the first 'double' of the body . . . . But when this stage has been surmounted, the 'double' reverses its aspect. From having been an assurance of immortality, it becomes the uncanny harbinger of death. (1985b, 356–7)

In this sense, the double operates like Derrida's 'dangerous supplement'. The representation, as supplement, appears as a secondary addition or surplus to that which is represented, but comes to function as a replacement, threatening to efface the 'thing itself'. In doing so, the supplement becomes an 'uncanny harbinger', foreboding the death of the 'original'.[3] The supplementary function 'adds only to replace. It intervenes or insinuates itself *in-the-place-of*; if it fills, it is as if one fills a void. If it represents and makes an image, it is by the anterior default of a presence' (Derrida 1976, 145). In the reactions to '*King Lear*' quoted above, this double takes the form of what Bradley describes as the 'twofold character of the play', an 'overwhelming' and 'huge' surplus that goes beyond the stage and returns to threaten the play 'as a whole', and which Knight calls a 'dualism at the root of this play'. Just as the 's' in the Quarto's 'kingdoms' retroactively signifies a political disintegration prior to Lear's ritual, an 'anterior default of a presence', the Freudian double represents to the subject its deathly otherness-to-itself. For both Bradley and Knight, this excess provokes in the mind of the spectator a corresponding split, another double. Freud, moreover, attributes an uncanny effect to both of the particular instances Knight offers of this schizophrenia, 'madness' and 'the demonic', since 'the layman sees in them the working of forces hitherto unsuspected in his fellow-men, but at the same time he is dimly aware of them in remote corners of his own being' (Freud 1985b, 366).

Another symptom noted by Bradley and Knight also appears in Freud's essay. The crossing of generic boundaries, between 'fiction' and 'real life', and between specific modes such as comedy and tragedy, can induce an uncanny sensation too, for example when the author begins in a realistic mode and then crosses over into the fantastic, or else when the transgression works in the opposite direction, so that 'an uncanny effect is often and easily produced when the distinction between imagination and reality is effaced' (Freud 1985b, 367, 374). Critics emphasise the peculiar power of '*King Lear*' to cross and recross precisely this boundary in both directions, between 'real life' and 'fantasy', between the stage and what goes beyond the stage. According to Bradley, following Samuel Johnson, the prime instance of this is the blinding of Gloucester. Johnson considered 'the extrusion of Gloucester's eyes. . . . an act too horrid to be endured in dramatic exhibition, and such as must always compel the mind to relieve its distress by incredulity' (Wimsatt 1969, 126). Bradley reinforces this remark, commenting that

> the mere physical horror of such a spectacle would in the theatre be a sensation so violent as to overpower the purely tragic emotions and therefore the spectacle would seem revolting or shocking. But it is otherwise in reading. . . . the blinding of Gloster belongs rightly to *King Lear* in its proper world of imagination; it is a blot upon *King Lear* as a stage-play. (Bradley 1991, 232)

Blinding, which Freud makes central to his reading of Hoffmann's 'The Sandman', becomes in Johnson's and in Bradley's comments the effect that most powerfully violates the boundary between imagination and reality, producing in the spectator a range of uncanny effects including horror, incredulity, shock and revulsion. The blinding is for Bradley too horrifyingly physical to take place on the stage, which should after all be the site of fantasy, and for Johnson too extravagantly fantastic to take place in drama, which must after all be life-like. It is moreover the *sight* – rather than the mere idea – of blinding that cannot be endured, for while Bradley condemns it as a 'blot' upon '*King Lear* as a stage play', he considers it acceptable in *King Lear* as a text to be imagined in reading (but which text?). Does blindness therefore provide simply an exemplary case of the play's transgression of generic boundaries, as well as the boundary between stage and audience? Or is the uncanniness aroused by blindness a more pervasive phenomenon altogether? This inquiry would put into question the status of blindness as a 'trope', a 'theme' or a 'meaning', and would focus instead on blindness as an unstable signifying movement, concentrating on its peculiar capacity to produce uncanny effects. The blinding, a blot upon the play, thus constitutes the *scotoma* or blind spot which psychoanalysis takes as its point of departure (Lacan 1979, 82–3).

In Bradley's account, the 'overwhelming' effect of the play returns upon the spectator, causing a duplication of vision, a twofold 'point of view' or 'regard'. This seeing double in itself represents blindness according to the psychoanalytic logic whereby the repetition of an organ or function betrays (through a defensive reaction-formation) the threat of its destruction. So in Freud, 'doubling . . . has its counterpart in the language of dreams, which is fond of representing castration by a doubling or a multiplication of the genital symbol' (1985b, 356–7). Freud's essay on the uncanny goes on to associate blinding intimately with castration:

> A study of dreams, phantasies and myths has taught us that anxiety about one's eyes, a fear of going blind, is often enough a substitute for the dread of being castrated. The self-blinding of the mythical criminal, Oedipus, was simply a mitigated form of the punishment of castration . . . (1985b, 356)

Derrida remarks, in reference to this passage from Freud, that dissemination – which 'entails, entrains, "inscribes", and relaunches castration' – represents 'that nonsecret of seminal division that breaks into substitution' (1981, 268 n. 67).

Blindness, then, occurs in Freud, and in *'King Lear'*, and in Derrida, as the locus of a play of substitutes (blindness–castration–substitution–supplementation–dissemination) among which the identification of a single or originary term again proves impossible. In these terms, it could be said that the blinding in *'King Lear'* threatens to 'castrate' its audience, in so far as it represents that process by which the play renders a singular and stable subject position untenable through the solicitation of conflicting responses, a multiplication of gazes, an excessive affect.

Doubling, madness, the demonic, generic uncertainty, castration, blinding. Already *'King Lear's'* critical repercussions resemble a Freudian case study. But one more exemplary feature of the uncanny may also be identified, to disturb any prematurely complacent recognition. For Freud, *das Unheimliche* derives, in the first place, from 'something which is secretly familiar . . . which has undergone repression and then returned from it' (1985b, 368). This discussion, therefore, will attempt to move beyond the familiar array

of psychoanalytic preoccupations to consider those 'secretly familiar' elements, repressed in both psychoanalytic accounts of the
'uncanny' and critical accounts of '*King Lear*', which may re-emerge
to produce the uncanny effects associated with both theatre and
psychoanalytic reading. We should therefore 'not be surprised to
hear that psychoanalysis' – like criticism – 'which is concerned with
laying bare these hidden forces, has itself become uncanny' (Freud
1985b, 366).

Out o' th' grave

To begin again. The disseminatory play of letters, inaugurated but
not initiated by Lear's display of cartographic division, delivers to
Lear's heirs a totally fragmented 'Britain'. Gloucester describes this
state early in the second scene of the play:

> Love cools, friendship falls off, brothers divide; in cities, mutinies;
> in countries, discord; in palaces, treason; and the bond cracked
> 'twixt son and father. This villain of mine comes under the pre-
> diction: there's son against father. The King falls from bias of
> nature: there's father against child. Machinations, hollowness,
> treachery, and all ruinous disorders follow us disquietly to our
> graves (F I.ii.104–12)

Gloucester's enumeration of division and double-dealing in the realm
might suggest the word 'uncannily' here as an appropriate substi-
tute for 'disquietly'. The disquiet of this land encompasses even
the graves themselves, for in such a disordered realm, where letters
and messages have such a tendency to follow detours and digres-
sions, the path of life 'to our graves' also becomes liable to reversal,
producing revenants from the grave. Characters banished from the
life of the play will return as their own doubles: Kent, Edgar, Cordelia
and eventually Lear himself.

In the first scene, Lear not only bisects the kingdom(s), but also
divides himself into his own double. Or else, according to our 'other'
reading (of the other text), the scene dramatises an anterior schism
in both the kingdom and its king. Of course, both these splits do
precede their dramatisation, for when the play was first performed,
the constitutional unification of England and Scotland under James
'VI and I' was only a few years old. Furthermore, early modern
theories of sovereignty did rely on a fundamental duplication in

the person of the king. The lawyers and judges of Elizabeth's reign described how the King had 'two Bodies':

> the one whereof is a Body natural, consisting of natural Members as every other Man has, and in this he is subject to Passions and Death as other Men are; the other is a Body politic, and the Members thereof are his Subjects, and he and his Subjects together compose the Corporation . . . as to this Body the King never dies, and his natural Death is not called in our Law . . . the Death of the King, but the Demise of the King, not signifying by the Word (*Demise*) that the Body politic of the King is dead, but that there is a Separation of the two Bodies, and that the Body politic is transferred and conveyed over from the Body natural now dead, or now removed from the Dignity royal, to another Body natural. (cited in Kantorowicz 1957, 12–13)

Lear, by seeking to divest himself of 'rule, / Interest of territory, cares of state', inaugurates a split between his body politic and his body natural, expecting that the latter may then 'unburdened crawl towards death' (F I.i.41–50). But according to the theory, only through his 'demise' can the king's two bodies be divided. Therefore, if Lear's body politic no longer inheres in his body natural, then indeed he must be 'constitutionally' dead, and hereafter his physical body can only represent a ghostly and extremely uncanny return *from* this death. The last scenes of the play make this increasingly clear, as Lear complains that 'You do me wrong to take me out o' th' grave' (F IV.vi.38). Furthermore, according to early modern theories of kingship, not only has Lear returned from the dead, but the kingdom itself has become a realm of the 'undead'. Since the subjects together with the King comprise the 'corporation' of the 'body politic', the person of the King does not merely represent, but actually performs the unity of the realm, a relationship indicated by the name 'Great Britain', suggested for the newly united kingdom of James I by Francis Bacon in 1603 as an expression of the 'perfect union of bodies, politic as well as natural' (Kantorowicz 1957, 24). 'Britain' is, of course, also the name of Lear's realm. Clearly, then, in dividing his own two bodies, Lear divides that kingdom just as the person of King James unites it. The body politic, the kingdom itself, also becomes caught in this zone between life and death.

All Lear's followers manifest this division, and this 'undead' revenance, by going into exile (Kent, Edgar, Cordelia, Gloucester), and then returning from it uncannily. 'You are a spirit, I know,' says Lear to Cordelia, 'Where did you die?' (F IV.vi.42). Edgar, similarly, returns in various guises: as a peasant, a fisherman, as one of Lear's fellow magistrates in the mock-trial of his daughters, and as a lunatic. In the figure of 'Mad Tom', Edgar most clearly expresses the nature of the revenant, with his continual invocation of the demonic. Edgar's demons, indeed, speak at several removes, for not only are they uttered by an actor pretending to take their part, but their names and attributes derive from another text, Harsnet's *Declaration* (Hunter 1972, 254). In more than one way, then, Edgar's 'Mad Tom' exists as a quotation, spoken by texts that are not his own.[4] Edgar's mad double is himself doubled by 'the foul fiend', condemned to 'course his own shadow for a traitor' (F III.iv.43, 54). Again, this possession brings the blindness associated with castration and dissemination: 'He gives the web and the pin' – that is, cataract – and 'squints the eye' (F III.iv.110).

Along with blindness, we have seen that Freud attributes the uncanny to the appearance of this 'demonic character', which he associates with 'the dominance in the unconscious mind of a "compulsion to repeat" . . . powerful enough to overrule the pleasure principle' (1985b, 360–1).[5] Jacques Lacan will later describe his category of the symbolic in these same terms, as being 'united with the diabolic' (1992, 92). The Lacanian symbolic in this sense takes over the functions of repetition compulsion, for in its entry into the signifying network, the human 'individual' becomes subject to a power that goes beyond it and 'speaks it', just as the demonic voice possesses Mad Tom.

So each of the main characters manifests in some way the uncanniness of their return. Kent describes the realm of banishment and his own place in it when he says, 'Friendship lives hence, and banishment is here' (Q 1.171). 'Britain' has become the place where identity is foreclosed, in exile, out of place. The intimate is cast out ('friendship lives hence'), and the alien 'banishment' irrupts within. Lacan coins a term for this inversion of the opposition between outside and inside, this state of intimate exteriority, calling it 'extimacy' (1992, 139). Freud would call it '*das Unheimliche*', the unhomely, a place ripe to produce revenants, ghosts, the return of the familiar in unfamiliar guise. This recurs once more at the end of the play, where Kent, having followed Lear into the uncanny zone between life and death ('from your first of difference and decay' (F V.iii.264)), has also been characterised, in the figure of his double Caius, as 'dead and rotten' (F V.iii.261).[6]

Furthermore, the 'Britain' on stage in '*King Lear*', remains 'gored', irremediably divided, even at the end, for no one will reign after the deaths of Lear and Cordelia. Here the play departs both from its sources and its most notorious adaptation, that of Nahum Tate – all of which have Lear and Cordelia survive and reign for some years – and also from the more usual Shakespearean practice of ending with some gesture of resolution:

> ALBANY.   Friends of my soul, you twain
> Rule in this realm, and the gored state sustain.
> KENT. I have a journey, sir, shortly to go:
> My master calls me; I must not say no.
> EDGAR. The weight of this sad time we must obey,
> Speak what we feel, not what we ought to say.
> The oldest hath borne most. We that are young
> Shall never see so much, nor live so long.
> *Exeunt with a dead march, carrying the bodies*
> (F V.iii.295–302)

Instead of a restitution of unity, Albany repeats Lear's inaugural abdication, splitting the realm once more between 'you twain'. But Kent declines, and Edgar's reply refuses to accept the crown, offering instead another series of doubles: old/young, speak/say, feeling/duty. The Quarto attributes this final speech to Albany – the texts, too, are as divided at the end as at the beginning – but 'we that are young' seems more appropriate to Edgar, and he would otherwise have no reply to Albany's offer. Kent will continue to follow his master, Lear, in this uncanny orientation towards death, as indeed they all do. For the final couplet, which would conventionally evoke some hope of renewal, predicts only a foreshortening of both sight and life. The play leaves the audience with the image of the survivors, weighed down with corpses, leaving the stage with a 'dead march'.

Lear's shadow

> FOOL. Dost know the difference, my boy, between a bitter fool and a sweet fool?
> LEAR. No lad. Teach me.
> FOOL. [*sings*] That lord that counselled thee
>   To give away thy land,
>   Come, place him here by me;

Do thou for him stand.
The sweet and bitter fool
Will presently appear,
The one in motley here,
The other found out there.
LEAR. Dost thou call me fool, boy?

(Q 4.132–43)

The 'difference' rehearsed at this point in the play conforms to the logic of repetition and the double. The Fool calls Lear fool, addressing him with his own title, employing the pejorative form of the second person pronoun, and calling him 'my boy', just as the King calls the Fool 'lad'. Furthermore, the Fool requires Lear to act in a brief 'play within the play'. Such moments are frequent in '*King Lear*': as in the mock-trial scene where the three 'madmen' act as magistrates, Edmond's staged conflict with his brother, and the charade of suicide Edgar directs for his father. Here, the Fool requires Lear to 'stand' for 'that lord that counselled thee', an imaginary figure who in turn stands for Lear's folly. Having placed this character beside himself, the Fool must represent the King receiving this counsel, so that this pair will then appear as 'the sweet and bitter fool'. Lear and the Fool thereby enact an irreducible supplementarity, simultaneously representing and taking the place of other, self, other, self, in an oscillation that confounds the occupation of any fixed locus within the specular or discursive order.

The passage thereby sets up a mirror identification between Fool and King. Allan Shickman has suggested that, in seventeenth-century performances of this play, the Fool actually carried a mirror on stage, 'because in the metaphorical sense *he* is one' (1991, 77); that is, he embodies the familiar iconography of the period (see Jacket illustration). According to Shickman's interpretation of this scene, rather than actually making Lear stand next to him, the Fool holds out his mirror to provide, in the form of his own reflection, the 'thou' which will stand for the 'lord that counselled' Lear. As he recites the verse, the Fool speaks to his own image, pointing to it to identify 'the other found out there'. Lear, turning to look where the Fool directs him, sees his own face appear in the glass, and as the realisation of the trick dawns on him, asks 'Dost thou call me fool, boy?'

For Lacan also, the subject's identification with a specular image involves the assumption of an alienating identity. Classically, however, in the 'mirror stage' this imaginary identification takes place with the other as the more masterful, co-ordinated and dominant image of the subject (Lacan 1977b, 1–7). The Fool, on the contrary, invites a mirror identification with a servant, one who slips out of fixed roles and subverts the dominant: with folly. Obviously, then, this scene stages precisely that which escapes from the Lacanian mirror stage, the troubling remainder that eludes or must be repressed by the imaginary identification between the 'ego' and its 'ideal ego' in the mirror.

Developing his theory of the mirror stage, Lacan describes this inherent possibility of reversal or decomposition in the relationship between the subject's ego and its specular other:

> The fundamental position of the ego confronted with its image is indeed this immediate reversibility of the position of master and servant. . . . The ego's fate, by its very nature, is to always find its reflection confronting it, which dispossess [*sic*] it of all it wishes to attain. This sort of shadow, which is simultaneously rival, master, sometime slave, keeps it at a distance from what is fundamentally at stake, namely the recognition of desire. (1988, 265–6)

While the imaginary provides an illusory dual relationship between ego and specular ideal ego, the symbolic introduces a supplementary play of substitution, effecting the subject with a radical instability. Introjecting or assimilating the specular ideal ego, the subject becomes other than itself. The Fool's miniature drama mimes that process whereby Lear is doubled and redoubled into his own mirror image or, as Shakespearean usage has it, his 'shadow'. Oscillating between master and slave, between subject and other, between ego, ideal ego and ego ideal, Lear's identity fractures into a series of uncanny *doppel-gangers*:

> LEAR. Does any here know me? This is not Lear.
> Does Lear walk thus, speak thus? Where are his eyes?
> Either his notion weakens, his discernings
> Are lethargied – ha, waking? 'Tis not so.
> Who is it that can tell me who I am?
> FOOL. Lear's shadow . . .
>
>   (F I.iv.208–13)

The decomposition of a stable relationship with his mirror image disrupts Lear's place in a visual economy, producing an uncertainty about both his own gaze (or lack of it) and that of the other: 'Where are his eyes?'

Again, these moments display not only the split inherent in 'King Lear', but the duplication endemic to '*King Lear*'. For the two texts diverge dramatically here. The Folio cuts out altogether the Fool's rhyme about the 'sweet and bitter fool', and its attendant 'mirror staging'. The comparison between King and Fool undoubtedly remains, pervading various parts of the play, but the later text excises this most explicit dramatisation of it.

Shickman's suggestion might point to one reason for this repression. The use of an actual mirror would exemplify the volatile impact of this passage, because it conveys most explicitly the destabilisation of a secure relationship between audience and stage. For instance, in order for the nearest spectators to see the Fool's face appear in the mirror, their own reflections would become visible in it from his oblique perspective. If, on the other hand, it turns directly towards the audience, the mirror shows them 'in the act' of looking, capturing them within the frame of the play. This incident therefore introduces to the position of the spectators an uncanny supplementarity, showing them represented as witnesses within the representation they witness. And what if, during the play's performance at court in 1606, the mirror were to catch the contours of the King, located no doubt in the best seat for a clear and unobstructed view? James I would make a cameo appearance within the play itself, as the bitter fool whose person and realm are split in two. Although we cannot know when these lines were cut, it seems most likely that the increasingly strong relationship between Shakespeare's company and the Stuart monarchy, including more and more frequent performances of his plays at court, would have made the presence of these 'speculative' lines uncannily ambiguous.

Envisaging this unsettling theatrical transaction – another moment, comparable with those described in the preceding chapter, in which the spectator finds a gaze returning from the stage – involves another aspect of the psychoanalytic uncanny, as it relates to the field of vision. In his discussion of 'Desire and the Interpretation of Desire in *Hamlet*', Lacan asserts that '*Das Unheimliche*, the uncanny', arises when 'something from the imaginary structure of the fantasy' – that is, the imagined relationship with the object in desire, the *objet a* – becomes 'placed in communication with . . . .

the image of the other subject, in the case in which that image is my own ego' (1977a, 22). The mirror stage, of course, provides the classic case in which the 'image of the other subject . . . is my own ego', inasmuch as the subject assimilates the masterful image of the specular other to provide the support and morphology of its own ego. Therefore, Lacan seems to be suggesting that the imaginary relation of the mirror stage, like the Fool's specular mime in '*King Lear*', is 'decomposed' by the irruption of the *objet a*, the object in desire, into an alienating dualism between ego and ego ideal. And, as Lacan points out, '*the* objet a *in the field of the visible is the gaze*' (1979, 105). In visual perception, then, the uncanny would occur when the gaze crosses over to, becomes inscribed upon, or maps across, the image of the subject's ego, which may take the form of its reflection in the mirror, or of another subject with whom it has a specular relationship. In short, it is the gaze which, added to the mirror image or ideal ego, creates the uncanny double.[7] Thus Lear becomes his own Fool, gazing at himself not in, but from, the mirror. The primary symptom of this proximity of the gaze is, of course, the blindness which becomes so evident in Lear's language as well as his actions.

Other figures in the play will come to embody this gaze for him. Most obviously, Lear desires recognition from Cordelia's gaze. However, at the moment he comes closest to apprehending this, Lear mistakes it:

> I fear I am not in my perfect mind . . .
>   Do not laugh at me,
> For, as I am a man, I think this lady
> To be my child, Cordelia . . .
>
>   (F IV.vi.56–63)

Becoming aware of the gaze of the other which Cordelia embodies, Lear typically misrecognises this moment as his own madness. For by definition, the *objet a* cannot be grasped. It slips away. Having construed his daughter as a ghost – 'You are a spirit, I know. Where did you die?' – Lear's entrance with her corpse in the final scene comes as no surprise.[8] Nor does his attempt to regain her again, as *objet a*, in a mirror:

> Lend me a looking-glass.
> If that her breath will mist or stain the stone,
> Why, then she lives.
> KENT. Is this the promised end?
> EDGAR. Or image of that horror?
>
> (F V.iii.236–9)

Lear once more seeks in the imaginary relation of the mirror stage that dreamt-of unity with the object of his desire, but of course he cannot find it, and is instead left only his own 'image', shadow, double. For the apprehension of the *objet a*, which belongs to the Lacanian 'real', is by definition impossible, because it constitutes exactly that which cannot be seen in the mirror:

> These objects have one common feature in my elaboration of them – they have no specular image, or, in other words, alterity. . . .
> It is this object that cannot be grasped in the mirror that the specular image lends its clothes. A substance caught in the net of the shadow, and which, robbed of its shadow-swelling volume, holds out once again the tired lure of the shadow as if it were substance. (Lacan 1977b, 315–16)

The *objet a* has no other ('alterity') because it functions as *nothing other than* alterity. As double, this object appears as a mirror image ('the tired lure of the shadow') which has escaped from the mirror and which therefore itself has no reflection (it 'cannot be grasped in the mirror').[9]

In the first productions of the play, critics have suggested, the same actor played both Cordelia and the Fool, and the audience would have recognised this (Howard 1991). Hence the references to a close relation between these two characters who never appear on stage together: 'Since my young lady's going into France, sir, the fool hath much pined away' (F. I.iv.71–2). Although in the opening scene Lear banishes Cordelia from his optical field – 'Hence, and avoid my sight!'; 'we / Have no such daughter, nor shall ever see / That face of hers again' (F. I.i.124, 262–4) – she returns uncannily, in the form of the Fool, Lear's 'shadow' in the mirror, representing what has been exiled from the King's imperious hold over the visual regime. Once madness takes hold, Lear becomes identified with folly, and the Fool fades away completely. Then Cordelia herself enters once more to incarnate this disembodied specular gaze, repudiated by Lear yet returning to him uncannily, the desired object which slips perpetually from his grasp. So, at the end of the play, when Lear calls for a looking-glass in which to seek Cordelia, he would of course be given the same one carried, earlier on, by the Fool. Immediately before her return from outside the realm of action in the play, the Quarto includes a scene in which Kent discusses with a Gentleman the effect of his letters about Lear's plight upon Cordelia.[10] The description of her reaction focuses repeatedly on her eyes. Not only are these imagined as gems emitting rays of light, but the tears that well from them are also precious stones, 'as pearls from diamonds dropped' (Q 17.23), suggesting a multiplication of eyes and a disseminated play of irradiation. The lustre of the jewel-as-eye provides a powerful instance of the gaze of the Other. 'In short,' says Lacan, 'the point of the gaze always participates in the ambiguity of the jewel' (1979, 96). This ambiguity resides, on the one hand, in the solicitation of the gaze of the subject by the jewel, and on the other, in this point of light emanating from the gem, which transfixes the subject as object in the sight of the world.[11] Later in the play, Edgar will also make reference to gems, when he describes his first view of Gloucester 'with his bleeding rings, / Their precious stones new-lost' (F V.iii.181–2). It is, of course, the increasingly uncanny figure of Gloucester who provides the primary focus for the play's preoccupation with sight and blindness.

Gloucester's glasses: an unsightly pair

The blinding, as discussed earlier, excites the most contradictory reactions of critics. And indeed this scene does seem especially designed to emphasise the physicality of Gloucester's ordeal, through the inclusion of the most graphic stage directions and dialogue. Yet the most uncanny feature of this blinding must be that, despite the unequivocal explicitness of the act of enucleation – 'Upon these eyes of thine I'll set my foot . . . . Out, vile jelly' (F III.vii.66–81) – performed not once but twice before the very eyes of the audience, Gloucester nevertheless afterwards *does keep looking*. The rest of the play suggests that the only possible reply to Cornwall's malicious question 'Where is thy lustre now?' must be 'still there'. For although Gloucester has lost his 'actual' eyes, his blinded face thereafter embodies the uncanny luminosity of the gaze.

When Edgar first sees the blinded Gloucester, he describes him as 'parti-eyed' (F IV.i.10), possessing a multiple, divided gaze, which in turn elicits partition in the object of its sight. Gloucester's own comments repeatedly suggest something other than a simple 'loss' of vision:

> I have no way, and therefore want no eyes.
> I stumbled when I saw. Full oft 'tis seen
> Our means secure us, and our mere defects
> Prove our commodities. O dear son Edgar,
> The food of thy abusèd father's wrath –
> Might I but live to see thee in my touch
> I'd say I had eyes again
>
> (F IV.i.18–24)

In Shakespearean usage, 'want no eyes' carries with it the meaning 'lack no eyes'. Continuing to employ the rhetoric of vision, the paradoxes here postulate Gloucester's blindness as another, prior form of visuality. As he utters the last two lines of this speech, Gloucester might stumble into Edgar, so that with the words 'see thee in my touch' he does indeed have 'eyes again', in the form of the sheer visibility of the gaze. Lear (mis)recognises this gaze when he meets Gloucester later in the play. 'I remember thine eyes well enough,' he remarks, 'Dost thou squiny at me?' (F IV.v.132). As 'blind Cupid', Gloucester's empty sockets might be compared to the mimetic *ocelli* on the wings of certain species of butterfly, the eye-shapes that embody the gaze – that which has become the object in Lear's desire.

It has become customary to comment of this play that the protagonists – Lear and Gloucester – both lose 'sight' but gain 'insight' in the course of the action.[12] However, my claim that Gloucester's blind face comes to embody the gaze represents the diametrically opposite view. For in so far as 'insight' would signify some consolidation of the stable position of the individual subject through the refinement of her or his perceptual or emotional sensibilities, what Lacan calls 'the gaze' is on the contrary characterised by the loss of these reassuring co-ordinates. The subject is dispossessed (or 'castrated', to use Lacan's terms) of precisely those guarantors of self-presence, self-consciousness and self-knowledge, and the gaze embodies this lack in the field of the visual. Gloucester does not therefore, according to this account, 'gain' anything but the capacity to represent brutally to others their deprivation of visual plenitude, their subjection to a mastering Other.

The blinded and blinding visuality which overflows or irradiates from the eyes of Cordelia and the sockets of Gloucester recalls Lacan's distinction between the geometrical structuring of vision and that which goes beyond it: the 'classic dialectic around perception' he asserts, remains misconceived, in so far as it only 'deals with geometral [*sic*] vision, that is to say, with vision in so far as it is situated in a space that is not in its essence visual'. But, he goes on to argue,

> The essence of the relation between appearance and being, which the philosopher, conquering the [geometrical] field of vision, so easily masters, lies elsewhere. It is not in the straight line, but in the point of light – the point of irradiation, the play of light, fire, the source from which reflections pour forth. Light may travel in a straight line, but it is refracted, diffused, it floods, it fills – the eye is a sort of bowl – it flows over, too, it necessitates, around the ocular bowl, a whole series of organs, mechanisms, defenses . . . . The eyelid, too, when confronted with too bright a light, first blinks, that is, it screws itself up in a well-known grimace. (Lacan 1979, 94)

This grimace characterises, I would argue, the subject's reaction to the uncanny – a gesture that shrinks back from the gaze in all its menacing excess. And just as the gaze escapes geometrical accounts of perception, it also seems to elude critical accounts of Shakespeare. The uncanniness, the excess and the multiplicity of the Shakespearean theatrical gaze escapes the modern reader precisely in so far as that reader inherits a visual regime which privileges a sovereign ego represented within a geometrically organised visual field by a monocentric point of view. By contrast, suggests Lacan, 'What we have to circumscribe . . . is the pre-existence of a gaze – I see only from one point, but in my existence I am looked at from all sides' (1979, 72).

This reappraisal of the place of the antecedent gaze recalls Hoffmann's story 'The Sandman', upon which Freud bases his account of the uncanny – in which the protagonist cannot escape his childhood fear of the Sandman who comes to pull out children's eyes.[13] Following Sarah Kofman, I would emphasise those instruments of artificial vision which precede and constitute Nathanael's point of view, from the 'glowing grains' with which Coppelius threatens him, to the spyglass through which he becomes subject to the gaze of the automaton Olympia (Kofman 1991, 151–4; Hoffmann

1969, 143–56).[14] These supplementary eyes are repeatedly described as fiery and bloody, characteristics which recall both the pearls that emerge from Cordelia's eyes (Q 17.23) and the 'sparks of nature' that Gloucester invokes during his own blinding (F III.vii.84). The gaze operates as a threat to the subject's sight through the proximity of an overabundance of vision, the surplus represented by a multiplicity of prosthetic eyes, like the 'spectacles' which Gloucester claims not to need in order to peruse the 'nothing' of Edmond's forged letter (F I.ii.35–6), or the 'glass eyes' which Lear will later urge him to procure, so that he may 'like a scurvy politician, seem / To see the things thou dost not' (F IV.v.166–8).[15] Glass eyes, like the jewel and the mirror, emit the rays of light or sight that dazzle the subject in its monocular blindness.

Returning to Gloucester, I would suggest that the lacking eyes of the blind man embody the gaze in two ways. First, because they inscribe the evidence of its own incapacity upon that part of the body concerned with sight, visibly displaying the subject as subject to, rather than as subject of, the transactions of the visual. Second, Gloucester's bleeding eyesockets represent the gaze from the other which exceeds the eye and always eludes the perspective of the Albertian viewpoint or the Cartesian ego. Lacan describes the operation of this blind gaze as follows:

> In the domain that I have called the geometral, it seems at first that it is light that gives us, as it were, the thread . . . .
>
> This is why the blind man would be able to follow all our demonstrations, providing we took some trouble in their presentation. We could get him, for example, to finger an object of a certain height, then follow the stretched thread . . . in the same way that we imagine, in pure optics, the variously proportioned and fundamentally homological relations, the correspondences from one point to another in space, which always, in the end, amounts to situating two points on a single thread. This construction does not, therefore, particularly enable us to apprehend what is provided by light.
>
> How can we try to apprehend that which seems to elude us in this way in the optical structuring of space? (1979, 93)

The blind man in Lacan's seminar demonstrates emblematically what is missing from the optical structure of the seeing Cartesian subject. Similarly, the blind man in *'King Lear'*, in his journey to Dover cliff, provides an allegory of what eludes the spectator in the theatrical structuring of reality. Edgar's panoramic speech performs the same demonstration Lacan describes: the blind man sees the world 'feelingly' (F IV.v.145), following the stretched thread of Edgar's 'lines' in order to construct in verbal rather than visual space a geometral mapping of images.

Critics as diverse as Jan Kott, Marshall McLuhan and Jonathan Goldberg have discussed how Edgar's elaborate descriptions of the surrounding scenery and the progress of the climb stage in a self-reflexive or parodic manner the very means by which Shakespearean theatre creates any landscape (Kott 1964, 114–17; McLuhan 1962, 15–17; Goldberg 1988). On a platform stage devoid of background scenery, the language of the characters must create what the audience are to imagine around them. But in this play, the audience are made aware – through his own asides, and through Gloucester's inability to hear the sea or feel the slope – that Edgar's 'landscape' is *nothing but* a discursive illusion.

Stephen Heath has described the essential elements of the perspectival organisation of the optical field as follows:

> The perspective system introduced in the early years of the fifteenth century in Italy (developing above all from Florence) is that of *central projection*: 'It is the art of depicting three-dimensional objects upon a plane surface in such a manner that the picture may affect the eye of an observer in the same way as the natural objects themselves.... A perfectly deceptive illusion can be obtained only on two conditions: (a) the spectator shall use only one eye, (b) this eye has to be placed in the central point of perspective (or, at least, quite near this point)'. The component elements of that account should be noted: the possible exact match for the eye of picture and object, the deceptive illusion; the centre of the illusion, the eye in place. What is fundamental is the idea of the spectator at a window, an *'aperta finestra'* that gives a view on the world – framed, centred, harmonious. (Heath 1976, 75–6; citing Doesschate 1964, 6–7)

Lacan will emphasise what must always be foreclosed by this geometrical ordering of the world: any gaze, perspective or viewpoint which might displace and destabilise the monocentric and sovereign eye, making the subject into an object inscribed in the picture rather than its origin and organising principle. This repressed function of the gaze can manifest, for example, as anamorphosis, the appearance within the picture of a distorted image which will only become legible from a perspective other than that of central projection. By introducing an alternative viewpoint, anamorphosis reveals the subject's position to be constructed rather than natural or given: 'I will go so far as to say that this fascination complements what geometral researches into perspective allow to escape from vision' (Lacan 1979, 87).

Jonathan Goldberg, following McLuhan, points out that Edgar's description of the view from the precipice adheres to the principles of Renaissance perspective painting in its creation of the illusion of a three-dimensional space with vanishing point:

> Blind Gloucester is positioned to have this illusionistic experience. Edgar roots him to 'the place' and insists that he 'stand still' [F IV.v.11]. Between the spot where they are supposed to stand and the dizzying prospect, a series of midpoints are marked, dividing the space into mathematical segments. Birds appear the size of beetles; a man at this distance 'seems no bigger than his head' [F IV.v.16]. Further down, they are even smaller; men become mice. The last objects seen are described in a kind of algebra that expresses a verbal version of a formula of proportion, a:b::b:c, 'yond [tall] anchoring bark / Diminished to her cock; her cock a buoy / Almost too small for sight' [F IV.v.18–20].
> (Goldberg 1988, 250)

The scene at 'Dover', then, offers a vertiginous staging of the delusion behind the 'reality' as presented by both the theatre and the visual art of its day. In doing so, the play once again puts on stage the spectatorial gaze, inscribing within the picture its own construction, so the audience see themselves, as blind, in Gloucester's place, at risk of falling into the abyss between the 'representation' and 'reality'. The uncanniness of the play derives once again from this permeability between what Freud calls 'reality' and the 'imaginary', or what Lacan terms the crossing of the fantasy through the limits assigned to it (1977a, 22). In this scene, these boundaries are doubly or trebly transgressed, through the play of multiple 'realities': Gloucester's (an ascent of, and a descent from, Dover cliff), Edgar's (that therapeutic illusion he perpetrates to 'cure' his father's 'despair' [F IV.v.33–4]), and the spectator's (situated in an audience, watching a play). None of these levels remains distinct, each becoming subject to deconstruction by a gaze which always already 'finds it out' in its illusory blindness.

However, the critics who discuss this scene fail to account for what takes place after Gloucester falls right through this perfect Albertian perspective painting, to be represented thereafter on the other side. He comes to embody this view from within the frame, looking back from the picture's vanishing point:

> GLOUCESTER. But have I fall'n, or no?
> EDGAR. From the dread summit of this chalky bourn.
> Look up a-height. The shrill-gorged lark so far
> Cannot be seen or heard. Do but look up.
>
> (F IV.v.56–9)

Prompted again by Edgar, Gloucester now occupies the locus of the gaze of the Other, which looks out of the perspective painting at the spectator. This position is, of course, impossible ('a miracle', as Edgar comments [i. 55]), like that of the ghost or the specular other escaped from the mirror.

This effect conforms strikingly to Lacan's discussion of perspective painting in relation to Holbein's *The Ambassadors*:

> The painter gives something to the person who must stand in front of his painting which, in part, at least, of the painting, might be summed up thus – *You want to see? Well, take a look at this!* He gives something for the eye to feed on, but he invites the person to whom this picture is presented to lay down his gaze there as one lays down one's weapons. This is the pacifying, Apollonian effect of painting. (1979, 101)

The picture in this account operates in two antagonistic ways. First, it provides a trap for the viewer's gaze, disarming the sovereign masterful gaze of the subject by offering it a lure, 'something to feed on'. At the same time, however, this process renders that subject position, and the gaze associated with it, vulnerable to deconstruction by the other function present in the painting, the pre-existent menacing gaze of the Other, which looks out at the viewer. Therefore the picture captures one gaze, but releases the Other. The pacifying, harmonising effect proves radically illusory.

Edgar's verbal perspective works in the same way. He says to his father, 'You want to see? Well, take a look at this!', and Gloucester seeks the Apollonian, pleasurable laying down of his gaze (in the Freudian sense of a pleasure which seeks annihilation): 'This world I do renounce, and in your sights / Shake patiently my great affliction off' (F IV.v.35–6). He relinquishes his gaze in the 'sights' of the Other. But Edgar's construction manifests the second function of the painting also, the instability of this illusion: 'How fearful / And dizzy 'tis to cast one's eyes so low!' (F IV.v.11–12). He associates this vertigo, as does Lacan, with 'the deficient sight' which threatens always to 'topple down headlong' (22–3). In Lacan's account of *The Ambassadors*, the realisation of this threat comes at the moment when the viewer leaves the painting and sees the alternative perspective of the anamorphic skull in the foreground coming into focus: 'you turn away, thus escaping the fascination of the picture . . . . It is then that, turning round as you leave . . . . you apprehend in this form . . . . What? A skull' (Lacan 1979, 88; see Figure 1, p. 54). Edgar turns away ('I'll look no more' [F IV.v.21]), and Gloucester, after his fall, has also escaped the fascination of the picture. The perspective painting from the top of the cliff has gone, to be replaced by another perspective, a reverse view which embodies that gaze of the Other looking out from the painting: the view from the bottom of the cliff. From this alternative location, just as the skull becomes visible in Holbein's picture, so the excess luminosity of the gaze appears in the image of 'some fiend' whose 'eyes / Were two full moons' (F IV.v.69–72). McLuhan and Goldberg both miss this perspective, turning away from the picture at the end of Edgar's view from the clifftop and remaining blind to what happens after Gloucester's 'fall'.[16]

The theatrical panorama, therefore, like Lacan's view of Holbein's painting, dramatises the split between the eye and the gaze. The spectator is invited in both cases to identify with two conflicting poles: either with the eye's illusory mastery of space through the geometrical composition of linear perspective, or else with the anamorphic gaze of the Other, which escapes the picture and displaces the subject from its centralised viewpoint. Kent Cartwright describes a performance of this scene entirely compatible with such a reading. During the 'climb' towards the clifftop, he suggests, Edgar and Gloucester make their way forward until they stand at the very edge of the platform, looking out towards the audience:

At the Globe, Edgar might speak looking out into the audience (front), yet directing the lines, with some glances, behind him

Figure 1. Hans Holbein, *The Ambassadors*

toward his father. . . . Edgar's description requires the actor imagina-
tively to locate objects in the middle and far distance: crows
and choughs in the 'midway air', samphire-gatherers '[h]alfway
down', fishermen 'upon the beach', and ship, cock, and buoy
anchored at sea. The actor's gaze might focus on a shallow point
in front of him, then lower and extend outward into the theater, further and further, until he himself appears dizzied. In so
doing, the actor must isolate 'spots' in the sea of people before
him that he can fix on or play against. (1991, 217)

Performed in this way, the mathematical precision of Edgar's lines
draws the audience within the Globe into an identification with
the centrally projected perspective he plots for them. If Gloucester
then casts himself into this word picture, tumbling off the stage,
the spectators will subsequently identify with his and Edgar's uncanny
gaze directed back 'up' at the cliff, towards the stage. The imaginary
fascination of the audience, caught within the 'painting', decomposes
into an uncanny alienation, in which they occupy the symbolic
locus from which the gaze returns out of the frame. The next scenes
take place upon the non-existent beach, beyond the borders of
'Britain', outside the realm of imaginary representation, where the
mad king re-enters to meet the gaze of both Gloucester's blinded
eyes and Cordelia's radiant ones, returning from exile.

What makes '*King Lear*' uncanny, then, is its repeated representation of the gaze as that radical alterity inhabiting the scopic field.
To the spectator in the theatre this gaze becomes apparent at several moments in the play: Lear's mirror image of folly, Gloucester's
blind gaze, the aftermath of the 'fall' from Dover cliff. At these
points the audience finds itself transfixed in the gaze of the Other,
where the play both looks back at the audience and shows itself
showing itself. 'The world is all-seeing, but it is not exhibitionistic
– it does not provoke our gaze. When it begins to provoke it, the
feeling of strangeness begins too' (Lacan 1979, 75). Provoking the
gaze of the spectator, reader or analyst, and returning it, this theatre displays intermittently what is excluded from a scopic economy
precariously constructed out of Euclidean geometry and Albertian
perspective. A reading of the uncanny moment suggests how an
illusory relationship between 'representation' and 'reality' can only
be maintained through certain repressions and the institution and
naturalisation of specific perceptual rubrics, and seeks to describe
how Renaissance theatre, criticism and psychoanalysis 'look', as their

various representational parameters – dramaturgic (between audience and stage), generic (between tragedy and what exceeds it), disciplinary (between psychoanalysis and theatre), and categorical (between literary and critical texts) – become liable to disintegration, duplication or reversal. The impossibility of these relations, of which the gaze is symptomatic, returns as an excess which psychoanalysis and theatre cannot name, describe or even gesture towards, except perhaps in the reverse of a movement, that shrinking away or warding off which characterises all reactions to the uncanny.

3
Othello: Black and White Writing

Skin deep

In *Hamlet*, 'woman' is the name for the frailty of the dramatic visual order; in *Othello*, it is 'Othello'. Shakespeare's stage cannot 'in truth' portray either a woman or a black man; instead, it can only play up the visual marks of identity – racial and sexual – in the forms of masquerade. In the same way, the figure of Oswald in *King Lear* embodies, in his presumptuous and extravagant dress, the incipient fragility of that social organisation which the Elizabethan sumptuary laws were designed to reinforce.

At the time *Othello* was first staged, the representation of 'blackness' on stage would have been highly stylised. Eldred Jones describes how Elizabethan and Jacobean theatre employed a variety of (dis)guises to represent racial difference, including soot, paint, velvet masks, gloves and wigs (1965, 120–3). For a modern audience, to envisage skin colour in such a denaturalised manner would be to question the relation between the representation of race and its 'essential nature', suggesting that any access to the latter involves an illusion perpetrated by the former. For Shakespeare's contemporaries, however, the reverse was probably true; their representation of 'blackness' could be extravagantly illusionistic precisely because it both relied on and produced specific preconceptions regarding the nature and behaviour of the character. Elliot Tokson refers to 'the Neoplatonic idea that associates inner being with outer appearance' in order to explain how the physical attributes of the black man on stage in sixteenth- and seventeenth-century drama 'would be used to create in the audience a readiness and an expectation for him to act in certain ways' (1982, 37–8):

> Simply stated, black skin almost invariably suggested the idea of sinfulness in one form or another . . . . Even in the most superficial function of this blackness – its capacity to conceal a blush – men found evidence of its inherent compatibility with sin. This inferred knowledge of the alliance between sin and its concealing shield of blackness is held by both blacks and whites. (41)

The striking aspect of Shakespeare's Othello, however, is that his moral hue oscillates wildly as the play progresses, so that at different moments his skin colour can be read either as incarnating, or as ironising, his internal disposition. In this way, the play further loosens the correlation between identity as conventionally represented within the symbolic and cultural organisation of the visual field, and identity as that incipient mode of interior consciousness represented by, for example, the tragic soliloquy.

In the first scene of the play, the conversation between Iago, Roderigo and Brabanzio projects an image of the Moor according to their darkest fears: bombastic, impetuous, lascivious, extravagantly alien. If, at his first entry, Othello's face conforms to this mask bestowed on him, he thereby incarnates the mark of those supposedly 'racial' characteristics produced by the anxiety of his detractors. Once the audience see him acting with obvious restraint and dignity in the face of these accusations, however, a competing representation of his character comes into effect. The play's destabilisation of any predetermined location of skin colour within the symbolic order – disturbing the conventional hierarchy of white over black, and the secure investment of those terms with positive and negative moral connotations – becomes apparent with the Duke's remark to Brabanzio that 'If virtue no delighted beauty lack, / Your son-in-law is far more fair than black' (I.iii.289–90). The visual manifestation of character appears to be challenged by virtue, which, like honour, 'is an essence that's not seen' (IV.i.16).

Yet later in the play Othello will himself reactivate and redeploy the accepted contemporary correlation between blackness and infamy, commenting that 'My name, that was as fresh / As Dian's visage, is now begrimed and black / As mine own face' (III.iii.391–3). Here, the identifications according to which the Moor defines his place within the dominant visual regime of the play appear thoroughly conflicted. His 'name', the verbal and literal signifier of his identity, has achieved representation within Venetian society by its association with the paradigm of white, European femininity:

the 'visage' of the goddess Diana, which in turn signifies purity. His marriage to Desdemona exemplifies this process. This identity, therefore, implies a perceptual divorce from his 'own face'. With his increasing estrangement from Desdemona, however, and his suspicion that her purity is not what it seems, his 'name' and identity return, alienated, to that from which he tried to separate himself. But of course he cannot see his own face, except via its reflection in the mirror of visual signification, coloured by the physiognomy of race and the conventional anatomy of sin. As Othello now looks at himself, according to a white, European, early seventeenth-century gaze, this face appears not merely 'black' but 'begrimed', dirty, sinful.

Othello thereby problematises the correlation between visual appearance and identity – whether that identity be racial or sexual – by revealing all such 'names' for the 'self' to be constructed according to a series of identifications and disidentifications, negotiated within a visual field dominated by oppositions between black and white, masculine and feminine, villainy and virtue, truth and falsehood. Perhaps the word 'complexion', as used recurrently in the play (III.iii.235, IV.ii.64), best illustrates the largely unnoticed collusion involved in any conventional equation between appearance and essence. In Elizabethan English, 'complexion' refers both to the superficial appearance and characteristic temperament of an individual.[1] The movement between these two distinct but always affiliated concepts will prove significant, not only in *Othello* itself, but also in the critical response to the play throughout its history.

Coleridge provides a famous starting place, with his remark that 'it would be something monstrous to conceive this beautiful Venetian girl falling in love with a veritable negro' (1969, 188). The phrase 'veritable negro' immediately identifies one recurrent preoccupation of the critical debate over this play: how could Othello possibly be a 'veritable Negro'? The attempts to determine Othello's precise colour – whether he was a 'tawny Moor' or a 'white Moor', an Arab or an Ethiopian – have, I suggest, reproduced exactly the doubts displayed in the play over the capacity of visual appearance to represent some 'deeper' racial character.[2] To pursue the issue in this way requires a somewhat different phrasing of the question: how can a 'Negro' be 'veritable'? That is, how can it be possible to locate either the verification (proof) or the veracity (truth) of racial identity? And how can we conceive the relationship between the 'evidence' of race and its imagined 'reality'? To begin looking for answers would involve an interrogation of the ways in which both play and critical texts deploy, on the one hand, certain perceptual manifestations of race – colour being the primary instance – and, on the other hand, its supposed substance or essence.[3]

One obvious place to pursue such an inquiry – since it precedes, literally, the modern reader's access to the play – is M. R. Ridley's editorial introduction to the Arden Shakespeare edition of the play.[4] His comments display an exemplary manoeuvre in the wider strategy of racial verification and veracity. Discussing the 'problem' of Othello's colour, Ridley remarks:

> a good deal of trouble arises, I think, from a confusion of colour and contour. To a great many people the word 'negro' suggests at once the picture of what they would call a 'nigger', the woolly hair, thick lips, round skull, blunt features, and burnt-cork blackness of the traditional nigger minstrel. Their subconscious generalization is ... silly .... There are more races than one in Africa, and that a man is black in colour is no reason why he should, even to European eyes, look sub-human. One of the finest heads I have ever seen on any human being was that of a negro conductor on an American Pullman car. He had lips slightly thicker than an ordinary European's, and he had somewhat curly hair; for the rest he had a long head, a magnificent forehead, a keenly chiselled nose, rather sunken cheeks, and his expression was grave, dignified and a trifle melancholy. He was coal-black, but he might have sat to a sculptor for a statue of Caesar, or, so far as appearance went, have played a superb Othello. (1958, li)

Ostensibly attempting to defuse the debate about Othello's racial identity, Ridley further ignites it. Apparently colour can be repressed if other anatomical features are sufficiently 'human' (that is, European): lips only 'slightly' thicker, hair only 'somewhat' curly. Employing a tactic familiar in racist rhetoric, he attempts to go beyond 'verification', or what might be called the ocular proof of race, sublimating colour by talking instead about universalised and essentialised human characteristics. These are, inevitably, qualities considered especially appropriate to any discussion of Shakespeare: gravity, dignity and tragic melancholia. But 'colour', the repressed perceptual evidence of race, returns as 'contour'. Othello, of course, has (indeed *is*, according to Roderigo's synecdoche) 'the thick-lips'

(I.i.66). And records of payments for 'curled head skulls of black lawn' in the accounts of the Office of Revels reinforce this suggestion that the visual representation of race on the Shakespearean stage was not confined to colour alone (Jones 1965, 123). Moreover, the resistance to such repression by the perceptual trace of ethnic difference becomes manifest in Ridley's phrase 'he was coalblack, *but . . .*'. The undecidability of any interior truth of race also re-emerges in the comment that 'he might . . . *so far as appearance went*, have played a superb Othello'. Even if the visual evidence of race can be neutralised, there remains always the suspicion that an interior reality, an essentialised quality, something like 'blood', will tell. Can this African American, no matter how grave and dignified he looks in other ways, really have it in him to play 'Shakespeare'?

Just before this passage, Ridley himself cites – and deplores – an even more extreme form of the tactic which he will then employ himself. In this case, the critic prioritises Othello's internal nobility so completely that she discounts 'the daub of black upon Othello's portrait' as a mistake on Shakespeare's part, 'one of the few erroneous strokes of the great master's brush':

> Shakespeare was too correct a delineator of human nature to have coloured Othello *black*, if he had personally acquainted himself with the idiosyncrasies of the African race. . . .
> Othello *was* a *white* man.[5]

Essential 'human nature' once again dominates, precedes and even erases the visual mark of difference, which becomes just a supplementary and incidental artistic decoration, a clumsy daub or erroneous stroke of the brush. In his ironic version of the same strategy, Wole Soyinka cites an Egyptian scholar's insistence that not only was Othello *not* a white man, but Shakespeare 'was in fact an Arab. His real name, cleansed of its anglicised corruption, was Shayk al-Subair . . .' (Soyinka 1988, 206). Again, as Soyinka points out, this assertion relies upon the internal authenticity of the character, a quality 'beneath the skin', to prove its point:

> the Moor's dignity even in folly has been held up as convincing proof that no European could have fleshed out this specific psychology of a jealousy complicated by racial insecurity but a man from beneath the skin – an Arab at the very least. (208)

Readers of the play thus tend to reflect its anxiety about how deep blackness actually goes. According to a racial psychology reading from the outside in, Othello represents an anomaly, either as a picture of a white man accidentally or incidentally painted black, or as a whitewash of a black man. Disconcerted by the disparity between appearance and inner authenticity, Shakespeare's critics seek to restore a correlation between the two: evidently Shakespeare was really black; or else Othello was really white; or, according to Ridley, even if Othello was black, he must not really have been *very* black.

The same uneasy dialectic remains troubling – although in a different way – even among some of the more politically engaged critics of recent times. Again, this manifests as the effacement of the apparent forms and signs of identity, and the privileging of an interiority or reality beyond them. For instance, in Stephen Greenblatt's seminal reading of the play, he writes of Othello that 'his identity depends upon a constant performance . . . of his "story", a loss of his own origins, an embrace and perpetual reiteration of the norms of another culture' (1980, 245). In spite of Greenblatt's insistence on the textuality of Shakespeare's characters, he seems incapable of avoiding reference to Othello's 'own origins'. This phrase reinstates the presupposition that a dramatic character can somehow be attributed with an anterior locus of origin, an essential and 'proper' self, as Karen Newman has pointed out (1987, 150). Instead of the crude oscillation, observed in the remarks of earlier critics, between the superficial marks of race and inherent character traits, Greenblatt's text displays a dichotomy between the 'performance' of a 'story', and the loss of Othello's 'own origins', his identity. The masquerade of performance or narrativity has replaced the mask of race. Instead of Tokson's 'concealing shield of blackness', Greenblatt envisages the character throwing up a smoke-screen of self-fashioning before the eyes of 'another culture'. Nevertheless, in doing so Greenblatt still implies – and fails to explore – some concept of self or ego to which is attributed priority and mastery over the fashioning it carries out. The relationship between outward sign and inward essence, between verifiable appearance and veridical truth, therefore remains a troubling one.

Ania Loomba criticises Greenblatt in a similar way, but even as she does so, her text repeats the same gesture for which she denounces him:

Greenblatt accounts for Othello's vulnerability to Iago's narrative by referring to the guilt that Christian orthodoxy imposes upon all forms of passion or sexual pleasure and specifically excluding racial difference: 'Nothing *conflicts* openly with Christian orthodoxy, but the erotic intensity that informs every word is experienced in tension with it. The tension is *less a manifestation of some atavistic "blackness" specific to Othello than a manifestation of the colonial power of Christian doctrine over sexuality*' [Greenblatt 1980, 241–2, Loomba's emphasis]. Why should Christianity, an adoptive religion for Othello, inform his psyche more fundamentally than the blackness which pervades every aspect of his history and identity? (Loomba 1989, 59)

The latter question itself presupposes a certain layering of identity, positing a 'fundamental' level, at which Loomba would locate colour. A blackness which thus 'pervades' from the bottom upwards suggests an epidermal racial mark that is somehow thicker than skin-deep. This deepening of appearance into substance continues when Loomba comments that 'evident in the imagery of black and white is Othello's *internalisation* of his own inferiority as well as the wickedness of women', and goes on to speak of the '*upsurge* of his non-European past, his pagan history' (59–60, emphasis added). As with Greenblatt, it is necessary to ask from where can this return of the repressed possibly originate, without granting Othello some form of precedent, essentialised racial and psychic interiority? The fact that these remarks follow directly after Loomba has pointed out that 'It is important, of course, to guard against reading dramatic characters as real, three dimensional people' bears out the difficulty of avoiding recourse to such interpretations (58). It would seem that any European representation of the racially other risks ignoring the extent to which, as Frantz Fanon has pointed out, 'what is often called the black soul is a white man's artifact' (1970, 12). For this reason, rather than speaking of the 'internalisation' by the black of an inferiority imposed by white culture, Fanon substitutes the neologism 'epidermalization' (10). In this sense the mark of race, although it comes to be envisaged as an interiority, always imposes itself from the outside.

This question of dimensionality raised by Loomba ought now to be articulated, for it is symptomatic of a troubled relation, pervading the debate surrounding Othello's race, between exterior form and interior reality, which manifests itself, in the critical texts mentioned so far, in a logic that belongs to the operation of the stereotype.

'Racism', as everyone knows, habitually works through the stereotype, a widespread prejudice against an entire group of people based solely on superficial characteristics: racial, sexual, religious, and so on. For instance Blackamoors, according to Renaissance convention, are murderously jealous, so that John Leo, who seems likely to be one of Shakespeare's sources for the play, asserts that 'whomsoever they finde but talking with their wives they presently go about to murther them' (Jones 1965, 22).[6] And of course *Othello* depicts a Moor roused to precisely such homicidal jealousy, on the slightest and least reliable of evidence. A stereotype of this sort therefore relies upon, and necessarily refuses to go beyond, traits restricted to the two-dimensional. But the word 'stereotype' has a hidden significance, an alternative and contradictory layer of meaning, for it derives from the Greek '*stereos*', meaning solid, *three*-dimensional. This etymology locates within the word a supplementary depth which fills out the conventional meaning of a flat or superficial image. The rediscovery of the solid repressed within the visual, perspectival plane suggests that the logic of the stereotype, as it operates in criticism and in racism, perpetrates an optical illusionism, consisting of a slippage between dimensions. The *trompe l'oeil* of stereotype would include both the covert move from the perception of a surface to the apperception or inference of depth and interiority, and from the colour of the skin to the behaviour of the individual via the collective. In so far as it permits an untroubled movement between, and an equation of, interior and exterior, the stereotype participates in the same ambiguity observed already in the word 'complexion', and operates in literary criticism as an alibi, a claim always to be in another place, a continuous movement or oscillation back and forth between colour and behaviour, psyche and skin.[7] This complicity between the visual signifiers of character and an imagined interiority or identity also relates to Derrida's discussion of the Platonic concept of mimesis, where he notes the 'historical ambiguity of the word *appearance* (at once the appearing or apparition of the being-present *and* the masking of the being-present behind its appearance)...' (1981, 211). For the audience in the theatre, though, there can be no 'actual' character behind the screen thrown up by the mimetic apparition of the play. In the acting of identity, race, nationality and gender are not merely represented but produced by their performance, by their visual signification within theatre.

To break down the operation of this stereotypical logic necessitates opening up a radical schism in this easy movement from two dimensions into three. By disarticulating the collaborative link between the mask of colour or gender and any hypostatised racial or sexual interiority, it may be possible to examine the operation of such differences within the visual economy by which they are produced and sustained. This process requires an exploration of the function of mimicry in the theatrical text, a move away from the collusion between appearance and reality to the examination of disguise, camouflage and travesty. Furthermore, by recalling another dormant meaning of the word 'stereotype', that of a metallic plate used in printing, I would also associate this approach with a movement from the reliance on psychological character to consideration of the production of character as letter, as signifier.[8] This rewriting of the stereotype, this stereo-typography, will therefore find its subject always already imprinted with the mark of certain textual, sexual, and racial traits and traces.

Looking through letters

Unsurprisingly, the slippage between external appearance and inner presence also preoccupies the psychoanalytic account of subjectivity. The emergence of this relation can be traced in Lacan's extrapolation, following Lévi-Strauss, of the primacy of the signifier over the signified. Lacanian analysis thereby changes its focus from an inferred psychic 'reality' within, to the shifting topology constructed by the signifiers of identity – glances, gestures, behaviours, words – as these play across the apparent body of the subject.

In his seminar on Edgar Allen Poe's 'The Purloined Letter', Lacan asserts that

> If what Freud discovered and rediscovers with a perpetually increasing sense of shock has a meaning, it is that the displacement of the signifier determines the subjects in their acts, in their destiny, in their refusals, in their blindnesses, in their end and in their fate, their innate gifts and social acquisitions notwithstanding, without regard for character or sex, and that, willingly or not, everything that might be considered the stuff of psychology, kit and caboodle, will follow the path of the signifier. (1972, 60)

The Lacanian subject actually comes into being through entry into language, or through the entry of language into her or him. It exists, therefore, only as an effect of the signifier, not as a referent. And for Lacan, the pun on the word 'letter' – as both epistle and typographical character – succinctly conveys this condition. As Jean-Luc Nancy and Philippe Lacoue-Labarthe point out, the letter in Lacanian theory

> designates *the structure of language in so far as the subject is impli-cated therein*. . . .
> This *literalization* of the subject is twofold. On the one hand, 'the structure of language exists prior to the entry that the subject makes there at a certain moment of its mental development'. . . .
> On the other hand, literalization stems from the fact that as a speaker, the subject borrows the *material support of its discourse* from the structure of language. Lacan writes: 'By letter we desig-nate that material support that concrete discourse borrows from language'. (Nancy and Lacoue-Labarthe 1992, 27–8)[9]

Subjectivity, then, will always and only take place as a 'purloined letter'. Being plurally named within language, human subjects appear irremediably dispersed across a wide constellation of identifications, desires, losses and exchanges, defined against a series of objects and others which perpetually oppose, reflect and escape them. 'Falling in possession of the letter – admirable ambiguity in language – its meaning possesses them' (Lacan 1972, 60). This total implication in the symbolic becomes manifest for Lacan in the subject's servitude to the Other and to the repetition automatism.

This emphasis on 'literality', I would suggest, therefore lends itself to a style of (typographical) character criticism, as opposed to the reading of character as interior presence. The subject of this approach would instead be the character-as-letter, and its itinerary would follow the transmission of this missive, and the effects of characterisation and narrative thereby produced. My discussion of the competing messages in *King Lear* in the preceding chapter has already provided a preliminary example of such a reading.

In *Othello*, then, it becomes evident that the 'character' of each character – in the sense of outward appearance, not inner motiva-tion, which remains perpetually in question, and actually decisive only in its absence – precedes and determines her or his role in the plot. As in Lacan's account of the Poe story, 'it is the letter and its diversion which governs their entries and roles' (1972, 60). *Othello* makes it explicit that the action occurs as it does, not because of the 'true natures' of the protagonists, but rather owing to the way in which they are read, how they are regarded, or how they are painted into the dramatic frame by the text. Iago best expresses this mechanism, for as Greenblatt suggests, he functions as a principle of narrativity or an embodiment of the plot (1980, 235–7). Iago's comments adumbrate for the audience a series of 'characters' – word portraits, collections of traits – whose 'typical' characteristics will determine the itinerary of his plot: Roderigo's foolishness (I.iii.375), Cassio's choler (II.i.271), Desdemona's honour (IV.i.16). Pre-eminently, Othello's nobility – and critics of the play have so often taken Iago's word here at face value – leaves him open to manipulation: 'The Moor – howbe't that I endure him not – / Is of a constant, loving, noble nature . . .' (II.i.287–8). The text establishes the pattern very early: 'Cassio's a proper man . . .', remarks Iago,

> He hath a person and a smooth dispose
> To be suspected, framed to make women false.
> The Moor is of a free and open nature,
> That thinks men honest that but seem to be so,
> And will as tenderly be led by th' nose
> As asses are.

> (I.iii.384–94)

Cassio's suave manner predisposes him to be seen in a certain way. This in turn 'frames', or draws into the picture, the falseness of 'women': in this case Desdemona. Othello's 'free and open nature' similarly determines the trajectory he will follow, drawn by Iago, 'led by th' nose'. In each case the characteristic functions decisively as an appearance to be perceived, rather than as an interior reality, and the trait therefore takes part in an intersubjective economy dominated by visual perception. Even Othello's 'noble nature', which should more than anything bespeak depth or integrity, relies on a perception of the honesty of others who 'but seem to be so'.[10]

Within this predetermined visual regime, of course, the most important masquerade will be performed by none other than Iago himself, portrayed repeatedly and blindly by himself, by Othello, and by all others as 'an honest man' (II.iii.260), 'honest Iago'

(II.iii.326), 'full of love and honesty' (III.iii.123), 'of exceeding honesty' (III.iii.262), 'direct and honest' (III.iii.383), 'Pricked to't by foolish honesty and love' (III.iii.417), 'brave Iago, honest and just' (V.i.32). He describes his camouflage of sincerity to Roderigo very early on in the play:

> Others there are
> Who, trimmed in forms and visages of duty,
> Keep yet their hearts attending on themselves,
> And, throwing but shows of service on their lords,
> Do well thrive by 'em, and when they have lined their coats,
> Do themselves homage. These fellows have some soul,
> And such a one do I profess myself...
>
> (I.i.49–55)

Iago turns the conventional relation between appearance and essence inside out, like the lining of the coat, which he shows to be of more importance than 'soul'. Money is the index of value here, associated through the metaphor of 'lined ... coats' with the superficial appurtenances of service and loyalty. Iago throws his 'forms and visages of duty', his 'shows of service' before the gaze of Othello like a cloak, so that outward appearance becomes both the sign of value and the means of attaining it, while the 'soul' that accrues from this display assumes the guise of a disguise:

> For when my outward action doth demonstrate
> The native act and figure of my heart
> In compliment extern, 'tis not long after
> But I will wear my heart upon my sleeve
> For daws to peck at. I am not what I am.
>
> (I.i.61–5)

Outward action, separated from the interior presence it is thought to represent, casts the actual existence of the latter into doubt. Always pre-empted by 'compliment extern', even what should be 'native' to Iago's 'heart' thereby becomes just another 'act and figure', a performance and a signifier only. The representation of identity produces it, as nothing but an effect of language. Iago's final comment here ironically betrays his total possession by the letter. 'I am not what I am': the 'I' of language, grammatical subject of the sentence, represents, pre-empts and replaces the 'self'.[11] The 'I' is nothing without language. At the end of the play, once his function as scriptwriter has been fulfilled, Iago falls totally silent, refusing to supply any explanation or motivation that might hint towards an internal consistency of character: 'Demand me nothing. What you know, you know. / From this time forth I never will speak word' (V.ii.309–10).

Iago's script, therefore, stages for the gaze the performance of a series of fixed roles, first of all by himself, and then by each other character. In this sense, he corresponds not only to the function of the playwright but also to that of the audience, for whom Cassio's 'smooth dispose', Othello's nobility, Desdemona's honour and Iago's own honesty are necessary prerequisites for the drama that must follow. Just as Othello's noble character is constituted through his apprehension of other men's 'seeming', so in the theatre the maintenance of the subject always returns to and from the perception of another.

In asserting the same to be true for psychoanalysis, Lacan insists upon the importance of the function of mimicry within the scopic drive. The structure of intersubjective imitation belongs to the Lacanian symbolic, inasmuch as it implies the introjection of the imagined gaze of the Other, to which the subject seeks to conform:

> That which is light looks at me, and by means of that light in the depths of my eye, something is painted ... something that is an impression .... which is in no way mastered by me. It is rather it that grasps me, solicits me at every moment, and makes of the landscape something other than a landscape, something other than what I have called the picture.
>
> The correlative of the picture, to be situated in the same place as it, that is to say, outside, is the point of the gaze, while that which forms the mediation from the one to the other, that which is between the two, is something of another nature than geometral, optical space, something that plays an exactly reverse role, which operates, not because it can be traversed, but on the contrary because it is opaque – I mean the screen. . . .
>
> And if I am anything in the picture, it is always in the form of the screen ... (Lacan 1979, 96–7)

The subject, grasped and solicited by the symbolic, paints itself into a picture seen from the perspective of the Other. Before this dominating gaze, the subject throws out its image like a screen. This defensive mimicry – for example, the 'shield' of race referred to by Tokson, the masquerade of gender, or Iago's 'forms and visages of duty' – functions at the point where the gaze of the Other and the eye of the subject intersect. In display, the subject 'gives off himself, or receives from the other, something that is like a mask, a double, an envelope, a thrown-off skin, thrown off in order to cover the frame of a shield' (Lacan 1979, 107).

Within the visual field, therefore, the subject's domination by, and dependence upon, the symbolic order consists of this mimicry, this adaptation to the gaze. Lacan refers to the parable of Choang-tsu, who dreams of his escape from the gaze of the Other in the form of 'that butterfly who paints himself with his own colours', 'a butterfly for nobody'. In the world of conscious perception, however, dominated by the symbolic order, such an escape can only be an impossible fantasy: 'It is when he is awake that he is Choang-tsu for others, and is caught in their butterfly net' (Lacan 1979, 76). In *Othello*, Iago employs a similar metaphor to anticipate the entrapment of the characters by the narrative network, and that of the actor within the visual field, remarking that 'With as little a web as this will I ensnare as great a fly as Cassio' (II.i.171–2).

If being looked at constitutes a mode of subjection to the symbolic, certainly the role taken by the actor provides an exemplary instance. But according to Lacan, even the position of the spectator gives only the illusion of being immune from such an experience. My discussion in earlier chapters has already located certain instances of this false security in Shakespearean tragedy. Both Claudius's guilty reaction to the play within the play staged by Hamlet, and Lear's madness in the face of the uncanny excess of vision represented by Cordelia and Gloucester, exemplify this disruption of the scopic mastery of the subject in the face of an alternative perspective deriving from the Other.

The relation between the camouflage assumed by the subject in the scopic field, and the letter or character which possesses the subject in language, becomes evident in Lacan's 'Seminar on "The Purloined Letter"'. Here, 'falling in possession of the letter' effects in each of the protagonists the assumption of an involuntary masquerade, which Lacan associates with a 'feminine' *ennui* or powerlessness. The Minister in Poe's story, therefore, 'in playing the part of the one who hides . . . is obliged to don the role of the Queen, and even the attributes of femininity and shadow, so propitious to the act of concealing' (Lacan 1972, 61). The assumption of this defensive mask in order to ward off the evil eye of the Other – by which process the subject negotiates its identity – calls into question the existence of a 'reality' or presence behind the mask. For this reason Lacan repeatedly associates the location of the subject within the symbolic with his version of castration, that is, with a lack which proves constitutive of the psyche. Thus the Minister in Poe's story, 'falling in possession of the letter' – that is, finding himself in the power of the symbolic order – assumes 'the attributes of femininity and shadow', giving out a masquerade, a placatory message to be read by the Other. However, if mimicry provides a condition of possibility for identity, then to associate it with 'femininity' only complicates and problematises the possibility of any stable or essential gender as well. In examining the mimetic structures of both *Othello* and psychoanalysis, therefore, the relation between gender and any other kind of masquerade – racial, cultural, social – begins to assume a primary importance.

Looking through lattice

When Lacan emphasises the decisive role of the signifier for the subject in his discussion of the gaze, he privileges the function of mimicry over any supposedly 'genuine' manifestation of identity. For the subject to participate in imitation, to assume a mask, is 'no doubt to reproduce an image. But at bottom, it is, for the subject, to be inserted in a function whose exercise grasps it' (Lacan 1979, 100). Inserted – according to the visual signs of race or gender, for instance – into the operation of the symbolic order, the subject is 'grasped' by the signifier – skin colour, sexual anatomy – whose fixation within that syntax situates and manipulates her or him. By locating this process 'at bottom', Lacan subverts the concept of the deep self, rendering it subject to the play of image or appearance, a ceaseless mimicry deprived of any original term. For the subject, there can be no substantial reality behind the masquerade, nothing accessible beyond appearance: 'Mimicry reveals something in so far as it is distinct from what might be called an *itself* that is behind' (Lacan 1979, 99). What is distinctive in Lacanian mimicry is that, through a successive play of images and gazes, 'it leaves the subject in ignorance as to what there is beyond the appearance'

(77). Beyond the veil of representation lies only the Other in whose eyes the image is produced: 'if beyond appearance there is nothing in itself, there is the gaze' (103).

The representation of Othello and Desdemona's love affair operates through just such an interplay of veils. Even a preparatory description of Desdemona locates her within an intersubjective economy in which her desire and identity are forged according to an inherent alienation. Her father describes her as

> A maiden never bold,
> Of spirit so still and quiet that her motion
> Blushed at herself – and she in spite of nature,
> Of years, of country, credit, everything,
> To fall in love with what she feared to look on!
> It is a judgement maimed and most imperfect
> That will confess perfection so could err
> Against all rules of nature, and must be driven
> To find out practices of cunning hell
> Why this should be. I therefore vouch again
> That with some mixtures powerful o'er the blood,
> Or with some dram conjured to this effect,
> He wrought upon her
>
> (I.iii.94–106)

To begin with, a scission appears between Desdemona's 'motion' – her impulses and desires – and her 'self'. But the 'blush' of shame which such a motion should evoke in its other, the self, is displaced instead back onto the urge. Super-egoic prohibition already crosses desire, the daughter's introjection of the law of the father pervading the 'feminine' psyche with the veiling flush of modesty or guilt. For of course, this portrait shows Desdemona's image from the viewpoint of the father. Rather than maintaining an internally consistent identity, Desdemona's nature 'err[s] from itself' as Othello will later describe, in terms echoing Brabanzio's own (III.iii.232). Desdemona's character is sundered by a desire for 'what she feared to look on': not a simple desire for the other, but a desire for her 'apprehension' of Othello: her perception of him, her seizure by this perception. Nor, according to Brabanzio, does this 'effect' even originate within Desdemona. Rather, it is elicited from without, 'wrought upon her' by means of love potions. Such potions, of course, as in *A Midsummer Night's Dream*, work most effectively when applied to the eyes.[12] Desdemona's gaze, from the start, appears to be solicited by a force external to her.

Othello does not deny that their attraction functions in this way. But rather than a literal (actual) witchcraft, he describes the process of the affair as a 'literal' magic, an art operating through the use of occult letters, a narrative. Through an interplay of revelations and secrets, verbosity and silence, 'dilat[ion]' and 'hint', Othello constructs the 'story' of his life (I.iii.127–68). Indeed this narrative, as the performance (in the theatre) of a performance (before the Senate) of a performance (to Desdemona and Brabanzio), already exemplifies the specular or echolaliac structure of mimesis. Within this *abyme*, the juxtaposition of episodes of revelation with periods of silence entices Desdemona into demanding more.[13] Spinning out his narrative 'by parcels', 'not intentively', Othello manages to 'beguile' his audience 'of her tears', which thus signify Desdemona's enlistment in the dialogue, her captivation within the mutual mimicry of desire (I.iii.153–5). Later, Iago will employ a similar hinting oscillation between loquacity and reticence to convince Othello of Desdemona's unfaithfulness.

At the end of this speech, Othello sums up the effect of this consummate display as follows: 'She loved me for the dangers I had passed, / And I loved her that she did pity them' (I.iii.166–7). Representation of the relationship in these two lines articulates Othello's version of why the other loves him, that is, because of the image he projects in his narrative, along with the reason for his love for her, that is, because she loves him in this way. He desires her desire, recognition in her eyes. Desdemona, as the audience for his narrative, draws him into Venetian society according to a dialectic comparable with Frantz Fanon's psychoanalytic version of the situation of the black man within white culture:

> I wish to be acknowledged not as *black* but as *white*.
>
> Now – and this is a form of recognition that Hegel had not envisaged – who but a white woman can do this for me? By loving me she proves that I am worthy of white love. I am loved like a white man.
>
> I am a white man.
>
> Her love takes me on the noble road that leads to total realisation. . . .
>
> I marry white culture, white beauty, white whiteness. (1970, 46)

Recalling Othello's earlier comparison of his name to 'Dian's visage', this passage suggests the kind of illusory mirror reflection performed by the Moor, who thereby identifies with 'white culture, white beauty, white whiteness'.[14] As a psychoanalyst, of course, Fanon explicitly draws his models of racial intersubjectivity from the 'dual narcissism' of the Lacanian mirror stage (Fanon 1970, 9).[15]

Lacan, in turn, might also be describing Othello's narrative mask when he writes that

> Modifying the formula I have of desire as unconscious – *man's desire is the desire of the Other* – I would say that it is a question of a sort of desire *on the part of* the Other, at the end of which is the *showing* (*le donner-a-voir*).
>
> How could this *showing* satisfy something, if there is not some appetite of the eye on the part of the person looking? (1979, 115)

This 'appetite' on the part of the other, the necessary correlative to Othello's 'showing', emerges in Desdemona's hungry, incorporative eagerness: 'She'd come again, and with a greedy ear / Devour up my discourse' (I.iii.148–9). Of course, when Lacan speaks of the desire of, or on the part of, the 'Other', the upper case proscribes any simple identification of Desdemona, or any one character, as Othello's Other. This term – in just one of its many senses – refers rather to the symbolic order to which they are both subject. Thus Desdemona, like Othello, manifests a desire constituted out of the archive of the Other: 'She wished she had not heard it, yet she wished / That heaven had made her such a man' (I.iii.161–2). Desdemona desires that heaven had made her both to be and to have such a man. This manifests a libido caught within the dominant patriarchal symbolic order, yet already split from itself, oscillating between 'feminine' masquerade and 'masculine' display, a Lacanian distinction which must be examined more closely later.

Desdemona's place in the patriarchal order of Venetian society remains a fractured one, even after her marriage. 'I do perceive here a divided duty' (I.iii.180), she comments, and later adds,

> My heart's subdued
> Even to the very quality of my lord.
> I saw Othello's visage in his mind,
> And to his honours and his valiant parts
> Did I my soul and fortunes consecrate . . .

> (I.iii.250–4)

Subject to desire, Desdemona assimilates and adapts to the identity of her 'lord', which in turn depends on his incorporation of a mask adapted to the gaze of the Other. For, of course, Othello's own mental picture of his 'name' relies upon his identification with 'Dian's visage'. Desdemona introjects an already alienated self-identity as she imagines it to appear in her lover's mind, consecrating her 'soul', an illusive or allusive interiority, to an image or 'visage', which has itself been already subjected to the portraiture of the Other. In Shakespearean tragedy, feminine identity defines itself through the incorporation of a male façade, which in turn relies on the assimilation of a female masquerade. And, of course, as I have discussed in relation to Ophelia and Cordelia, the 'woman' in the Shakespearean theatre is already a male actor in disguise.[16]

The framing of Desdemona's 'guilt', in the dialogue between Othello and Iago, will repeat exactly the strategy followed in the courtship: that of a narrative which entraps its interlocutor through the juxtaposition of silence and loquacity, veiling and disclosure. Iago functions always as the holder – and partial or gradual discloser – of secrets. Roderigo's 'Tush, never tell me!', the first line of the play, constitutes his companion immediately in this role, which Iago will later claim explicitly: asked by Brabanzio 'What profane wretch art thou?', Iago replies 'I am one, sir, that comes to tell you . . .' (I.i.116–17).

In his scenes with Othello, Iago deploys this role constantly, hinting at information that he must withhold:

> IAGO. Ha! I like not that.
> OTHELLO. What dost thou say?
> IAGO. Nothing, my lord. Or if, I know not what.
> (III.iii.33–5)

By the tactical interpolation of silences pregnant with potential meaning, Iago provokes Othello's imagination, implanting a suspicion before expressing any overt accusation.[17] Along with this fraudulent discretion, Iago makes use of a verbal mimicry, echoing Othello's questions, reflecting his doubts back to him and thereby reinforcing them:

> OTHELLO. Is he not honest?
> IAGO. Honest, my lord?
> OTHELLO. Honest? Ay, honest.
> IAGO. My lord, for aught I know.

OTHELLO. What dost thou think?
IAGO. Think, my lord?
OTHELLO. 'Think, my lord?' By heaven, thou echo'st me
As if there were some monster in thy thought
Too hideous to be shown! Thou dost mean something.
I heard thee say even now thou liked'st not that,
When Cassio left my wife. What didst not like?
And when I told thee he was of my counsel
In my whole course of wooing, thou cried'st 'Indeed?'
And didst contract and purse thy brow together
As if thou then hadst shut up in thy brain
Some horrible conceit. If thou dost love me,
Show me thy thought

(III.iii.105–20)

Othello begs Iago to 'show' his thought, to display the secret, to unveil the truth.[18] The secret, indeed, becomes 'true' only in so far as the veil obscuring it constitutes it as such. Iago's ostensible unwillingness to disclose what he knows predetermines Othello's belief in it, marking a return to the decisive function of the mask with its inferred gaze behind. The doubt about how to interpret Cassio's apparent 'honesty' also participates in this return:

IAGO. Men should be what they seem,
Or those that be not, would they might seem none.
OTHELLO. Certain, men should be what they seem.
IAGO. Why then, I think Cassio's an honest man.
OTHELLO. Nay, yet there's more in this.
I prithee speak to me as to thy thinkings...

(III.iii.131–6)

And just as Desdemona proved a greedy listener to his own narratives, Othello's appetite for verbal confirmation of his suspicion will grow with what it feeds on.

The speed of this process is also compatible with the psychoanalytic theory of mimicry discussed so far. Critics have often been troubled by the compression of time in the play, and the rapidity of Othello's so-called 'descent' from nobility through suspicion into murderous jealousy, occurring within 'some thirty-three hours', according to Ridley (1958, lxviii).[19] Certainly, Shakespeare does compress the time scheme of his source, a tale from Cinzio's *Gli*

Ecatommiti. According to my reading of the play, however, the swiftness of Othello's involvement in Iago's plot simply participates in a temporal elision typical of the scopic drive. The act of mimicry sees the subject compress linear time in order to project itself forward as an image in the eye of the Other, pressing to inscribe itself in the picture. As Lacan puts it,

> The moment of seeing can intervene here only as a suture, a conjunction of the imaginary and the symbolic, and it is taken up again in a dialectic, that sort of temporal process that is called haste, thrust, forward movement, which is concluded in the *fascinum*. (1979, 118)

A suture takes place between the subject's imaginary location within the optical field, the place from which it deludes itself that it has clear sight, and the 'terminal moment' of the gaze, the *fascinum*, in which the subject is arrested as an element pictured by the gaze in the symbolic. Mimicry occurs at the juncture of these two moments: the subject is always already preceded by its image, seen in the eyes of the Other. This conflation or reversal of linear temporality, which recurs in Lacan's emphasis on repetition, deferred action, the return of the repressed, and retrospective construction, also features in Derrida's consideration of classical mimesis: 'The difficulty lies in conceiving that what is imitated could be still to come with respect to what imitates, that the image can precede the model, that the double can come before the simple' (Derrida 1981, 190).

Othello hastens to draw himself within the frame of Iago's picture, as the two construct, through their dialogue, various imaginary voyeuristic scenarios. At one point, the actors represent to the audience Iago's re-presentation to Othello of Cassio's dream representing his affair with Desdemona, another play of substitutions which can only find its 'origin' in the fantasy of a fantasy, a dream of Cassio's invented by Iago. This seductive progression leads Othello to visualise himself before the door of Desdemona's chamber, beyond which she is pictured in bed with Cassio:

IAGO. Would you, the supervisor, grossly gape on,
Behold her topped?
OTHELLO. Death and damnation! O!
IAGO. It were a tedious difficulty, I think,
To bring them to that prospect. Damn them then

If ever mortal eyes do see them bolster
More than their own! What then, how then?
What shall I say? Where's satisfaction?
It is impossible you should see this,
Were they as prime as goats, as hot as monkeys,
As salt as wolves in pride, and fools as gross
As ignorance made drunk. But yet I say,
If imputation, and strong circumstances
Which lead directly to the door of truth,
Will give you satisfaction, you might ha't.

                                        (III.iii.400–13)

Othello's imagination of the scene, as provoked by Iago's speech, still takes part in a simultaneous veiling and disclosure. He arrives at 'the door of truth', the last veil between him and the 'ocular proof' that will confirm his suspicion (III.iii.365). But of course, Iago's speech then glosses over any distinction between such 'truth' and its veils or 'strong circumstances'. Satisfaction gained from the latter replaces the former: the veil, the door, becomes the revelation. Concealment, and not disclosure, elicits and sustains scopic desire, as in Lacan's version of the fable of Zeuxis and Parrhasios, the two painters who held a competition to produce the most effective *trompe l'oeil*. Zeuxis' grapes were so deceptive that they even attracted the birds, but nevertheless his rival beat him by painting a veil 'so lifelike that Zeuxis, turning towards him said, *Well, now show us what you have painted behind it'*. Lacan describes this moment as 'A triumph of the gaze over the eye', because the veil represents the enslavement of the subject within the economy of the gaze, always wanting to see more than it does (1979, 103).

Even when seeming to present explicitly the naked 'facts' – 'to be naked with her friend in bed / An hour or more, not meaning any harm?' (IV.i.3–4) – Iago's provocations remain necessarily enveloped by the veil of an imagined gaze, a covering interpretation or fantasy. For psychoanalysis, nudity will often be portrayed in precisely this way, as a representation, a metaphor covering a further revelation:

> Is nudity purely and simply a natural phenomenon? The whole of psychoanalytic thought is designed to prove it isn't. The thing that is particularly exalting about it and significant in its own

right is that there is a beyond of nudity that nudity hides. (Lacan 1992, 227)[20]

Recalling Fanon's discussion of 'epidermalization', my reading of *Othello* finds once more that apparently profound features of identity – race, gender, sexuality – are turned inside-out, pre-empted by the superficial markers that represent them. Nothing could be more naked than skin itself, yet even Othello's face, or Desdemona's nudity, constitute a form of masquerade.

According to Lacan, what the voyeur therefore desires is not the naked object, but the gaze itself:

> The gaze is this object lost and suddenly refound in the conflagration of shame, by the introduction of the other. Up to that point, what is the subject trying to see? What he is trying to see, make no mistake, is the object as absence. What the voyeur is looking for and finds is merely a shadow, a shadow behind the curtain. (1979, 182)

This shadow represents the veil behind the veil, the endless succession of masks, endlessly exciting to the eye of the voyeur. So, when Othello overhears Iago in dialogue with Cassio, the revelation is necessarily screened off by that which enables it to be witnessed at all: the intervening wall, fence or curtain behind which Othello hides. On stage, the part of this mediating obstacle would best be played by some kind of lattice, through which Othello can catch only glimpses and hear only snatches.

This play of veil and disclosure comes to a focus most decisively, of course, on the handkerchief, which condenses all the associations which have emerged so far, evoking a narrativity symbolised by the web or weave, playing its part by knitting together the occult and the revelatory:

> There's magic in the web of it.
> A sibyl that had numbered in the world
> The sun to course two hundred compasses
> In her prophetic fury sewed the work.
> The worms were hallowed that did breed the silk,
> And it was dyed in mummy, which the skilful
> Conserved of maidens' hearts . . .

(III.iv.69–75)

Sibylline, interweaving revelation with a proverbial obscurity, the handkerchief is imbued with that feminine libido – 'maidens' hearts' – which psychoanalysis will also insistently associate with the masquerade. Even its design of strawberries hints at an ambivalence between honesty and deceit:

> In the Renaissance, strawberries signified virtue or goodness, but also hypocritical virtue as symbolised by the frequently occurring design and emblem of the strawberry plant with an adder hiding beneath its leaves . . . . Iago's description of the napkin as 'spotted' constitutes for Othello a new meaning to the handkerchief – the strawberries become signs of Desdemona's deceit. (Newman 1987, 156)

This ambivalent design hints toward another emblem of disguise, another morphological mimicry: Lady Macbeth's advice to 'look like the innocent flower, / But be the serpent under't' (*Macbeth* I.v.64–5)

Patricia Parker traces this play of disclosure and secrecy in *Othello* through a series of puns on 'suits'. Signifying both clothing and the attempt at verbal argument or persuasion, the recurrence of this word suggests 'a gap between descriptive or subordinate "circumstance" and substance or essence . . .' (Parker 1985, 71 n. 9). The Duke's description of Brabanzio's accusation against Othello as 'thin habits' first invokes the trope of verbal rhetoric as a cloth or veil (I.iii.108). Parker finds this metaphor

> repeated in Iago's 'this may help to thicken other proofs / That do demonstrate thinly' in the temptation scene [III.iii.435–6]. The figure of 'circumstances' as not the essence or substance but its clothing was conventional . . . (71 n. 9)[21]

My reading suggests that a transubstantiation takes place, or rather a desubstantiation, of 'essence' into 'circumstances', of truth into its clothing. More than just a 'gap' between the two, *Othello* stages the priority of circumstance in relation to substance, the determination of the latter by the former, as suggested by Iago's substitution of 'imputation, and strong circumstances' for the naked reality, of the 'door of truth' for the truth itself.

Discussing the implantation and elicitation of Othello's suspicions through the undulation of this textual weave, Parker also emphasises the partiality of the scopic drive, its reliance upon a complicity between blindness and sight to construct a vision:

> The link in French (as in several languages) between jealousy and 'jalousie' or lattice . . . may indeed be part of the subtle link, in *Othello*, between the emphasis on the eye, or on what Lacan calls the invidious desire to see, in the jealousy plot of the play and its exploitation of the language of 'close dilations' as only partial glimpses. (1985, 72 n. 15)

Following this suggestion, the rhetorical structure of the text might be envisaged as a lattice or fretwork of language which eroticises and reifies the fantasy scene it dis/covers, or as Iago calls it, a 'net / That shall enmesh them all' (II.iii.352–3). The chiaroscuro of Orson Welles' 1952 film of the play conveys precisely this effect. The protagonists – especially Desdemona – are recurrently crossed or barred by stripes of shadow and light, and Othello's face will often emerge from or merge into a surrounding darkness, emphasising the placement of such lines as 'Put out the light, and then put out the light' (V.ii.7) within the same tropic economy as the racial metaphors.[22] Like the spots on the handkerchief (III.iii.440), or the sheets which, 'lust-stained, shall with lust's blood be spotted' (V.i.37), the narrative web itself comes, in psychoanalytic terms, to represent the mottled camouflage adopted by the subject under the gaze of the Other, 'the primal stripe marking his being . . . with the grid of desire' (Lacan 1979, 76). In the final scene of the play these tropes recur in the repeated drawing of the curtain back and forth across the bed, and the ultimate disclosure of the details of Iago's plot in letters disinterred from the pockets of the dead Roderigo's clothes.

Emaskulation

An exploration of the transactions of mimicry in *Othello*, therefore, suggests that race and gender, and their respective signifiers, both participate in a dominating scopic topology, within which they are prone to displacement, one onto the other. Moreover, any masquerade performed by the subject in the gaze of the Other always presupposes – while problematising – the assumption of gender identity, in so far as Shakespearean tragedy will consistently associate the concept of masquerade itself with the feminine. The same tendencies, I suggest, can be traced within psychoanalysis itself.

For Freud, femininity subsists always in opposition to masculinity, with the latter repeatedly if tentatively established as the originary and normative term. However, Freud's own text renders this assertion highly questionable by stressing the lability of any binary signification of gender. Hence the conditional tone in the following passage from 'Three Essays on Sexuality':

> Indeed, if we were able to give a more definite connotation to the concepts of 'masculine' and 'feminine', it would even be possible to maintain that libido is invariably and necessarily of a masculine nature, whether it occurs in men or in women and irrespectively of whether its object is a man or a woman. (Freud 1986, 355)

The prodigality of Freud's footnotes always provides an index of how problematic, but also how integral, certain points in his argument will prove to be. The comments added to this passage in 1915 are typical in this respect: 'It is essential to understand clearly that the concepts of "masculine" and "feminine", whose meaning seems so unambiguous to ordinary people, are among the most confused that occur in science' (1986, 355 n. 1). In order to elucidate this 'confusion' more 'clearly', Freud goes on to distinguish 'at least three uses' of these concepts: the activity/passivity opposition, biological difference, and sociological difference.[23] Of these, Freud insists upon the first as 'the essential one and the most serviceable to psycho-analysis'. Characteristically, however, he complicates the issue further still, by suggesting that observation of the third category, sociological gender,

> shows that in human beings pure masculinity or femininity is not to be found either in a psychological or a biological sense. Every individual on the contrary displays a mixture of the character-traits belonging to his [sic] own and to the opposite sex ... (355 n. 1)

Following Freud, both Joan Riviere and Jacques Lacan will pursue the question of how these 'character-traits' belonging to each sex are found in both: that is, through a dual mimicry, the mutual assumption of the signifiers of sexual difference.

In 1929, Riviere introduced to psychoanalysis the term 'masquerade' in order to describe the female relationship to the libido. For Riviere, femininity always comes into being in a complex relationship to masculinity, negotiated through a play of mimicry and disguise. The woman adopts an apparent masculinity in order to assume power or to participate in intellectual (and other 'traditionally male') pursuits, but she alternates this with a mask of exaggerated femininity designed to dispel the anger or anxiety aroused in men by the initial imposture. Consequently the question arises of what might be considered the reality or essence of femininity, lying beneath these veils:

> Womanliness therefore could be assumed and worn as a mask, both to hide the possession of masculinity and to avert the reprisals expected if she was found to possess it – much as a thief will turn out his pockets and ask to be searched to prove that he has not the stolen goods. The reader may now ask how I define womanliness or where I draw the line between genuine womanliness and the 'masquerade'. My suggestion is not, however, that there is any such difference; whether radical or superficial, they are the same thing. (Riviere 1986, 38)

Behind the masquerade of womanliness, Riviere finds a (male) thief, who turns out his pockets in a kind of theatrical strip-search, a display of naked honesty, much as Iago inverts the lining of his coat or Roderigo yields up letters from his garments. In each case, the looking behind, the very gesture of removing a covering veil, constitutes in itself a further act of concealment.

Lacan, however, not only assimilates Riviere's suggestion of masquerade, but takes it a step further, by hinting that both femininity and masculinity are constructed in this way. 'It is no doubt through the mediation of masks that the masculine and the feminine meet in the most acute, most intense way' (Lacan 1979, 107):

> Carrying things as far as they will go, one might even say that the masculine ideal and the feminine ideal are represented in the psyche by something other than this activity/passivity opposition of which I spoke earlier. Strictly speaking, they spring from a term that I have not introduced, but of which one female psycho-analyst has pin-pointed the feminine sexual attitude – the term *masquerade*. (Lacan 1979, 193)

The activity/passivity opposition, 'the essential one' for Freud, proved to be as far as he could go with gender. But Lacan can carry things further still, can even take them 'as far as they will go', asserting that the masculine and feminine ideal 'spring from' the masquerade. Earlier in *The Four Fundamental Concepts* he uses the term 'travesty' to designate that mimetic function in which 'a certain sexual finality is intended' (Lacan 1979, 100). For Lacan the superficial transactions of mimicry provide the last word in the construction of gender. As I have shown so far, his treatment of the gaze consistently rejects any possible access to an essence – and therefore to either a masculine libido, or to the activity/passivity opposition – beyond the veil of representation.

In spite of this development, there also persists in Lacan's work a distinction between the masculine and the feminine manifestations of sexual mimicry, implied by his use of differential terms. For he applies the word 'masquerade' to the feminine version, and 'display' to the masculine.[24] This division itself, however, already indicates an asymmetry which has pervaded the entire psychoanalytic discourse on gender. 'Display', like the French '*parade*' which it translates, avoids the connotations of guile or counterfeit implicit in 'masquerade'. Anxieties about such fraudulence, therefore, insistently coalesce around the feminine side of the transaction. This is evidently the case for Shakespearean tragedy as well. Iago's comment that women are 'pictures out of door' supplies one example (II.i.112), and Othello's condemnation of Desdemona's distress as a 'well painted passion' (IV.i.259) another:

> Sir, she can turn and turn, and yet go on
> And turn again, and she can weep, sir, weep,
> And she's obedient, as you say, obedient,
> Very obedient

> (IV.i.255–8)

Othello sees obedience and repentance as two more misleading performances: the woman can turn over layer after layer of display, 'and yet go on'. Desdemona plainly becomes the focus for the play's uneasiness with the masquerade, just as Ophelia does in *Hamlet*, according to my reading of that play in Chapter 1.

Lacan's essay on the 'Signification of the Phallus' provides an important instance of the inheritance of this tendency by the psychoanalytic tradition:

it is in order to be the phallus, that is to say, the signifier of the desire of the Other, that the woman will reject an essential part of her femininity, notably all its attributes through masquerade. It is for what she is not that she expects to be desired as well as loved. (Lacan 1982, 84)

Conversely, however, I would suggest that the ubiquity of the mimetic strategy, which Lacan finds to be constitutive of the subject's position in the scopic drive, suggests inexorably that masculinity must also be constructed according to its assumption of a mask of identity or self-presence. The masculine seeks to fix its location within the symbolic order, however, by valorising and defining itself against the mendacious superficiality of the woman. Nevertheless the duplicity of this manoeuvre puts it in constant jeopardy of deconstruction, a risk which emerges at the end of Lacan's essay:

The fact that femininity takes refuge in the mask, because of the *Verdrängung* [repression] inherent to the phallic mark of desire, has the strange consequence that, in the human being, virile display itself appears as feminine. (Lacan 1982, 85)

At the climax of an essay which seems to reinstate the mark of a normative male libido, 'virile display' itself, the phallus, the apparition of masculine potency, becomes estranged from itself, begins to look feminine. As the pre-eminent signifier and the founding term of the patriarchal symbolic order, the phallus 'can only play its role as veiled': that is, by assuming the supposedly 'feminine' tactic of masquerade (Lacan 1982, 82).

My dual reading of *Othello* and psychoanalysis, therefore, suggests that the postulate of an essentialist libido or identity merely supplies another tactic, another mimetic strategy, in the dialectical negotiation of subjectivity. Derrida describes the specular logic of this uncanny theatrical duplicity:

We are faced then with mimicry imitating nothing; faced, so to speak, with a double that doubles no simple, a double that nothing anticipates, nothing at least that is not itself already double. There is no simple reference. It is in this that the mime's operation does allude, but alludes to nothing, alludes without breaking the mirror, without reaching beyond the looking-glass. . . . This speculum reflects no reality; it produces mere 'reality-effects'. For this double that often makes one think of Hoffmann . . . reality, indeed, is death. It will prove to be inaccessible, otherwise than by simulacrum, just like the dreamed-of *simplicity* of the supreme spasm of the hymen. In this speculum with no reality, in this mirror of a mirror, a difference or dyad does exist, since there are mimes and phantoms. But it is a difference without reference, or rather a reference without referent, without any first or last unit, a ghost that is the phantom of no flesh, wandering about without a past, without any death, birth, or presence. (1981, 206)

Doubling one another, the masculine and the feminine, the black and the white, the actor and the spectator, produce only a mimetic play of simulacra, denying the possibility of identifying an original term. As in *King Lear*, the uncanniness of the gaze – 'this double that often makes one think of Hoffmann' – arises from the spectre of a supplementary representation which rivals and replaces the referential presence of gender, race or identity.

Appropriately, Derrida's discussion of the mime leads him to the metaphor of the hymen. Again, the 'feminine' attribute of the veil – that which 'desire dreams of piercing, of bursting, in an act of violence that is (at the same time or somewhere between) love and murder' (Derrida 1981, 213) – offers a locus for the deconstruction of the masculine scopic relation exemplified by the stage. For ultimately, Derrida's text cannot find its way through the masquerade of sexuality, or that of the theatrical moment. In the drama upon which 'The Double Session' hinges, even the murder of his wife and his own suicide are mimed by Pierrot rather than acted 'realistically', so that the reference is ultimately to another reference and not to a referent. And in one of his throwaway lines, Pierrot admits to a particular mimetic identification not without relevance to my discussion: 'I'm too white to be aping Othello' (Derrida 1981, 204). Moreover in both *Othello* and the Pierrot mime, death occurs by suffocation, so that the veil remains ultimately in place.

For although the murder of Desdemona has many of the resonances of a rape, the play nevertheless emphasises that there can be no penetration of the veils which represent her sexuality. She dies from smothering, not stabbing; from an excessive covering over, rather than the opening of a wound. And when, in turn, Othello does actually stab himself, he in turn only discloses an empty gap between the masks he has worn, an aporia into which his identity (as actor) vanishes. In the act of stabbing he conflates his own role with that of the Turk who 'traduced the state' (V.ii.363). For Othello himself has also 'traduced' – which can mean translated or transgressed – 'the State', by moving between racial, social and political worlds, adopting the guise of Venetian culture. So even this final affirmation of loyalty confirms that Othello's own identity, sexual and racial, has been composed through a series of masquerades with which he cannot dispense. 'I am overdetermined from without: I am the slave not [of] the "idea" that others have of me but of my own appearance' (Fanon 1970, 82).

In this way, the anxieties about identity, projected onto the feminine, return upon the person of Othello, who represents himself in the end according to the same (dis)appearance of veils. Anxiety about the groundlessness of the masculine libido is thereby displaced onto, and represented by, the problem of race. This suggests an alternative interpretation of why the black man, like the woman, elicits so much sexual disquiet in white European culture.[25] Embodying the visual evidence of a mimicry implicit in the establishment of the libido, the woman and the black man both provoke the castration anxiety which psychoanalysis insistently finds to be integral to the formation of identity. According to my reading, however, this 'castration' appears as a form of blindness, the mark of an anxiety deriving from the operation of a restless mimicry, the lability of the signifiers of identity, and the consequent failure of any fixed location of the subject within the visual field. Hence Lacan equates castration in the field of vision with the function of the gaze:

> The gaze is presented to us only in the form of a strange contingency, symbolic of what we find on the horizon, as the thrust of our experience, namely, the lack that constitutes castration anxiety.
> The eye and the gaze – this is for us the split in which the drive is manifested at the level of the scopic field. (1979, 72–3)

The incommensurable gap between the eye, with its imaginary mastery of the visual field, and the gaze returning from the Other, from the 'horizon' of the symbolic order, constitutes a subjectivity fundamentally out of place, lacking, 'castrated'. Mimicry represents the subject's vain attempt to draw itself into the symbolic picture.

To trace a certain complicity within the scopic structure – as psychoanalysis understands it – between the visual construction and subjection of the woman and that of the racially other, is not to conflate the differences between the operations and effects of these oppressions in history or today. There can be no question of 'racism' and 'sexism' being simply 'the same thing'. My point is rather that a dominant visual order, through the strategic implantation of certain types of difference (male/female, white/black), and the stereotypical repression of alterity, constructs an oppositional subjection which can be filled with any available other, indeed must be filled in order for the binary order to sustain itself. The specificity of this other – racial, sexual or otherwise – is necessarily disavowed in order to promulgate the system.

Finally, if Derrida's mimetic fantasy of an eternal echolalia devoid of reference or origin seems too complete, too self-enclosed, a consideration of the audience will provide a destabilising third term, another other beneath whose gaze the play is always subject. And of course, that gaze has never actually been absent. Obviously, the narrative rehearsals of Othello and Desdemona's courtship, like the voyeuristic scenes in which Othello and Iago construct their monstrous fantasy of female guilt, all mimic the position of the spectator. Hearing of Desdemona's hunger for the unfolding of her lover's plot, imagining Othello approach in fantasy to the 'door of truth' or watching him observe and misinterpret the scene between Cassio, Iago and Bianca, the spectators are drawn into the scene/seen by viewing the representation of their own function on stage. The audience hear each of the protagonists in turn proclaim themselves as actors, foregrounding their artifice and their masquerade: Iago asking 'what's he then that says I play the villain . . .?' (II.iii.327), Othello asserting that 'Were it my cue to fight, I should have known it / Without a prompter' (I.ii.84–5), Desdemona insisting that 'I am not merry, but I do beguile / The thing I am by seeming otherwise' (II.i.125–6).

Each of the transactions described so far – between Othello and Desdemona, Othello and Iago – travesty the intersubjective relation between spectator and stage, relying as they do upon narrative tension, the alluring juxtaposition of display and absence, and the plausibility of costume and act. The effect of this self-referential play must be in turn to face the audience with the contingency of their own position. This occurs most powerfully at the end of the play as the spectators perceive Othello's rapid transition between multiple racial identities and roles, a wild adoption and discarding of various stock early modern foreigners, re- (or rather de-)constituting himself once more as the 'extravagant and wheeling stranger / Of here and everywhere' (I.i.138–9). He takes on in turn the guises

Of one not easily jealous but, being wrought,
Perplexed in the extreme; of one whose hand,
Like the base Indian, threw a pearl away
Richer than all his tribe; of one whose subdued eyes,
Albeit unusèd to the melting mood,
Drops tears as fast as the Arabian trees
Their medicinable gum. Set you down this,
And say besides that in Aleppo once,
Where a malignant and a turbaned Turk
Beat a Venetian and traduced the state,
I took by th' throat the circumcisèd dog
And smote him thus.
He stabs himself

(V.ii.354–65)

The 'one' that begins the speech divides and subdivides according to the alien locations in which the passage places him. One after another, his identities are 'being wrought' – that is, produced – as Indian (or perhaps, since a textual disagreement proliferates the possibilities still further, as 'Iudean', or Jew), as Arab, Turk and Venetian. Othello's final masquerade paints him, as this chapter began by envisaging, many different shades. He dies dyeing his clothes with his own blood, mottled by the stains of racial difference. The audience will be left with this violent disintegration, sharply reminiscent of Frantz Fanon's description of the effect of the white gaze upon himself as a black man:

the occasion arose when I had to meet the white man's eyes. An unfamiliar weight burdened me. The real world challenged my claims. In the white world the man of colour encounters difficulties in the development of his bodily schema. Consciousness of the body is solely a negating activity. It is a third-person consciousness.... Below the corporeal schema I had sketched a historico-racial schema. The elements that I used had been provided for me... by the other, the white man, who had woven me out of a thousand details, anecdotes, stories. I thought that what I had in hand was to construct a physiological self, to balance space, to localise sensations, and here I was called on for more.

'Look, a Negro!'... assailed at various points, the corporeal schema crumbled, its place taken by a racial epidermal schema. . . .

On that day, completely dislocated, unable to be abroad with the other, the white man, who unmercifully imprisoned me, I took myself far off from my own presence, far indeed, and made myself into an object. What else could it be for me but an amputation, an excision, a haemorrhage that spattered my whole body with black blood? (1970, 78–9)

4

Troilus and Cressida: Space Wars

Prologue: the author's drift

'I'll interrupt his reading.' In the middle of *Troilus and Cressida*, Ulysses wanders with studied nonchalance, book in hand, in front of Achilles' tent, pretending to ignore him and hoping thereby to shame him into joining battle against Troy. As he passes, Achilles calls out to him: 'What are you reading?' Ulysses answers that

> A strange fellow here
> Writes me that man, how dearly ever parted,
> How much in having, or without or in,
> Cannot make boast to have that which he hath,
> Nor feels not what he owes, but by reflection –
> As when his virtues, shining upon others,
> Heat them, and they retort that heat again
> To the first givers

> (III.iii.87–97)

Agonising over the identity of Ulysses's 'strange fellow', critics have assembled a wide range of possible authors from classical, medieval and early modern texts. The *Oxford Shakespeare* editor suggests Plato, Davies, Cicero and Montaigne (Muir 1982, 126). The *Arden* adds Erasmus, Persius, the parable of the talents from the Gospels, and, for good measure, Shakespeare himself, offering the first 17 sonnets as examples of prior formulations of the conceits employed in Ulysses' 'reading' (Palmer 1982, 210). It is particularly tempting to embrace this last suggestion, and to envisage the playwright staging the pre-emptive reading of his own verses by Homer's, and Chaucer's, Trojan war heroes.

Dismissing all other speculations, however, any reader familiar with recent psychoanalytic theory can now conclusively identify Ulysses' book as Jacques Lacan's *Four Fundamental Concepts of Psychoanalysis*, in the English translation by Alan Sheridan. In fact, Achilles' reply makes it evident that they are discussing, specifically, the four chapters entitled 'Of the Gaze as *Objet Petit a*' (Lacan 1979, 67–119):

> This is not strange, Ulysses.
> The beauty that is borne here in the face
> The bearer knows not, but commends itself
> To others' eyes. Nor doth the eye itself,
> That most pure spirit of sense, behold itself,
> Not going from itself; but eye to eye opposed
> Salutes each other with each other's form.
> For speculation turns not to itself
> Till it hath travelled and is mirrored there
> Where it may see itself. This is not strange at all
>
> (III.iii.97–106)

The passage duplicates, with startling clarity, Lacan's description of the structure of the scopic drive, split between the eye of the subject and the gaze from the Other, mediated by the ego's imaginary mirror identification with its ideal image. The two Greeks are evidently well acquainted with Lacan's version of psychoanalysis as well as his idiosyncratic style since, like most of his readers, they 'do not strain at the position – / It is familiar – but at the author's drift . . .' (III.iii.107–8).

This scenario, therefore, stages nothing other than the double project of my own text: both the reading of psychoanalysis by the early modern literary text, and its more usual converse, the reading of Shakespeare according to psychoanalytic theory. But in doing so, it questions the practices of a critical mode in which the psychoanalytic 'position' has become too 'familiar' and comfortable; in which the 'author's drift' – the movement of the signifier, the textuality of the relation between Shakespearean play, Lacanian seminar, and Freudian article – is either disregarded or homogenised into psychoanalytic 'truth'.[1]

Troilus and Cressida enjoys – or suffers from – an exemplary relationship with both poststructuralist and psychoanalytic critical practice. Despite its previous unpopularity – it was seldom if ever staged in Shakespeare's time, and subsequently unperformed for nearly three hundred years – recent critics and producers have privileged the play, frequently employing it as a paradigm for modernist and postmodernist interpretations of subjectivity, politics and language.[2] According to Jan Kott, for instance, '*Troilus and Cressida* is from the outset a modern play' in which Cressida features as 'a teen-age girl of the mid-twentieth century' (1964, 65–6). More recently, the play has become a focus for numerous poststructuralist, psycho-analytic, deconstructive and cultural materialist appropriations of Shakespeare, including readings by Elizabeth Freund (1985), René Girard (1985), Malcolm Evans (1986, 139–40), Joel Fineman (1986, 22, 23), Carol Cook (1986), John Kopper (1988), William O. Scott (1988), Jonathan Dollimore (1989, 41) and Linda Charnes (1993).

All these critics, furthermore, emphasise the same three moments in the play: first, the above discussion between Ulysses and Achilles concerning the specular structure of vision; second, the oath taken by Troilus, Cressida and Pandarus – 'Let all constant men be Troiluses, all false women Cressids, and all brokers-between panders' (III.ii.198–200) – in which they guarantee their faithfulness to each other by citing the pre-existing proverbial status of their names; and finally, Troilus's speech about 'bifold authority' (V.ii.140–63), in the context of a multiple metatheatrical perspective: the audience watching Thersites watching Troilus watching Cressida. Moreover, these selected scenes are prone to receive the same treatment by all these critics, since – for obvious reasons – each provides a perfect opportunity to rehearse certain favourite preoccupations of recent psychoanalytic theory. These could be paraphrased, respectively, as the subject's relation to the gaze and the Lacanian mirror stage; its location within the symbolic order, represented by its naming within a language that precedes it; and the fragmentation and dispersal of its psyche into a series of conflicting perceptual identifications.

Such summary treatment obviously does violence, in various ways, to a sophisticated and complex series of theoretical texts. But the fact that in recent criticism, this reduction of 'poststructuralist theory' to a set of formulae, an easily recognisable shorthand, is now both possible and common, in itself signals a danger that besets such modes of reading wherever they occur.

My own approach to Shakespearean tragedy in the first three chapters of this volume has also, of course, been consistently con-cerned with the topics outlined above. Obviously, therefore, I would seek neither to invalidate nor to dismiss out of hand the readings derived from such an emphasis. But I do wish to explore the possibility that such critical appropriations of psychoanalysis, when divorced from an accompanying theorisation of the effects of their own position, risk presupposing that Freud and Lacan provide a series of precepts which may be fruitfully and unquestioningly 'applied' to the Renaissance text, and that in exchange the Shakespearean play offers a series of 'illustrations' of psychoanalytic theories of subjectivity.[3] For this reason, I have attempted to problematise, in the preceding chapters, the critical as well as the dramatic texts with which I have been concerned. Gender, mimicry, theatricality, the uncanny and the gaze have each in turn provided points from which the theoretical viewpoint that articulates them must be scrutinised just as rigorously as *Hamlet*, *King Lear* or *Othello*. None the less, the nature of the historical and textual relation between Shakespeare and psychoanalysis concerning the above topics has not yet been specifically addressed.

Reading the many critical interpretations of *Troilus and Cressida* mentioned above, the question arises whether the imposition upon the play of a postmodern sensibility might be taking place too comfortably, and whether the Renaissance text and psychoanalysis have not become slightly over familiar with each other.[4] Whenever the relation between Shakespeare and psychoanalysis seems, as Ulysses finds it in my scenario, no longer 'strange at all', it is necessary to re-emphasise the textual and historical materiality of psychoanalytic theory, its constitution as a skein of derivations, attributions, references, allusions and interpretations. For these reasons, the second half of this study will attempt to relocate its discussions of the gaze – Lacanian, Freudian or Shakespearean – more explicitly within the historical and textual milieux appropriate to them. This chapter will begin that process by scrutinising the cycle of derivation and influence linking the Lacanian scopic drive to the Freudian, which will in turn throw frequent glances back towards the Shakespearean text. For *Troilus and Cressida* itself dramatises precisely the need to take into account such intertextual relations, which it will characterise as voracious, infectious and antagonistic.

Framed to the life

Before anything else, then, '*Enter the Prologue armed*', to announce the following: 'In Troy there lies the scene.' Summarising the rape of Helen and the first seven years of the war in less than 20 lines, the Prologue brings its audience to a theatrical present tense with anticipation:

> Now expectation, tickling skittish spirits
> On one and other side, Trojan and Greek,
> Sets all on hazard. And hither am I come,
> A Prologue armed – but not in confidence
> Of author's pen or actor's voice, but suited
> In like conditions as our argument –
> To tell you, fair beholders, that our play
> Leaps o'er the vaunt and firstlings of those broils,
> Beginning in the middle, starting thence away
> To what may be digested in a play.
> Like or find fault; do as your pleasures are;
> Now, good or bad, 'tis but the chance of war.

$$(1–31)$$

Any prologue provides a paradoxical frame for what follows. Because *Troilus and Cressida* incorporates the most formidable of sources, including Homer (perhaps directly, but also through Chapman), Ovid, Chaucer, Caxton and Lydgate, it appears more than usually conscious of its location within a powerful and extensive textual matrix (Palmer 1982, 22–38). Although enabling it to begin *in medias res*, assuming the audience to have a thorough knowledge of 'the vaunt and firstlings of these broils', this very familiarity of the story nevertheless poses a threat to the play. Like the situation it narrates, any treatment of the Trojan War immediately encounters the prior 'expectation' of its audience, which 'sets all on hazard'. Therefore the play comes 'armed', in the wary anticipation of conflict, 'not in confidence / Of author's pen or actor's voice, but suited / In like condition as our argument'. The text's relationship with the 'beholders', and thereby with the literary field into which it ventures, appears from the start as one of antagonism and menace, inasmuch as the audience's judgement of the play will participate in 'the chance of war'. Furthermore, the process of re-presenting received material features for playwright, audience and players alike as the question of 'what may be digested in a play'. This phrase, as the first a great many gastronomic tropes, associates the intertextual relationship in advance with a certain degree of voracity as well.[5]

In its concern with the dramatic assimilation of sources, and the reception in turn of the play by its audience, the Prologue therefore manifests the troubling permeability of the textual 'frame', that supplementary surround which – both extraneous and intrinsic to the text it seeks to contain – introduces that text to, orients it towards, and locates it within, its context(s). Structures of this sort have been discussed by Derrida in relation to the Kantian 'parergon', the 'outside-the-work', of which the typical instances are the frames of paintings, the garments on statues, and the columns outside buildings. As that which separates the play from, and yet involves it with, both its audience and its sources, the Prologue here constitutes just such a parergon, problematising the relationship between the 'outside' of the text (audience, sources, authorship, production) and its 'inside' (content, action, character, rhetoric), and symptomatic of the corruption of any boundary between them.

> A parergon comes against, beside, and in addition to the *ergon*, the work ... but it does not fall to one side, it touches and cooperates within the operation, from a certain outside. Neither simply outside nor simply inside. Like an accessory that one is obliged to welcome on the border, on board. (Derrida 1987c, 54)

Is the Prologue a character in the play or the mouthpiece of its author? Is it part of the action or apart from it? Narrative or commentary? Should it be seen as essential to the play or not? As text or not? 'Art' or not?

Appropriately, the Prologue comes 'not in confidence' of the attributes of any of these, 'author's pen or actor's voice'. It does however come 'suited / In like condition as our argument', 'armed' in a form that suggests participation in the play's militaristic interior or content. However, just as the clothing on statues provides Kant with a prime example of the parergon, the Prologue's armour must be considered ambivalent as a signifier of either its involvement in the action or its indispensability to the work. Standing outside the play, the Prologue claims to plunge into it immediately: the narrative 'leaps o'er the vaunt ... Beginning in the middle'. Both the inflated rhetoric of the Prologue and its military garb seem to contribute to this.

According to Derrida, by outlining the limits – both internal and external – of the work, framing devices partake of a critical lack at its centre:

What constitutes them as *parerga* is not simply their exteriority as a surplus, it is the internal structural link which rivets them to the lack in the interior of the *ergon*. And this lack would be constitutive of the very unity of the *ergon*. Without this lack, the *ergon* would have no need of a *parergon*. The *ergon's* lack is the lack of a *parergon*, of the garment or the column which nevertheless remains exterior to it. (1987c, 59–60)

The apparel of the Prologue in *Troilus and Cressida* creates a structural complicity of this sort, between an internal lack, constitutive of the work, and the undefinability of its border. The armour of the Prologue, like that of the characters, constructs for the play a chivalric and classical façade, but simultaneously betrays the hollowness of those conventions. Participating in the kind of 'characterisation' discussed in the preceding chapter, *Troilus and Cressida* parades its personae and plots before the audience in a way that foregrounds external appearance and denies the possibility of any interior consistency or reality.

This operation of armour as parergon becomes evident if considered in relation to a character from the midst of the play's climactic skirmishes, albeit one who has no 'character', whose function seems characteristically emblematic, the 'one in sumptuous armour' pursued by Hector to his death during the battle scenes. It would be appropriate if, in performance, this was recognisably the same actor who played the Prologue, wearing the same costume. Described as a 'Most putrefièd core, so fair without' (5.9.1), this enigmatic figure embodies the link between internal lack and parergonal excess of which Derrida speaks. Led astray by the mere adornment of sumptuous armour, Hector ceases to represent the epitome of heroic integrity, becoming instead the vacuous emblem of a lethal avarice. He doffs his own armour in order to plunder that of his victim, and is promptly killed in a thoroughly unchivalrous manner by Achilles and his Myrmidons. The Prologue's attire, therefore, prefigures the emptiness or fragmentation of the classical and chivalric ideals represented by the 'heroes' of the play: the avarice of Hector, the pride and treachery of Achilles, the envy and stupidity of Ajax, the devious cynicism of Ulysses. Consequently, it is not surprising that the question of genre has preoccupied critics approaching the play. In so far as genre can be thought of as the relationship between a given text and a series of literary conventions which precede it, or a set of audience expectations confronting it, the Prologue exemplifies the hollowness which this play finds in the elaborate themes and forms essential to its generic predecessors. *Troilus and Cressida* lacks the honour associated with the chivalric or epic tragedy, the integrity demanded by the romance, and the final resolution which makes the comedy.

The play seems to be plagued by a succession of such frames, which are repeatedly replaced, and thus appear, like Derrida's parerga, both detachable and vital. Eighty years on, Dryden's renovation substitutes a new prologue, 'Spoken by Mr Betterton, Representing the Ghost of Shakespear' (Dryden 1984, 13: 249). Aware, like Shakespeare, of the prestige of his textual predecessors, Dryden invokes, incorporates and executes them in a single passage, summoning the author of the source text to champion his own version – whether Shakespeare's or Dryden's becomes blurred in the process – in a combat implied by mention of 'Homers angry ghost' (250). The complex relationships between author, sources, text and audience retain a significantly aggressive tenor, which Dryden emphasises – by means of an appropriately involuted allusion – when he adds yet another frame in the form of a preface: 'I will conclude my reflexions on [Shakespeare's play] with a passage of Longinus [*On the Sublime*], concerning Plato's imitation of Homer':

> We ought not to regard a good imitation as a theft; but as a beautifull Idea of him who undertakes to imitate, by forming himself on the invention and the work of another man; for he enters into the lists like a new wrestler, to dispute the prize with the former Champion. This sort of emulation, says Hesiod, is honourable . . . when we combat for Victory with a Hero, and are not without glory even in our overthrow. (1984, 13: 228)

This antagonism, endemic to any mimetic relation within the visual field, will prove to be of primary relevance to my discussion of the relationship between texts.

Meanwhile, the frames proliferate further still. The Quarto and Folio versions of Shakespeare's play were both printed with a prefatory 'Epistle' of unknown authorship, which some critics have identified as the descendant of an older prologue (Taylor 1982b, 119). The writer witnesses to the excellence of 'this author's comedies, that are so framed to the life, that they serve for the most common commentaries of all the actions of our lives' (Muir 1982, 193). Again, the frame constitutes an ambivalent relation between play, audience and readers. 'Framing' their lives, taking place as a commentary on their society, the play is in turn framed by their lives, since these provide the context in which the comedy may be seen as relevant, well received, life-like.

As a text, then, as well as a performance, the play seems once again threatened by constant pre-emption, and repeated violence. The Epistle warns of an impending 'scramble' to acquire such 'comedies', and by imagining this sudden demand as a 'new English Inquisition' it also compares the reception of the text to torture, and the process of reading as the sadistic extraction of a confession (194). In its abuse of certain 'dull and heavy-witted worldlings', moreover, the Epistle itself also appears notably belligerent. And in addressing the play's 'eternal readers' rather than its 'beholders', it claims to introduce 'a new play, never staled with the stage, never clapper-clawed with the palms of the vulgar' (193). While 'clapper-clawed' in this context presumably refers to applause, the phrase more usually signifies thrashing or beating, echoing Thersites' description of the Greeks and Trojans 'clapper-clawing one another' (V.iv.1). The repetition of the word in the Epistle thereby equates the action within the play with the reactions of the audience, who respond with aggressivity to the representation of aggressivity.

As the preceding chapters have suggested, this supposed power of the stage to elicit emulation in its audience is far from unique to this play. The Puritan anti-theatrical pamphleteers of Shakespeare's time repeatedly compared the appeal of plays with contagion. In his pamphlet of 1580 Anthony Munday calls them 'filthie infections' and a 'common plague' (Munday 1972, 54, 73). In *Troilus and Cressida* such tropes of disease are also frequent, and are also associated with the contagious power of imitation, so that the parodic impersonation by Achilles and Patroclus of the Greek generals inspires an epidemic of mimetic insubordination in the camp: 'in the imitation of these twain / . . . many are infect' (I.iii.185–7). This conventional metaphor was prompted by the common belief that playhouses facilitated the spread of bubonic plague, as Thomas White concludes in his *Sermon preached at Pawles Crosse on Sunday the thirde of November 1577 in the time of the Plague*:

> But I vnderstande they [public plays] are nowe forbidden bycause of the plague. I like the pollicye well if it holde still, for a disease is but bodged or patched vp that is not cured in the cause, and the cause of plagues is sinne, if you looke to it well: and the cause of sinne are playes: therefore the cause of plagues are playes. (Chambers 1974, 4: 197)

Stephen Gosson, in fact, considered plays a greater pestilence than the plague itself (1974, 156–7), while some pamphleteers were more explicit still in drawing a connection that seems less like an analogy and more like a diagnosis. *This World's Folly* (1615) describes players, 'whose garbe is the Plague-sore of Iudgement, and Common-sewer of Obscaenities . . .':

> who are faine to produce blinde *Impudence*, to personate himselfe vpon their stage, behung with chaynes of Garlicke, as an Antidote against their own infectious breaths, lest it should kill their Oyster-crying Audience. (Chambers 1974, 4: 254)

The Epistle prefacing the Quarto *Troilus and Cressida* similarly describes the effect of a play's public reception as 'being sullied with the smoky breath of the multitude' (Muir 1982, 194). The contagion of theatre goes both ways, passing from player to beholder and returning from audience to stage, as it breaks down the dramatic frame constitutive of the relationship between the play and the circumstances of its reception. The frame shows up as a disease, an ill fit between text and context.

The Epilogue spoken by Pandarus, as the final frame of *Troilus and Cressida*, has again proven semi-detachable, and again manifests most clearly the contaminating borders of the work.[6] Towards the end of the play the multitude of tropes associated with plague, venereal disease and pestilence infect Pandarus, who already operates idiomatically as the figure of whatever one lover passes on to another – 'let all pitiful goers-between be called to the world's end after my name: call them all panders' (III.ii.196–8). Troilus complains at one point, 'O gods, how you do plague me! / I cannot come to Cressid but by Pandar . . .' (I.i.94–5), and the go-between himself will complain later in the play of 'a whoreson rascally phthisic. . . . I have a rheum in mine eyes too, and such an ache in my bones . . .' (V.iii.104–8). Both symptoms are associated with venereal disease, and recall Thersites' references to syphilis as the 'Neapolitan bone-ache' (II.iii.18, V.i.17–21). As representative and 'goer-between' for the affair between Troilus and Cressida, Pandarus becomes diseased from the moment the 'truth' of that relationship is thrown into doubt.[7] And when he speaks the epilogue, the role played by Pandarus becomes further symptomatic of the infectious relationship between the audience and stage, and therefore participates in the ambivalent operation of the parergon.

Caught for a moment in this uneasy space between character and epilogue, Cressida's uncle wanders inappropriately onto the battle-field after Hector's death and Troilus' final speech, like the love plot invading the fighting scenes, or the military politics of the play contaminating the romance. Troilus exits with a curse, leaving the stage to Pandarus, who now turns towards the audience, perhaps descending from the stage into the pit and walking among the nearest spectators, touching them, embodying the contagious unconstraint of the frame as he speaks his epilogue.[8] This is given in the Oxford *Complete Works* as an 'additional passage', after the end of the play 'proper' (Wells and Taylor 1988, 748):

> Good traders in the flesh, set this in your painted cloths:
> As many as be here of Pandar's hall,
> Your eyes, half out, weep out at Pandar's fall.
> Or if you cannot weep, yet give some groans,
> Though not for me, yet for your aching bones.
> Brethren and sisters of the hold-door trade,
> Some two months hence my will shall here be made.
> It should be now, but that my fear is this:
> Some gallèd goose of Winchester would hiss.
> Till then I'll sweat and seek about for eases,
> And at that time bequeath you my diseases.

Pandarus transforms from character into parergon, and the text in turn determines, instead of being determined by, its context, so that the theatre becomes a brothel or 'Pandar's hall'. Now the spectators occupy the appropriately liminal position of prostitutes in open doorways, 'brethren and sisters of the hold-door trade', constituted as commodities and objects of the gaze rather than consumers and viewing subjects. As Pandarus 'sweats' and 'seeks about' among the audience, they have a vivid tactile, auditory and visual experience of being bequeathed his diseases. With their eyes 'half out', they already display the partial blindness symptomatic of infection by Pandarus' venereal disease; symptomatic also, as discussed in earlier chapters, of the spectator's subjection to the gaze. The tragedy predetermines their contamination by it: for even if they will not weep, and instead express their displeasure with groans or hisses, these are also taken as symptoms of contagion, 'Winchester goose' being a slang term for both a prostitute and a sore from venereal infection because, according to the Arden editor, 'The brothels of

Southwark stood on land under the jurisdiction of the bishops of Winchester' (Palmer 1982, 303). William Prynne will later make the same connection between the actor's role as pander, and the close geographical relation between playhouses and sources of venereal infection: 'our Theaters if they are not Bawdy-houses (as they may easily be, since many Players, if reports be true, are common Panders), yet they are Cosin-germanes, at leastwise neighbours to them' (Bentley 1968, 6: 49–50).

What infectiously itself affects

In short, *Troilus and Cressida* stages the infectious, incorporative and aggressive relationship between texts, between author and source, and between player and spectator. For this reason alone, any critical commentary which seeks to frame this text with its own interpretation should be more than usually wary. Yet the psycho-analytic reading ought to be even more sensitive to this tendency towards the corruption of borders between criticism and its object – between analytic 'truth' and literary 'example' – in so far as the texts of psychoanalysis are themselves characterised by the same instability.[9] The texts of Lacan's seminars are shot through with the same aggressive incorporations or exclusions that I have found to characterise the intertextual relationships in *Troilus and Cressida*. 'The Meaning of the Return to Freud', the second section of which is entitled 'The Adversary', is no exception.

In this paper, Lacan directs his antagonism towards American psychologists, whom he accuses of departing from the guidelines laid down in the Freudian text. They have given in to the temptation, as analysts, 'to reduce one's function to one's difference' from the analysand, thereby employing 'the reactionary principle operant in the duality of the sick and the healer, the opposition between someone who knows and someone who does not'. Describing this as the 'most corrupting of comforts', Lacan attacks the complacency of any misleadingly secure discrimination between therapist and subject (1977b, 115–16). In contrast, obedient to (the Lacanian reading of) Freud's text, the practitioners of the 'return' must remain aware of the perilous instability and corruptibility of the boundary between the analysis and its 'object'.

Lacan goes on to describe this insecurity in terms already familiar from my discussion of the frame: he compares it with infection. He does so by means of a famous and apocryphal quotation from

Freud, whom he thereby summons to champion the Lacanian 're-turn' against its American opponents.

> Thus Freud's words to Jung – I have it from Jung's own mouth – when, on an invitation from Clark University, they arrived in New York harbour and caught their first glimpse of the famous statue illuminating the universe, 'They don't realize we're bringing them the plague'... (1977b, 116)

Lacan quotes Jung quoting Freud, an unusual digression for the return to (of, from) Freud given Jung's genealogical status as wayward son, but one which none the less exemplifies the voracious and infectious transmission of the psychoanalytic text. Lacan has Freud's words from Jung's mouth, the place from which a disease might be caught, or into which food is ingested. The quotation itself, moreover, is not in fact substantiated anywhere else.[10] Does Lacan then actually put his own words into Freud's mouth (via Jung), or does he simply infect Freud's words with his own tendentious interpretation? Either way, by incorporating into his argument a representation of psychoanalysis as the plague, Lacan places the analyst and analysand, 'the sick and the healer', in a contagious relationship which disintegrates the secure 'difference' between them (allegedly) asserted by American psychology. Psychoanalysis, then, as Thersites might put it, constitutes a 'dry serpigo on the subject' (II.iii.73). Analysis infects its subject, by which it is in turn contaminated.

This reversal or displacement of opposed positions – of subject and object, reading and text, or spectator and spectacle – has of course been characteristic of the various theatrical transactions I have discussed in relation to *Hamlet, King Lear* and *Othello*. The same structure, of a mutually reactive feedback, also features in *Troilus and Cressida* on more than one occasion. For example, when Troilus remarks that 'Helen must needs be fair, / When with your blood you daily paint her thus', he describes an involuted trajectory of desire, according to which every action of the Trojan War retroactively constitutes, as its own origin or cause, Helen's desirability (I.i.90–1). In the meeting of the Trojan Council, Hector offers a similar assessment, commenting that 'the will dotes that is in-clinable / To what infectiously itself affects / Without some image of th'affected merit' (II.ii.57–9). This formulation makes the source of the 'infection' indistinguishable from what it affects, so that the will, inclining to its object, attributes to it a value not inherent, but rather deriving from the desire it provokes. But it is Agamemnon who most closely paraphrases Lacan when he remarks of Ajax that 'He will be the physician that should be the patient' (II.iii.210–11).

The many images of plague and venereal disease in the play are given dramatic form most clearly during a number of parallel scenes in which one character is 'passed around', like an infection, among a group of others. Thersites, for example, a 'crusty botch of nature', passes from Ajax to Achilles (V.i.5). During Hector's meeting with the Greek generals, he is also circulated between the various members of the group (IV.vii). This itself provides a powerful visual echo of a scene preceding it, in which each of the Greeks in turn extracts a kiss from Cressida.

Just as Lacan contracts Freud's words – 'the plague' – from Jung's mouth, each of the Greeks takes the kiss of his predecessor from Cressida. Cressida thereby figures, like Pandarus, as an embodiment of infection, and the medieval tradition that she died of leprosy seems implicit here as in other parts of the play. Achilles, kissing her after Nestor, remarks 'I'll take that winter from your lips, fair lady' (IV.vi.25), which has been taken as an allusion to the transmission of disease through oral contact (Palmer 1982, 245). The scene stages the establishment of identity as itself occurring through a contagious intersubjective identification and displacement, so that Patroclus 'contracts' Paris's role, intercepting the kiss meant for Menelaus, as though Cressida were Helen. In his reluctance to join in this game, Ulysses confirms the representation of Cressida as symptom of a promiscuous infection, and he makes this a metaphor for the relationship of texts to one another, or that of the reader or spectator to a text or performance:

> ULYSSES.   Fie, fie upon her!
> There's language in her eye, her cheek, her lip;
> Nay, her foot speaks. Her wanton spirits look out
> At every joint and motive of her body.
> O these encounterers so glib of tongue,
> That give accosting welcome ere it comes,
> And wide unclasp the tables of their thoughts
> To every ticklish reader, set them down
> For sluttish spoils of opportunity
> And daughters of the game
>
> (IV.vi.55–64)

The body of Cressida, as a set of heterogeneous signifiers only too ready to infect and affect the reader, pulls apart like a text separating into its various interpretations or its constituent sources. Cressida's (masculine) 'reader' finds himself both encountered and encountering, welcomed and welcoming, accosted and accosting. Both 'tickling' and 'ticklish' – the two alternatives given in the Quarto and Folio texts (Muir 1984, 153) – the reader actively participates in an interpretive relation that incites and arouses the text, but finds himself prone to the same stimulation. Cressida's readers are men, moreover, since here and throughout the play she functions, like Helen, as an object of desire and exchange between the male protagonists, in order that a masculinist scopic and aggressive economy can be played out.[11] However, this textual and dramatic 'object' is not simply passive before the reader. On the contrary, the ambiguity of the reader's 'tickling', provoking and provoked by an 'accosting welcome', calls into question the conventional allocation of attributes such as activity and passivity within that gendered economy.

The reversals of cause and effect, of subject and object, which emerge here are insistently associated with the visual sense. For according to Ulysses, Cressida's 'eye' has language in it: it gives out a message. Rather than seeing, it gives itself to be seen. Similarly, her 'wanton spirits look out' not to see, but to display themselves, to incite the gaze of the other. This curious reversal of the role of the optical organ – from an act of seeing to an active being seen – would be associated in Shakespeare's time with both witchcraft and prostitution, as in the following passage from Reginald Scot's *Discoverie of Witchcraft*:

> The vertue conteined within the bodie of an harlot, or rather the venome proceeding out of the same maie be beheld with great admiration. For hir eie infecteth, entiseth, and (if I maie so saie) bewitcheth them menie times, which thinke themeselves well armed against such maner of poeple. Hir toong, hir gesture, hir behaviour, hir beautie, and other allurements poison and intoxicate the mind: yea, hir companie induceth impudencie, corrupteth virginitie, confoundeth and consumeth the bodies, goods, and the verie soules of men. And finallie hir bodie destroieth and rotteth the verie flesh and bones of mans bodie. (1930, 172)

According to the accepted Renaissance physiology of vision, the eye here operates as the organ by which infected spirits are transmitted from the body of the harlot to that of the observer. As the agent of infection or bewitchment, the eye forms the point at which sight transforms from passivity to activity, and where subject and object exchange places.

In dealing with either psychoanalysis or Shakespearean theatre, therefore, it becomes evident that no analytic method can claim immunity from this inextricable and mutual reversibility of cause and effect. My reading so far suggests the need, first of all, to pay close attention to the operations of infection, incorporation, aggression and violence implicit in this relationship as it occurs within the psychoanalytic tradition. For the same corrupting reversal will contaminate the Freudian discussion of scopophilia and exhibitionism.

Wars and lechery

According to Thersites, the plot of *Troilus and Cressida* consists of 'Lechery, lechery, still wars and lechery! Nothing else holds fashion' (V.ii.196–7). In the same way, within the psychoanalytic tradition, the disruption and contamination of oppositions – especially those of subject and object, spectator and spectacle – occurs most explicitly in the discussion of aggressivity and the drive. My examination of these themes, therefore, in relation to the treatment of visual perception, will trace certain lines of influence passing between Lacan and Freud. In this process, suggestions will also emerge about the historical and textual kinship between this psychoanalytic conception of the scopic drive, and the early modern or Shakespearean understanding of vision, a relation to be extrapolated further in the two chapters that follow.

In order to focus, then, upon the psychoanalysis of aggressivity and the drive, it is necessary to consider Freud's 'Civilization and Its Discontents' (1930) and 'Instincts and Their Vicissitudes' (1915), in conjunction with Lacan's reading of these two texts in various of his seminars. The link between Freud's two essays, which Lacan will emphasise and develop, lies in that reversal of the subject-object relationship discussed above. In describing the trajectory of the drive, 'Instincts and Their Vicissitudes' takes its primary examples from two pairs of apparent opposites: sadism–masochism, and voyeurism (or 'scopophilia')–exhibitionism.

In each case, however, Freud deconstructs the security of the opposition and reverses the direction of the drive, repeatedly exchanging the apparently 'active' partner with the 'passive'. This 'reversal into its opposite', of course, constitutes one of the four 'vicissitudes' to which Freud considers the drive liable. Accordingly, in each of the two examples, 'the active aim (to torture, to look at) is replaced by the passive aim (to be tortured, to be looked at). . . . The essence of the process is thus the change of the *object*, while the aim remains unchanged' (Freud 1984, 124). However, as the discussion progresses, it becomes obvious that the change of the object demands also a certain transmutation of aim, and of subject, which Lacan will emphasise, but which remains problematic in Freud's text. In the case of scopophilia, then, the reversal of the drive results in the following stages:

> (a) Looking as an *activity* directed towards an extraneous object.
> (b) Giving up of the object and turning of the scopophilic in-
> stinct towards a part of the subject's own body; with this,
> transformation to passivity and setting up of a new aim – that
> of being looked at. (Freud 1984, 127)

The aim changes from activity to passivity, while the subject becomes the object. In order for this to take place, however, there must also occur '(c) Introduction of a new subject to whom one displays oneself in order to be looked at by him' (127). The substitutions involved here provoke a footnote added to Freud's text by the editor:

> Though the general sense of these passages is clear, there may
> be some confusion in the use of the word 'subject'. As a rule
> 'subject' and 'object' are used respectively for the person in whom
> an instinct (or other state of mind) originates, and the person
> or thing to which it is directed. Here, however, 'subject' seems
> to be used for the person who plays the active part in the rela-
> tionship – the agent. (Freud 1984, 125 n. 1)

The subject, the one who desires to look, becomes an object, while subjectivity or agency is displaced onto the one who carries out the looking in her or his place.

Lacan, however, interprets the 'new subject' introduced here,

> not in the sense that there is already one, namely the subject of
> the drive, but in that what is new is the appearance of a subject.
> This subject, which is properly the other, appears in so far as
> the drive has been able to show its circular course. (1979, 178)

For Lacan, this circular, reversible play of the drive actually constitutes subjectivity, which comes into existence only in this structure.
As such, this 'new subject' of the drive cannot be thought of as in
any way self-sufficient or self-originating; rather it is always already
'other'. Freud's text (if read through Lacanian eyes) does seem to
gesture in this direction, in remarking that

> we can recognise in the case of the scopophilic instinct a yet
> earlier stage than that described as (a) [i.e. the activity of the
> subject looking at an object]. For the beginning of its activity
> the scopophilic instinct is auto-erotic: it has indeed an object,
> but that object is part of the subject's own body. It is only later
> that the instinct is led, by a process of comparison, to exchange
> this object for an analogous part of someone else's body – stage (a).
> This preliminary stage is interesting because it is the source of
> *both* the situations represented in the resulting pair of opposites,
> the one or the other according to which element in the original
> situation is changed. (1984, 127)

This structure, I suggest, in turn provides the source for both sides
of Lacan's scopic dialectic: that of the imaginary apprehension of a
subject which imagines itself '*seeing itself seeing itself*', and that of
the gaze of an Other, prior to and constitutive of the subject (Lacan
1979, 82). In fact, the entire argument of Freud's article proves
central to Lacan's seminars on the gaze and the drive in the *Four
Fundamental Concepts*. Freud's proposal here provides for Lacan's
discussion an object from which it derives, to which it returns,
and around which it circles. In Lacan, furthermore, the two examples (sadism–masochism and scopophilia–exhibitionism) seem to
infect each other, so that the scopic drive becomes contaminated
with what he calls 'aggressivity'.[12]

This latter term is offered as a complement, if not an opposite,
to 'aggression' (Lacan 1953, 16). Aggressivity – which turns into
aggression only 'At the limit, virtually' – indicates precisely this
complicity between the sadistic and scopic drives, which are intimately related in the antagonistic rivalry between the subject and
its imaginary other (Lacan 1988a, 177). In the mirror stage, the
subject's fascination with its reflection as ideal ego always includes
an attitude of malevolence. The body in the mirror, appearing more
co-ordinated and masterful than its original, excites the envy of
the latter, whom it threatens to replace. The mirror relation there-

fore inaugurates the formulation of the subject's identity in a fundamentally paradoxical manner, as Teresa Brennan points out:

> Because identification forges a unity with another, it also poses an imaginary threat. To maintain a separate identity, one has to define oneself against the other: this is the origin, for Lacan, of that aggression towards the other who threatens separateness, and thereby threatens identity. (1989, 11)

The ego will attempt to forge identity or unity out of separateness by aiming to destroy, replace or incorporate the image of the other: hence the dual modes of projection and introjection, which seek either to map the spectator onto its reflection or to devour it.

The 'drama' of the intersubjective scopic relation therefore always manifests envy or, according to the pattern of the reversed drive, its antithetic counterpart, jealousy:

> This moment in which the mirror-stage comes to an end inaugurates, by the identification with the *imago* of the counterpart and the drama of primordial jealousy ... the dialectic that will henceforth link the *I* to socially elaborated situations. (Lacan 1977b, 5)

In the essay 'Aggressivity in Psychoanalysis', Lacan remarks that St. Augustine offers the classic instance of an invidious spectacle when he describes a child, 'pale and with an envenomed stare', watching a younger brother take its place at the mother's breast. Here, Lacan tells us, 'are the psychical and somatic co-ordinates of original aggressivity' (1977b, 20). The example returns in the *Four Fundamental Concepts*, where the Latin of Augustine's account also prompts an etymological justification for Lacan's conception of the position of the subject in the scopic drive as one of envious, imitative aggressivity: '*invidia* comes from *videre*' (1979, 115–16).

Another of Augustine's images of envy, that of the wolf which eats itself, appears in *Troilus and Cressida* (Palmer 1982, 131). Ulysses' famous speech on order climaxes with the description of how, when 'Each thing meets / In mere oppugnancy ...'

> Then everything includes itself in power,
> Power into will, will into appetite;
> And appetite, an universal wolf,

> So doubly seconded with will and power,
> Must make perforce an universal prey,
> And last eat up himself
>
> (I.iii.110–24)

Here the paradoxical reversibility of appetite brings about the incorporation of the subject as its own object, just as the gaze turns upon itself in the Lacanian drive. This similarity seems less surprising in so far as the Shakespearean and the psychoanalytic models of the scopic drive draw upon a common precursor in their search for images of envy.

As Ulysses' speech concludes, moreover, it participates in the conventional association – also found in Augustine, and also repeated by Lacan – of envy with pallor:

> The general's disdained
> By him one step below; he, by the next;
> That next, by him beneath. So every step,
> Exampled by the first pace that is sick
> Of his superior, grows to an envious fever
> Of pale and bloodless emulation
>
> (I.iii.129–34)

As with mirror-stage aggressivity, each person in the Greek camp simultaneously envies and disdains, loves and hates, their immediate rival or superior. The play recurrently dramatises the oxymoronic ambivalence of this relation, as in the meeting between Diomedes and Aeneas, during which the latter remarks that 'No man alive can love in such a sort / The thing he means to kill more excellently'. The chivalrous platitudes exchanged by these two plainly display this antagonistic passion, or what Paris calls 'the most despitefull'st gentle greeting, / The noblest hateful love' (IV.i.24–34).

The meeting between Hector and Achilles manifests a similar oscillation between desire and hatred. As Achilles has previously claimed,

> I have a woman's longing,
> An appetite that I am sick withal,
> To see great Hector in his weeds of peace,
> To talk with him and to behold his visage
> Even to my full of view.
>
> (III.iii.230–4)

This 'woman's longing' for his opponent may imply either a desire which transforms Achilles into a woman, or which operates as if Hector were a woman. When they do meet, this 'appetite that I am sick withal' – an eroticism simultaneously charged with menace, hunger and disease – emerges as a stylised or ritualistic fascination:

> ACHILLES. Now Hector, I have fed mine eyes on thee.
> I have with exact view perused thee, Hector,
> And quoted joint by joint.
> HECTOR. Is this Achilles?
> ACHILLES. I am Achilles.
> HECTOR. Stand fair, I pray thee, let me look on thee.
> ACHILLES. Behold thy fill.
> HECTOR   Nay, I have done already.
> ACHILLES. Thou art too brief. I will the second time,
> As I would buy thee, view thee limb by limb.
> HECTOR. O, like a book of sport thou'lt read me o'er.
> But there's more in me than thou understand'st.
> Why dost thou so oppress me with thine eye?
> ACHILLES. Tell me, you heavens, in which part of his body
> Shall I destroy him . . .
>
>   (IV.vii.114–27)

In this moment of identification and rivalry, Hector becomes for Achilles successively a joint of meat to be consumed, a commodity to be bought, a quarry to be hunted, a book to be read, and a body to be dismembered.

This 'face-off' offers a striking representation of pure scopic fascination and malignancy. The expectations of the audience regarding this meeting would be considerable, and would arise both from its notoriety, as it occurs in the many other versions of the Trojan War story, and the degree of negotiation and anticipation which goes into preparing for it in this play. Each of these two characters enters the scene as a pre-existing text, a legend if not a cliché, who therefore requires incorporation into the Shakespearean play. Unsurprisingly, then, in their speeches the process of reading again manifests as a violent and ravenous appetite, and Hector figures as a menu. Achilles' eye takes in Hector, both as a prospective meal and as a citation, as though assimilating him into a document, 'quoting' him. He scrutinises Hector like a joint of meat, but also reads him like a hunting manual.

As a mode of incorporation, the scopic drive makes the eye function like a mouth, so that each man beholds his 'fill' of the other. The relationship between audience and play partakes of the same voracity. In *Troilus and Cressida*, the actor can imbibe the gaze of the spectator like a drink, and have it forced in like food: 'how his silence drinks up this applause' (II.iii.199), 'Farce him with praises' (II.iii.220). For Elizabethan theatregoers the reverse also applies. Anthony Munday describes them as insatiable consumers, 'alwaies eating, & neuer satisfied; euer seeing, and neuer contented; continualie hearing, & neuer wearied; they are greedie of wickednes...' (1972, 69-70).

Fragments, scraps, bits and greasy relics

The voracious antagonism which consumes the subject in its iden- tification with a rival also involves a desire for the fragmentation or breaking down of the mirror-image. Achilles quotes Hector 'joint by joint', views him 'limb by limb', piecemeal, until by the end of the dialogue he can see only anatomical portions and not the whole: 'in which part of his body / Shall I destroy him – whether there, or there, or there...' (IV.vii.126–7). Similarly, in the psychoana- lytic account of imaginary aggressivity, the subject's ideal-ego breaks down into what Lacan lists as

> images of castration, mutilation, dismemberment, dislocation, evisceration, devouring, bursting open of the body, in short, the *imagos* that I have grouped together under the apparently struc- tural term of *imagos of the fragmented body*. (1977b, 11)

These *imagos* become manifest at the point at which 'the movement of the analysis encounters a certain level of aggressive disintegra- tion of the individual' (Lacan 1977b, 4). In analysis, the subject, through the establishment of this antagonistic dual relationship with the analyst, experiences the breakdown of the various fragile bound- aries which the ego has fabricated in order to maintain the illusion of an individual self. Lacan describes a long series of belligerent forms, including poison, evil spells, physical intrusion, abuse, theft, persecution, defamation and revenge, 'in which we find all the successive envelopes of the biological and social status of the person...' (1977b, 16–17). The ego's successive boundaries between itself and its objects, like enveloping skins or garments, are shed during the disintegrating process of the analysis, thereby manifesting a certain discord between man's organization and his *Umwelt* [which] is the very condition that extends indefinitely his world and his power, by giving his objects their instrumental polyvalence and symbolic polyphony, and also their potential as defensive armour. (17)

The progressive fragmentation of the imaginary body reveals a sequence of identifications which have established the subject's relation to its environment, but which themselves provide nothing more than precarious barriers between ego and other.

Again, it is instructive to trace in Freud's texts possible sources for this emphasis in Lacan. At the beginning of 'Civilization and Its Discontents', for example, Freud comments on the illusion that the ego

appears to us as something autonomous and unitary, marked off distinctly from everything else. That such an appearance is deceptive, and that on the contrary the ego is continued inwards, without any sharp delimitation, into an unconscious mental entity which we designate as the id and for which it serves as a kind of façade – this was a discovery first made by psychoanalytic research . . . (1985a, 253)

Envisaging the ego as a 'façade', like the parergonal columns outside a building, marks the borders of the psyche with an instability between conscious and unconscious, self and world, subject and object. On one hand, the ego comes into existence according to this illusion of 'clear and sharp lines of demarcation' around itself. On the other, however, Freud goes on to describe one state in which 'the boundary between ego and object threatens to melt away. Against all the evidence of his senses, a man who is in love declares that "I" and "you" are one . . .' (1985a, 253).

The relationship of transference between analyst and analysand constitutes, for both Freud and Lacan, the typical instance of love, and as such it manifests pre-eminently this dissolution of intersubjective boundaries. Moreover, each step of the analytic relation can be most directly apprehended in dreams, because as Freud describes it, sleep involves a state of psychic undressing, which divests the subject of the 'defensive armour' or 'façade' of the ego, just as people each night remove 'the wrappings in which they have enveloped their skin, as well as . . . their spectacles, their false hair and teeth, and so on' (Freud 1917, 222). However, as Lacan remarks, no clear demarcation can be made between this and the 'hideous picture of a disintegrating being':

> We thus come upon this partially decomposable, collapsible character of the human ego, whose limits are so imprecisely defined. Surely false teeth are not a part of my ego, but to what extent are my real teeth? – if they are so easily replaced. (1988a, 151)

This ambiguity of what Lacan calls the 'defensive armour' of the ego recalls my earlier discussion of the corruption of the parergon, of which the armed Prologue in *Troilus and Cressida* provided an example. Thus Derrida remarks that although 'We think we know what properly belongs or does not belong to the human body, what is detached or not detached from it . . . the parergon is precisely an ill-detachable detachment' (1987c, 59).

Psychoanalysis therefore imagines the formation of the ego to take place through a series of identifications, the assumption of various masquerades. This performance is envisaged as more or less theatrical in mode:

> Freud states in a thousand, two thousand different places in his writings . . . that the ego is the sum of the identifications of the subject, with all that that implies as to its radical contingency. If you allow me to give an image of it, the ego is like the superimposition of various coats borrowed from what I would call the bric-à-brac of its props department. (Lacan 1988b, 155)

For this reason, it is not surprising that theatre offers plentiful opportunities to explore the psychoanalytic notion of the subject, or that the latter provides a model for the operation of the transaction between audience and stage. In relation to *Othello*, for example, the preceding chapter has discussed that the succession of masks by which the characters are constituted, and the way in which this mimicry, like the façade of the Freudian ego, is 'continued inwards, without any sharp delimitation' between its own processes and some definite internal reality. Consequently, even skin and flesh can be seen as masks to be manipulated, covered over or penetrated.

The threat of corporeal decomposition – of the body in the text, the body of the text, and the body into a text – therefore pervades *Troilus and Cressida*, in its tropes, plot and dramaturgy. Near the beginning of the play, a cast of Trojan heroes marches over the stage before the audience, to whom they are already literary icons, and each is labelled and characterised by Pandarus as such: brave Aeneas, shrewd Antenor, gallant Paris, and so on (I.ii).[13] In the same way, Iago displayed the 'characters' according to his own predetermining script in *Othello*. But *Troilus and Cressida* undercuts this parade of famous figures by preceding it with a more satirical and compromised description of the textual process which constitutes them. This is described as a form of theft, for Ajax, another heroic name familiar to the audience, appears to be patched together out of attributes stolen from various sources. Alexander remarks that 'They say he is a very man *per se*, / And stands alone' (I.ii.15–16). The description which follows, however, totally disintegrates this tautological and self-sufficient identity:

> This man, lady, hath robbed many beasts of their particular additions: he is as valiant as the lion, churlish as the bear, slow as the elephant – a man into whom nature hath so crowded humours that his valour is crushed into folly, his folly farced with discretion. There is no man hath a virtue that he hath not a glimpse of, nor any man an attaint but he carries some stain of it. He is melancholy without cause and merry against the hair; he hath the joints of everything, but everything so out of joint that he is a gouty Briareus, many hands and no use, or purblind Argus, all eyes and no sight. (I.ii.18–29)

Ajax's composite identity fragments in the very process of its construction. Like Hector before the dissecting gaze of Achilles, his body falls apart into so many useless 'joints', into its supplementary 'additions', which – like the 'additions' of which Kent accuses Oswald in *King Lear* – have been purloined or copied from other sources. As Carol Cook points out,

> Ajax's disjointedness is partly a matter of his being composed of the 'additions' of two literary precursors, the Ajax Telemon and Ajax Oileus of Homer, additions which are further disseminated through the many medieval retellings of the Troy story. (1986, 45)

Hector's speech to Ajax will commingle this textual ancestry with references to heraldry and to fictional genealogy. According to Ovid and Lydgate, Ajax was the son of Hector's aunt, a relationship expressed in the following convoluted passage:

> HECTOR. Were thy commixtion Greek and Trojan so
> That thou couldst say 'This hand is Grecian all,
> And this is Trojan; the sinews of this leg
> All Greek, and this all Troy; my mother's blood
> Runs on the dexter cheek, and this sinister
> Bounds in my father's', by Jove multipotent,
> Thou shouldst not bear from me a Greekish member
> Wherein my sword had not impressure made
> Of our rank feud
>
> (IV.vii.8–16)

According to the Arden editor, this speech in itself comprises a hybrid conceit. On the one hand, according to the heraldic metaphor, 'the arms of a husband and his (armigerous) wife were divided *party-per-pale* (i.e. along the vertical axis), with the husband's achievement on the *dexter* side'. On the other hand, the passage employs the conventional Elizabethan understanding of physiology, which proposed that

> certain parts of the body – bones, gristle, ligaments, membranes, fibres – developed in the foetal stage from the father's seed (= spermatic parts), whereas fat, flesh, and skin derived from the blood of the mother (= sanguine parts). (Palmer 1982, 252)

Metaphorically, then – that is, as a walking metaphor – Ajax embodies the composition and decomposition of 'character' as textual corpus.

The play represents this fragmentation with a multitude of other images of dismemberment. Like Ajax, other protagonists break down into their disparate components, or they feature as incomplete parts only, or reassemble into hybrid forms: Achilles calls Thersites a 'fragment' (V.i.8), Menelaus turns into 'both ass and ox' (V.i.56), and Ajax 'a very land-fish, languageless, a monster' (III.iii.255–6). The action begins and ends with disintegration, from the 'many hollow factions' that beset the Greek camp (I.iii.79), to the slaughter of the last act, where the choreography ruptures into numerous short, confused scenes, and the players are no longer rhetorically but actively 'mangled . . . hacked and chipped' (V.v.33–4).[14] Even the relationship between Troilus and Cressida disintegrates into 'fragments, scraps . . . bits and greasy relics' (V.ii.162); and her character into a torn up letter: 'Words, words, mere words, no matter from the heart' (V.iii.111).

The play's spectators and critics have reflected this fragmentation in various ways. Response to the text has, for example, been characterised by a shattering of the categories into which its audiences have tried to place it. Generic labels undergo a peculiar proliferation, and give birth to curious mongrels, on coming into contact with *Troilus and Cressida*. The Quarto begins by calling it a history, while the accompanying Epistle classifies it as comedy, and the Folio opts for tragedy. Since then critics have responded with various permutations (tragicomedy, comical satire, tragical satire . . .) until at the end of the nineteenth century the term 'problem play' gained an enthusiastic response, if only as an admission of defeat (Taylor 1991, 244–5). Swinburne perhaps came closest in his exasperated (and extra-aspirated) classification of the play as a 'hybrid and hundred-faced and hydra-headed prodigy' (Muir 1982, 37).

Similarly, those writing about the play seek to divide its audience into factions appropriate to their generic proclivity, variously maintaining that it was written for an Inns of Court audience, most likely to enjoy satire, or for the public at the Globe, thought to be happier with conventional comedy or tragedy.[15] If opting for the latter, critics subdivide the implied audience even further. René Girard, for instance, remarks tellingly, if patronisingly, that 'Part of that audience must have been highly sophisticated, endowed with a great sense of humour; the other part must have been stodgy and crude' (1985, 191).

Critics also insist that the action of that play has a peculiar capacity to fragment and split the gaze of its spectators.[16] In the second scene of Act V, for instance, when the audience observes Thersites watching Ulysses and Troilus spying on Cressida and Diomedes, its attention becomes irremediably fractured by the competition between the different focal points associated with each group. These coalesce around three dialogues: between Cressida and Diomedes, Troilus and Ulysses, or Thersites and the audience. Conflicting pockets of activity produce the 'bifold' (or for the audience, multifold) authority which Troilus himself finds so shattering. Each focus threatens to 'swagger' the spectator 'out on's own eyes' (V.ii.139), to bully the audience into 'taking part' in three senses: partaking (in Troilus's confusion), taking sides (for or against Cressida), and taking apart (the action, attempting to disentangle or make sense of it).

Dryden criticised precisely this generic and choreographic fragmentation of the play, and sought to correct it in his rewriting:

two different independent actions, distract the attention and con-
cernment of the Audience, and consequently destroy the intention
of the Poet: If his business be to move terror and pity, and one
of his Actions be Comical the other Tragical, the former will
divert the people, and utterly make void his greater purpose.
Therefore as in Perspective, so in Tragedy, there must be a point
of sight in which all the lines terminate: Otherwise the eye wanders, and the work is false. (1984, 13: 230)

Dryden employs a figure appropriate to the Restoration obsession
with pictorial illusionism in drama: the play must conform to the
compositional rubrics of Albertian perspective painting. The singular
viewpoint of the theatrical spectator corresponds to the vanishing
point within the painting, an intersubjective scopic relation mediated by the geometrical positioning of the frame. However, as Norman
Bryson points out, the clarity of focus in all parts of the oil painting
actually disseminates the vision of the spectator:

> Although composition addresses itself to a gaze of Argus, with a
> thousand foveae held motionless to a thousand points on the
> canvas, the practice of viewing must necessarily approach such
> simultaneous knowledge through deferral: the material construction
> of the eye permits only one area of the image to clarify at each
> moment. . . . Composition drives a wedge between a moment of
> full presence, when the abundance of the image is released in
> complete effusion; and a series of partial and provisional views
> closer to the labours of Sisyphus, than the splendours of Argus.
> (1983, 121)

'Purblind Argus' has, of course, already featured as the exemplifica-
tion of the dissecting power of the gaze on the textual body of
Ajax. Bryson's discussion derives its emphasis from Lacan, for whom
the shifting anamorphic perspectives of the painting offer a paradigm for the dissolution of the ego's imaginary gestalt. Remarking
that 'in front of the picture, I am elided as subject of the geometrical frame', Lacan emphasises the reverse view to that of Dryden's
monocentric spectator: the role of the anamorphic gaze in disconcerting the geometrical optical economy (1979, 108).
    In both psychoanalysis and Shakespearean tragedy, therefore, the
texts under discussion move towards a decomposition of the regula-
tions and limits of conventional geometrical space: linear perspective,

mathematical composition, the singular focus and a series of strict oppositions between inside and outside, spectator and spectacle, subject and object. The early modern stage, the modern subject, and the postmodern psychoanalysis of the gaze each address this figuration of space in Euclidean or Albertian geometrical terms, although of course each does so differently – as, respectively, an emergent, a dominant and a residual cultural formation. The demand for an increased attentiveness to historicity and textuality with which this chapter began, may therefore begin to be addressed by a reading attentive to the establishment and disintegration of these structures within and between texts: Shakespearean, critical and psychoanalytic.

The eternal city and the Trojan horse

As described so far, the identificatory dialectic of the scopic drive manifests what Lacan describes as 'The aggressiveness involved in the ego's fundamental relationship to other people', based upon 'the intra-psychic tension we sense in the warning of the ascetic that "a blow at your enemy is a blow at yourself"' (1953, 16). This transitivism – which Lacan also finds pertinent to the relation between 'actor and audience' – itself participates in the drive's tendency towards reversal, so that a blow at the self can also replace a blow at the other. The same double displacement informs Freud's discussion of the antagonism between the ego and the superego in 'Civilization and Its Discontents'.

According to Freud, the drives are subject to two overruling categories, the life instinct (Eros), which aims to 'preserve living substance and join it into ever larger units', and the death instinct (Thanatos), which on the contrary seeks to 'dissolve those units and bring them back to their primaeval, inorganic state' (1985a, 309–10). Aggressiveness and destructiveness occur as manifestations of the death instinct. In describing the source, aim and object of these drives, however, Freud's text manifests the same circularity and involution that pervaded his discussion of the scopic and sadistic drives in 'Instincts and Their Vicissitudes'. In both cases the argument turns and returns upon itself, undergoing a similar displacement of oppositions and describing the same oscillation between subject and object.

In 'Civilization and Its Discontents' Freud starts with his 'assumption' that 'the death instinct operated silently within the organism towards its dissolution . . .' (1985a, 310). To begin with, then, the postulate of the death instinct and its associated aggressivity appears self-contained, deriving from and operating upon the 'organism' itself. It is only secondarily that a 'more fruitful idea' occurs, according to which

> a portion of the instinct is diverted towards the external world and comes to light as an instinct of aggressiveness and destructiveness. In this way the instinct itself could be pressed into the service of Eros, in that the organism was destroying some other thing, whether animate or inanimate, instead of destroying its own self. (310)

Through this diversion, the death drive seems to be brought under the dominion of the life instincts, but only as a subsequent and subsidiary modification of the original narcissistic structure. Control over it remains incomplete and incapable of preventing the deleterious effect on the self: 'any restriction of this aggressiveness directed outwards would be bound to increase the self-destruction, which is in any case proceeding' (310).

The third stage of modification undergone by the death instinct also parallels the vicissitudes of the other drives. This comes about through the sublimating influence of 'civilization', which Freud considers to be 'a process in the service of Eros, whose purpose is to combine single human individuals . . . into one great unity . . .' (313). In order to inhibit the destructive thrust of the death drive, which opposes this programme of unification, the aggressiveness of the individual

> is introjected, internalized; it is, in point of fact, sent back to where it came from – that is, it is directed towards his own ego. There it is taken over by a portion of the ego, which sets itself over against the rest of the ego as super-ego, and which now, in the form of 'conscience', is ready to put into action against the ego the same harsh aggressiveness that the ego would have liked to satisfy upon other, extraneous individuals. (315)[17]

The death drive therefore follows the same circuit described by the earlier essay in relation to the scopic and sadistic drives. From an original narcissism, it moves outside the subject's own ego, but then returns upon it as its own double, in a potentially destructive reversal.

The change of trajectory, and the splitting off and alienation of agency, are common to both.

As such, the drive constitutes precisely that movement – examined already in relation to the frame, the tropes of infection and voracity, the gaze between stage and audience and the relationship between texts – which violates the boundaries between inside and outside, source and object, subject and other.[18] In the incorporative oral drive, for instance, the outside is consumed and taken inside; in the excretory anal drive, the inverse process occurs. As with the aims of sadism – penetration, evisceration, violation or mutilation – the mechanism of the drive aims to disfigure the body through the paradoxical meeting of impossible spaces, contingent upon undecidable boundaries.

As Freud's discussion progresses, he offers one of his frequent spatial metaphors to picture this relationship between ego and superego. Civilization, he remarks, 'obtains mastery over the individual's dangerous desire for aggression by weakening and disarming it and by setting up an agency within him to watch over it, like a garrison in a conquered city' (1985a, 316). The garrison of the superego governs from within the very walls by which the ego is constituted. For Lacan, similarly, this occupying army, which he renames the *nom-du-père*, the phallic name and prohibition of the father, appears 'outside' the ego, and yet infiltrates it. As discussed in Chapter 1, he uses the term 'introjection' to indicate that process whereby 'something like a reversal takes place – what was the outside becomes the inside, what was the father becomes the super-ego'. He implicitly compares this with the oral drive, relating introjection of the superego to cannibalism and the Eucharist, joking that '*the child devours his father*' (1988a, 169). Continuing the psychoanalytic preoccupation with the disruption of space, and adapting Freud's metaphor to Lacan's emphasis, the superego or the law of the father might also be imagined as a kind of Trojan horse, bringing the outside (army) within (the city) through an eruption from the inside (of the horse) outwards.

The first lines of *Troilus and Cressida* participate in a similar spatial inversion. After the Prologue, whose armour stands in parergonal relation to the play's corrupted 'core', Troilus opens the first scene with the intention to 'unarm again'. He then asks: 'Why should I war without the walls of Troy / That find such cruel battle here within?' (I.i.1–3). These walls, moreover, occupy their legendary place in the Western literary tradition precisely because of the manner of their breaching. The text plays with this knowledge ironically, so that Cressida can invoke a future

> When time is old and hath forgot itself,
> When waterdrops have worn the stones of Troy
> And blind oblivion swallowed cities up...

> (III.ii.181–3)

The incorporative appetite of time repeats the same reversal: 'blind oblivion' swallows the city, but in turn, the disappearance of every trace of Troy's architecture represents the loss of the capacity for memory itself, of the mnemic archive for which the form of the city stands, so that in devouring Troy time forgets itself.

The intra- (and inter-) psychic relationships between the ego and its others are repeatedly formulated by both Freud and Lacan through reference to such architectural, topographical and textual representations. Freud begins 'Civilisation and Its Discontents' with a discussion of how the ego, though it 'originally... includes everything' later 'separates off an external world from itself' (1985a, 255). As in Lacan's discussion of the successive 'envelopes' by which the ego performs this partition, Freud insists that each of the different stages of the process is not erased once it has been superseded, but survives in the form of a psychic trace. This assertion 'brings us to the more general problem of preservation in the sphere of the mind' (256). Psychoanalysis insists that 'in mental life nothing which has once been formed can perish...'. Therefore, 'in suitable circumstances (when, for instance, regression goes back far enough) it can once more be brought to light' (256). In the attempt to describe this phenomenon, Freud has recourse to another of his many spatial conceits, comparing the preservation and potential re-examination of psychic memory-traces to an archaeology of the architectural transformations undergone by a city like Rome in the course of its history.

However, the comparison requires certain imaginative adjustments, which in fact reconstruct what Freud aptly refers to as the 'Eternal City' according to an architecture of impossible space:

> Now let us, by a flight of imagination, suppose that Rome is not a human habitation but a psychical entity with a similarly long and copious past – an entity, that is to say, in which nothing that has once come into existence will have passed away and all

the earlier phases of development continue to exist alongside the latest one. . . . In the place occupied by the Palazzo Caffarelli would once more stand – without the Palazzo having to be re-moved – the Temple of Jupiter Capitolinus; and this not only in its latest shape, as the Romans of the Empire saw it, but also in its earliest one, when it still showed Etruscan forms and was ornamented with terracotta antefixes. Where the Coliseum now stands we could at the same time admire Nero's vanished Golden House. On the Piazza of the Pantheon we should find not only the Pantheon of today, as it was bequeathed to us by Hadrian, but, on the same site, the original edifice erected by Agrippa; indeed, the same piece of ground would be supporting the church of Santa Maria sopra Minerva and the ancient temple over which it was built. And the observer would perhaps only have to change the direction of his glance or his position in order to call up the one view or the other. (1985a, 257–8)

Ultimately, however, Freud claims to be disappointed by this archi-tectural fantasy, dismissing it as an 'idle game', only justifiable to the extent that it shows 'how far we are from mastering the charac-teristics of mental life by representing them in pictorial terms' (258). In spite of this admission, however, he does persist with such 'topologies' in his description of psychical apparatuses, although at times this usage borders on abuse, pushing spatial models beyond the limits of their signifying repertoire.[19]

With the suggestion that the observer of this city could 'call up' the different views simply by altering 'the direction of his glance or his position', Freud locates one of the limits fundamental to the representational structure of geometrical optics. As long as the single, privileged viewpoint of the spectator is maintained, temporally and spatially fixed, 'the same space cannot have two different contents' (1985a, 258). This same crisis in visual perspectivism recurs, for both Renaissance painting and Lacanian psychoanalysis, in the form of anamorphosis. According to this device, as I have previously described it in reference to *The Ambassadors* and to *King Lear*, the adoption by the spectator of a different viewing trajectory, directed from a peripheral position, reveals the same area of the picture to contain more than one 'content'. Freud's conceit, however, represents an anamorphic effect more radical still, for he imagines it taking place not within the frame of a painting, outside which the sub-ject stands, but in the environment of concrete architectural space surrounding the viewer. In this way, the constraining and determining paradigms of two-dimensional representational conventions are shown to leak into the optical perception of supposedly 'real' or three-dimensional space as well. The spectator's grasp on 'reality' itself encounters the limits imposed by geometrical representation.

Again, this can be compared with the changes of perspective and attention demanded of the audience during the scene of Cressida's 'betrayal'. Apart from the fragmentation of focal points remarked upon earlier, there are several trajectories or layers of observation struggling to dominate. Along with that of Thersites, Ulysses, and Troilus, there is also Cressida's own, which bifurcates in turn: 'One eye yet looks on thee, / But with my heart the other eye doth see' (V.ii.109–10). Whichever gaze the audience identifies with will involve them in a certain perceptual 'reality'. Each viewpoint – associated with, and emanating from, one of the characters onstage, looking in a certain direction, from a given position – implies an accompanying ethical, emotional or interpretive perspective.

This 'co-acting' of multiple visions produces in the action itself a radical fragmentation. Cressida performs more than one role, betraying Troilus by giving Diomedes the sleeve, staying true to him by snatching it back. Troilus himself describes the struggle of the spectator to cope with the perception of a spectacle that cannot be contained within the bounds of reason or representability. In his eyes, two Cressidas, one belonging to Diomedes and one to him, appear anamorphically superimposed across the same body:

> This is and is not Cressid.
> Within my soul there doth conduce a fight
> Of this strange nature, that a thing inseparate
> Divides more wider than the sky and earth,
> And yet the spacious breadth of this division
> Admits no orifex for a point as subtle
> As Ariachne's broken woof to enter
>
> (V.ii.149–55)

Two spatial comparisons are in conflict here: the double Cressidas are divided wider than sky and earth, and yet so intimately related that not even a needle could penetrate the gap between them. The texture of the 'woof' represents this, as a material made up of gaps, like a web or net. The name 'Ariachne' similarly constitutes a hybrid reference to two separate stories: Arachne's weaving competition with Athena, and Ariadne's thread in the Minotaur's labyrinth. Like the mongrel version of Ajax which Shakespeare conceives from conflicting accounts, the name 'Ariachne' offers an exemplary crux in which the text combines two sources that cannot 'fit' into the same space, an impossible juxtaposition which perpetually threatens the disintegration of the entire play into its disparate components.[20] Troilus follows his reference to threads and weaving, developing a metaphorical knot. On one hand, 'Cressid is mine, tied with the bonds of heaven', but on the other, 'The bonds of heaven are slipped, dissolved, and loosed, / And with another knot, five-finger-tied, / The fractions of her faith . . . are bound to Diomed' (V.ii.157–63).

The intricacy and convolution of the knot make it a valuable metaphor for the paradoxes of textual and psychical space. For this reason, Lacan will increasingly refer to topologies of impossible space in describing the activity of the drive, frequently employing paradoxical knots to reconfigure the representation of the internal and external space of the subject.[21] As Barbara Johnson points out, Lacan 'has been seeking to displace the Euclidean model of understanding (*comprehension*, for example, means *spatial inclusion*) by inventing a 'new geometry' by means of the logic of knots' (1977, 481). Johnson goes on to relate this emphasis in Lacan to Derrida's similar concern with the limits of spatial logic, in his reference to various paradoxical 'borderline cases': the tympanum, the hymen and, most relevantly for this discussion, the frame. In order to 'write on the frame', a reading must follow the consequences of what Derrida calls 'this infectious affection' of the parergon, working at

> a certain repeated dislocation, a regulated, irrepressible dislocation, which makes the frame in general crack, undoes it at the corners in its quoins and joints, turns its internal limit into an external limit, takes its thickness into account, makes us see the picture from the side of the canvas or the wood . . . (1987c, 74)

Just as the dislocation of conventional 'painterly' perspective occurs through the identification of another anamorphic gaze within the painting – looking from within the canvas 'out' at the spectator, or peering askew from beside the frame – the limits of theatrical space become visible in the reversal, disintegration or proliferation of dramatic viewpoints.

Returning to Freud's example of the 'Eternal City', as with the competing perspectives and focal points on stage in *Troilus and Cressida*, the coexistence of different buildings on the same site makes evident the inadequacy of the structures of a geometrical conception of vision to represent perception. For as Freud himself remarks, the problem with such metaphors lies in the limitations of spatial representation. 'If we want to represent historical sequence in spatial terms we can only do it by juxtaposition in space: the same space cannot have two different contents' (1985a, 258). Yet this discussion (Freud's, as well as mine) precisely concerns itself with the 'discontents' of the psychic processes, those features of the drive – aggressivity and the gaze – that are neither contented nor contained within the boundaries and restrictive structures of the ego. The pervasive use of metaphors of impossible space in psychoanalysis, as emphasised and developed by Lacan, evinces a desire for the deconstruction of those very oppositions – container and contained, inside and out – upon which the secure and realistic deployment of Euclidean geometry and Albertian perspective depend. The dramaturgical movement and rhetoric of *Troilus and Cressida* also challenges the limits of these same conventions of spatial and representational comprehension, at the very moment – that is, at the turn of the sixteenth century – at which they are coming to exert considerable influence on the dominant modes of perception and representation in all areas of art, science and philosophy.

Lacan, of course, will always emphasise the points at which psychoanalysis exposes the perceptual rubrics governing the subject's symbolic and imaginary universe. Following Freud's architectural and urban representations of the relation between the ego and the superego, and of the preservation of the ego's prototypes, Lacan describes how

> the formation of the *I* is symbolized in dreams by a fortress, or a stadium – its inner arena and enclosure, surrounded by marshes and rubbish-tips, dividing it into two opposed fields of contest where the subject flounders in quest of the lofty, remote inner castle whose form (sometimes juxtaposed in the same scenario) symbolizes the id in a quite startling way. (1977b, 5)

The inner castle of the id and the fortress of the ego, like the buildings of Freud's 'Eternal City', are 'juxtaposed in the same scenario'. This representation is 'startling' for a number of reasons: not only because the ego and the id occupy the same ground, one space with two different contents, but also because the subject is located in both of these 'two opposed fields of contest'. Occupying both the marshes and rubbish-tips outside and the inner arena and enclosure, the psyche constructs its ego as a barrier which it besieges, but from beyond which it is itself under siege. Similarly, the lofty inner castle of the id represents the enemy camp, which the subject seeks to penetrate and from which it is simultaneously under attack.

The word Sheridan translates here as 'stadium' recurs in the title of the essay, '*Le stade du miroir...*' (Lacan 1966, 97). As I mentioned in my first chapter, *stade*, like its English counterpart 'stage', can signify both a temporal phase in development and a theatrical platform on which drama takes place. Evidently, the decomposition of spectatorial geometry undertaken by these recurrent architectural and spatial metaphors can also be read in relation to the topology operating in the dramatic arena. Similarly, the juxtaposition of subsequent 'stages' of psychical development and their preservation as memory-traces suggests a possible reconfiguration of the problematic relation between texts, their sources and their audiences.[22] Both the Shakespearean and the Lacanian mirror/stage thereby provide the site upon which layer after layer of identification construct an entity which will always, subsequently, be liable to decomposition: an ego, a text.

Formed in th' applause

Wherever theatrical space does feature explicitly in Lacan's explorations of the gaze, it comes to exemplify the misrecognition implicit in geometrical representation. Lacan associates the dramatic 'gesture', for example, with a dissolution of the Euclidean spatial economy. He refers on more than one occasion to the Peking Opera, in which

> two characters move about the same stage, really giving the impression that they are in two different spaces. With an acrobatic agility, they literally pass through one another. These beings reach one another at every moment through a gesture which could not miss the adversary and nonetheless does pass by him, because he is already elsewhere. This truly sensational demonstration suggests to one the *miraginary* character of space... (1988b, 264–5)

Theatrical space is 'miraginary', not simply because it reconfigures the area of the stage according to the fictional co-ordinates of the performance, but specifically at those moments when it illustrates the illusionism inherent in the visual regime. Lacan also explicitly compares this type of gesture with the function of the dramatic aside which, as seen already in the competing focal points of *Troilus and Cressida*, verbally parallels the simultaneous display of more than one visual perspective or perceptual 'reality' (Lacan 1988b, 264). Those moments where the characters in the play 'pass through one another', like the acrobats of the Chinese theatre, would therefore include the extended play of asides during the conversation between Ajax, Agamemnon, Ulysses, Nestor and Diomedes regarding Achilles' pride.

The arrogant assertions made by Ajax, encouraged by the flattery of the others, establish one discursive grid, while the series of satirical asides between the Greek generals simultaneously institutes another. Each comment is thereby revealed to be part of an aggressive identification by Ajax with Achilles as ideal image:

> AJAX. A paltry insolent fellow.
> NESTOR. (*aside*) How he describes himself!
> AJAX. Can he not be sociable?
> ULYSSES. (*aside*) The raven chides blackness.
> AJAX. I'll let his humour's blood.
> AGAMEMNON. (*aside*) He will be the physician that should be the patient.
>
> (II.iii.205–10)

The triangular exchange between Ajax, Agamemnon and Ulysses intersects with a quadrangle formed by lines passing between Diomedes, Nestor, Ulysses and Agamemnon. As Ajax delivers his self-important remarks he turns from one member of the group to another, undercut each time by a sarcastic quip between the characters on his blind side. Like a mirror, the aside alienates each observation made by Ajax, so that it then reflects upon himself. Of course, the audience hears and contributes, with derisive laughter, to both fields.

As another instance of scopophilia, the fascination of Ajax with his rival participates once again in the hunger to assimilate the image of the 'other self': 'Your mind is the clearer, Ajax, and your virtues the fairer. He that is proud eats up himself. Pride is his own glass, his own trumpet, his own chronicle . . .' (II.iii.152–5). In its reversal, through this voracious drive, of outside and inside, container and contained, the optical paradox of the mirror also participates in the decomposition of the geometrical optical regime. The reflected image occupies an 'imaginary' space 'within' the mirror, corresponding to a 'virtual' location beyond the surface of the glass, diametrically opposed to the subject's position in 'real' space, a structure which parallels the symmetry of the viewing eye and vanishing point on either side of the frame in perspective painting. According to Lacan's 'Mirror Stage', the subject's ego can only reach towards its ideal in the mirror 'asymptotically' but never actually meet it (Lacan 1977b, 2). However, through a series of 'experiments' with a spherical mirror, a vase and a bouquet of flowers, Lacan seeks to demonstrate that, because of 'the strict intrication of the imaginary world and the real world in the psychic economy', the viewing subject subscribes to the illusion of being at one with this imaginary other (1988a, 78). Placed in a given position, the eye sees the reflected image of the flowers, which are actually hidden upside down beneath the table, appear as if placed in the vase. Through the superimposition of a 'real' object before the mirror and a 'virtual' object within it, the same location appears to house two different contents, and 'the imaginary space and the real space fuse' (1988a, 76, 78). Similarly, Lacan points out that if a plane mirror operates like a pane of glass, simultaneously transparent and reflective, it will superimpose an image mirrored on its surface with another seen through it, representing 'a coincidence between certain images and the real' (1988a, 141).

The next scene in the Greek camp stages another deployment of gestures, a theatrical display of aggressivity designed to disturb the imaginary correspondence between Achilles and his ideal image of himself. In the virtual space provided by the glass of his pride, Achilles sees the reflection of his own importance. By ignoring him or regarding him with disdain, the Greek generals cross through the zone of this imaginary conceit and establish a competing reality, from which the trajectory of their gaze looks right past Achilles instead of back at him admiringly, superimposing an antagonistic and anamorphic perspective over the image of his ideal ego:

ULYSSES. Achilles stands i' th' entrance of his tent.
Please it our general pass strangely by him,
As if he were forgot; and, princes all,
Lay negligent and loose regard upon him.
I will come last. 'Tis like he'll question me

Why such unplausive eyes are bent, why turned on him.
If so, I have derision medicinable
To use between your strangeness and his pride,
Which his own will shall have desire to drink.
It may do good. Pride hath no other glass
To show itself but pride . . .

(III.iii.38–48)

Ulysses sets up an alternative 'glass', a tableau of indifference in conflict with the inflated image Achilles perceives reflected in the glass of his arrogant self-esteem: a conflict 'between your strangeness and his pride'. This theatrical masquerade of negligence enacted by the Greek princes aims to upstage Achilles, displacing him from the limelight and positioning him as a spectator with a peripheral viewpoint, rather than a heroic cynosure. Bending 'unplausive' eyes upon Achilles will display his reliance upon the approving gaze of the audience, thereby moving him from an imaginary fascination with his own ideal image to a symbolic subjection to the gaze. Provoking his appetite for the desire of the Other elicits a performance from him in turn.

Achilles observes this new and disconcerting diversion of the gaze:

I do enjoy
At ample point all that I did possess,
Save these men's looks – who do methinks find out
Something not worth in me such rich beholding
As they have often given.

(III.iii.82–6)

In this scene, therefore, the strategy of the Greek generals operates according to the same logic as Lacan's 'gesture', which 'is not a blow that is interrupted. It is certainly something that is done in order to be arrested and suspended. . . . as a threatening gesture it is inscribed behind' (1979, 116). Lacan differentiates 'between the gesture and the act' by placing the former in the context of scopic antagonism. Theatrically menacing, the performance of this 'gesture' remains deliberately incomplete, seeking thereby to elicit the anticipated gaze of the Other, which remains 'inscribed behind' it. The gesture operates as a signifier within the visual field. Just as Cressida has 'language in her eye', as her 'wanton spirits look out / At every joint and motive of her body' (IV.vi.56–8), the gesture employs the vocabulary of the 'look', that is, both the appearance of the subject and the gaze it elicits and answers. Here the word 'motive', in Shakespearean usage a moving limb, can also suggest the inscription of significance behind the gesture, 'the element of motive in the sense of response, in so far as it produces, behind it, its own stimulus' (Lacan 1979, 114).

The theatrical gesture, in displaying itself to the gaze, obviously has much in common with mimicry as it operates in Shakespearean drama – in *Othello*, for example. In my discussion of that play in the preceding chapter, the butterfly provided the exemplary case of an adaptive camouflage which found itself always already caught in the net of visual perception. In the same way, Achilles observes that

> What the declined is
> He shall as soon read in the eyes of others
> As feel in his own fall; for men, like butterflies,
> Show not their mealy wings but to the summer,
> And not a man, for being simply man,
> Hath any honour, but honour for those honours
> That are without him – as place, riches, and favour...
>
> (III.iii.70–6)

The 'place' assigned to the subject within the symbolic order is indicated by certain 'honours', 'riches, and favour', which mark the character externally like a mottled camouflage, the 'mealy wings' of the butterfly. 'It is through this dimension that we are in scopic creation – the gesture as displayed movement (Lacan 1979, 117). In so far as the subject comes into being through this 'creation' of the scopic dimension, it participates in a pervasive theatricality, styling its look according to the gaze of the Other.

It is at this point that Ulysses, as author and director of the gestural theatre confronting Achilles, introduces the book with which this chapter began, quoting a 'strange fellow here' who in turn describes so accurately the scopic structure already created on stage. The vocabulary employed by the two characters in their interpretation of Ulysses' book evidently derives from the visual economy of the theatre, portraying a position created and maintained through an identification with the gaze of the spectator. The author's 'circumstance', his text,

> expressly proves
> That no man is the lord of anything,
> Though in and of him there be much consisting,
> Till he communicate his parts to others.
> Nor doth he of himself know them for aught
> Till he behold them formèd in th'applause
> Where they're extended – who, like an arch, reverb'rate
> The voice again; or, like a gate of steel
> Fronting the sun, receives and renders back
> His figure and his heat . . .

(III.iii.109–18)

This passage, like so many others in Shakespeare, envisages the transaction between audience and stage in terms of the mirror relation,
characterised by the reflection of heat, light and voice. The theatrical
conceit thereby undergoes what Freud calls, in relation to the drive,
a reversal. Instead of first learning a role and then communicating
it to the audience, the player here does not know his 'parts' – his
attributes, but also his roles, the sum of his identifications – until
he 'behold[s] them formed in th'applause / Where they're extended'.
The metaphor of a spectatorial gaze preceding and constituting the
performance of the actor would no doubt have seemed consider-
ably more familiar in the Shakespearean theatre, which relied upon
a willing collaboration between audience and players for the establishment of any theatrical illusion – setting, action and character –
far more explicitly than a more naturalistic drama might.[23]

Concluding his paraphrase of the 'author's drift', Ulysses remarks
that 'I was much rapt in this' (l. 118), describing both his fascination with the concepts involved, and his participation in the structure
being delineated. 'Rapt' in the words he reads, Ulysses enters into
the mirror relation between text and reader, captivated by the speculative and spectacular identification he describes. However, like the
theatrical gesture described by Lacan, this apparently self-contained
rapture nevertheless displays itself histrionically to the scrutiny of
another. Ulysses, staging this reading in order to catch the eye of
his spectators – both Achilles and the audience – thereby precipi-
tates it into what Lacan calls the symbolic, the register characterised
by an intrusion of a third gaze to destabilise the imaginary duality
of the mirror relation.

Ulysses's reading, therefore, according to the model of theatrical spectatorship, follows the trajectory of the scopic drive, proceeding from an imaginary narcissism – which is nevertheless apprehended only through the assimilation of the image of the other – into the field of the symbolic, and thereby returning reflected, augmented, reverberated. Even when 'rapt' in this intersubjective antagonism of reading, the text at no moment exists in and for itself, but always performs for the eye of the Other, which takes in the perspective escaping the false mastery of the imaginary register.

Epilogue – to an ever reader: news

Confronting analysis with Shakespeare demonstrates that the means by which a text seeks to establish its own identity uncannily doubles the psychoanalytic description of the formation of the ego. The reading incorporates its speculative text just as the subject of the mirror stage assimilates the image of its reflected ideal-ego. And that 'reading' always thereby constitutes a 'work' (in both the literary and analytic sense) of its own: a play incorporating sources from classical and medieval poets, a critical discussion of that play and those sources, a critique of such a commentary which assimilates those predecessors in turn. Writing consists of the delineation of a series of boundaries between itself and its others, of identification with certain ideal models, and of the expression of aggressivity in regard to various rivals. Moreover, as with the ego, those boundaries, identifications and antagonisms will all be subject to the fragmentation of subsequent analysis, revealing that the multiple stages (phases, platforms) of the formation of the 'reading-ego' are not lost or erased but survive as traces within the text.

The meeting between the bodies of Shakespearean and psycho-analytic writing therefore forms an agonistic dual relation comparable to that occurring between analyst and analysand, as well as to the performative transaction between audience and stage. Criticism seeks to follow the unfolding of the successive 'envelopes' of the text's formative identifications with its others: audiences, sources, readers, critics. But as both Lacan and Freud would emphasise, the position of the analyst, or the critical text or commentary, cannot be considered immune from the fragmenting and disintegrating effects of this relation. Writing, reading and analysis are different stages of the same 'work'. Shakespeare consumes the Freudian and Lacanian readings voraciously, just as Freud incorporates Shakespeare, and the problematics of theatrical gesture and Renaissance geometry overflow into Lacan's discussion of the gaze. Lacan ingests Freud, and any reading of Freud becomes infected by Lacan's. Yet, to change to another metaphor common to all the texts discussed in this chapter, the archaeology of each text remains alongside, within or against its critical superimpositions.

My approach to psychoanalytic criticism and the Shakespeare text therefore attempts the incorporation, juxtaposition and superim-position of texts which would appear not to be contained within, alongside or across one another. However, this very 'incapacity' of the reading, its 'discontents', forces a simultaneous breakdown of its various elements and the emergence of an excess, an overflow between and within the boundaries of each text, a series of cross-references infiltrating both the Shakespearean stage and modern (or postmodern) psychoanalysis. These allusions may occasionally appear as actual sources held in common – for example, Augustine's descriptions of envious pallor and voracity infiltrating both Ulysses' speech and Lacan's seminar – but more often they appear where the texts invoke shared perceptual structures, literary devices or deeply embedded tropes: the frame, the aside and the gesture; geometrical and perspective optics; envy, rivalry and aggressive desire; images of the fragmented body, incorporation and infection.

The historical and epistemological 'stages' of the visual phenom-enology shared by both Shakespearean theatre and psychoanalytic theory must therefore now be explored in greater detail. The role of a geometrical ordering of space, which has emerged so insis-tently in the deployment of linear perspective in the Shakespearean, Freudian and Lacanian texts under discussion, will provide the itin-erary for the next chapter. Finally, following the reversals and infections occurring between the gaze of the observer and that of the observed – for example in the 'language' spoken by Cressida's looks, or again in Achilles' description of the eye as emitting a 'most pure spirit of sense' – the final chapter will trace the rela-tionship between the Lacanian dialectic of eye and gaze, and early modern beliefs in the physical and metaphysical powers of vision.

5
Mapping Histories

Now do you not see that the eye embraces the beauty of the whole world? It is the lord of astronomy and the maker of cosmography; it counsels and corrects all the arts of mankind; it leads men to the different parts of the world; it is the prince of mathematics, and the sciences founded on it are absolutely certain. It has measured the distances and sizes of the stars; it has found the elements and their locations... it has given birth to architecture, and to perspective, and to the divine art of painting.... It moves men from east to west. It has discovered navigation...

(Leonardo da Vinci, in Richter 1970, 2: 67–8)

I have forgot the map!

From the fifteenth to the seventeenth centuries, a powerful cartographic paradigm emerges alongside the early modern developments in linear perspective, mathematics and optics that have been the focus of this study so far. The fundamental principles of this cartography derive from the same sources as these other developments: Euclidean geometry and its Ptolemaic applications, as modified by practitioners such as Abraham Ortelius and Gerard Mercator in the Netherlands, and John Dee, John Davis, Richard Hakluyt and Edward Wright in Britain. In the cartographic transactions of Shakespeare's time, therefore, it is possible to glimpse, inextricably caught up in the development of this visual and representational economy, one ancestor of that 'modern' subjectivity typified by and reliant upon its occupation of a single, fixed and centralised viewpoint.

Jacques Lacan insists that this subjectivity, as manifest in Europe and European-influenced cultures since Descartes and Pascal, constructs an ego which speaks, thinks or sees – these being its most characteristic functions – according to the displacements, elisions and distortions of precisely those principles at work in, and derived from, early modern experiments in perspective painting: hence his lengthy discussion, in relation to what he calls the 'dawn of the historical era of the "ego"' (Lacan 1977b, 71), of the operation of linear perspective in Holbein's *Ambassadors*, or his repeated exhortations to his listeners to study optics and the Euclidean, geometrical visual regime (Lacan 1979, 79–119; 1988a, 74, 76):

> Euclid's geometry is precisely founded on this, that one can employ in an equivalent way the two symbolised realities which have no common measure. . . . It took a world of surveyors, of practical procedures . . . learning to fold things on to others, to match up outlines, to begin to conceive of a space structured in an homogeneous way in three dimensions.
>
> In the same way, the images of our subject are buttoned down [*capitonnées*] in the text of his history, they are enmeshed in the symbolic order . . . (1988b, 256–7)

The subject is 'buttoned down' into the text of this historically produced visual field: situated opposite and fixated upon the vanishing point of the painting or the map, it functions as 'itself a sort of geometrical point, a point of perspective' (1979, 86). And the same principles are at work, instituting the same subjectivity according to the same operations, in the dissemination throughout Elizabethan culture of an innovative cartographic idiom, which has a critical influence upon the rhetoric and dramaturgy of Shakespearean theatre.[1]

Why else would Shakespeare choose to begin *King Lear* by shocking his audience with the most vivid available image of a kingdom divided: the old man, peremptorily demanding 'the map there' (*King Lear* F I.i.37), and proceeding to reduce the political and phenomenal world to a cartographic representation? Lear translates a land 'With shadowy forests and with champaigns riched, / With plenteous rivers and wide-skirted meads', into a set of geometrical divisions, 'these bounds even from this line to this' (F I.i.63–5).[2] The mastery of his gaze over this realm appears explicit in Lear's imperious dissection of the map and, by extension, the kingdom itself. Such scenes actually occurred in Renaissance Europe with increasing frequency, as land was carved up and served out by politicians with no knowledge of the territory outside of its representation on maps and globes, one famous example being the arbitrary line of demarcation drawn by Pope Alexander VI in 1493 to divide Columbus's recently 'discovered' New World between Spain and Portugal (Edgerton 1987, 46).

For Lear, however, it soon becomes apparent that his stable, potent and central symbolic position in this opening scene is illusory, dependent upon an imaginary correlation between his own unified image as king, and its reflection, the unified image of the kingdom. By dividing one, he inadvertently fragments both, as my earlier discussion of the play argued. Towards the middle of the play, this dehiscence of king and kingdom reaches its climactic expression in Lear's madness and the storm. Interestingly, however, although Lear seems to embrace this double disintegration, he does so in terms that seek to reconstitute the world precisely according to that device of cartographic representation which he employed to perform the initial division:

> ... thou all-shaking thunder,
> Strike flat the thick rotundity o'th' world,
> Crack nature's moulds, all germens spill at once
> That makes ingrateful man
>
> (F III.ii.6–9)

Lear demands that the three-dimensional world, with all its wealth of sensory and perceptual composition, be 'struck' flat, like an engraving, text or map, like an image on a coin, an engraver's mould or a printer's type. This translation from three dimensions into two would put the phenomenal world, in all its 'thick rotundity' once more under the sway of (his own) sovereign geometrical vision, as it was in the first scene when he unrolled, read and redrew his map. The three-dimensional here acts as an unsettling irruption, into imaginary and symbolic space, of what Lacan would call the 'real', that which resists representation and disrupts the illusory correlation between ego and ideal image, king and map.

In another famous scene of map reading, the leaders of the factions rebelling against the king in *1 Henry IV* discuss the trisection of the realm (sanctioned, like the division of the Americas between Spain and Portugal, by the Church):

> GLYNDWR. Come, here's the map. Shall we divide our right,
> According to our threefold order ta'en?
> MORTIMER. The Archdeacon hath divided it
> Into three limits very equally.
> England from Trent and Severn hitherto
> By south and east is to my part assigned;
> All westward – Wales beyond the Severn shore
> And all the fertile land within that bound –
> To Owain Glyndwr; (*To Hotspur*) and, dear coz, to you
> The remnant northward lying off from Trent
>
> (III.i.67–76)

Once again, however, what frustrates or conflicts with the representation of the map are the geographical contours of the land itself, what Lear calls its 'thick rotundity'. In this case, the course of the River Trent elbows into the picture, marking an intrusion by something the map would rather ignore:

> HOTSPUR. See how this river comes me cranking in,
> And cuts me from the best of all my land
> A huge half-moon, a monstrous cantle, out.
>
> (95–7)

Moreover, instead of the cartographic representation adapting itself to provide an accurate and innocent representation of the land it purports to reflect, the country itself is to be carved up by the redirection of the river. The map institutes strict lines of geometrical propriety ('three limits very equally') with which the geographical reality must be forced to comply:

> HOTSPUR. I'll have the current in this place dammed up,
> And here the smug and silver Trent shall run
> In a new channel fair and evenly.
> It shall not wind with such a deep indent,
> To rob me of so rich a bottom here.
>
> (98–102)

The arbitrariness of such transactions – for Hotspur changes his mind again within 30 lines – again recalls the division of the New World according to cartographic abstractions, as it was taking place in the palaces of Europe at the time.

Marlowe also dramatises the violence of these transactions when Tamburlaine boasts that with his sword as a pen, he will 'reduce' those regions as yet unconquered, the New World, 'to a map', and remarks that 'here at Damascus will I make the point / That shall begin the perpendicular' (Marlowe 1981, 1: IV.iv.75–84). The perpendicular or prime meridian, originating at the 'point' from which he surveys the area to be conquered, signifies both his own privileged viewing position and the central vanishing point around which he will reorganise the lines of perspective on the map of his empire. By the end of Part Two, Tamburlaine's imminent death reflects the disintegration of the world he has subjected. 'Give me a map, then let me see how much / Is left for me to conquer all the world' (Marlowe 1981, 2: V.iii.123–4). With the same command used by Lear to signify his mastery over the realm and to inaugurate its dissection, the dying Tamburlaine enumerates his conquests, constructing a verbal map of an empire that disintegrates as he speaks. Again, 'symbolic' geography seeks to dominate the 'real': Ethel Seaton has shown that Tamburlaine's world map follows the contours of Ortelius's *Theatrum Orbis Terrarum* (1570), faithful even to its errors, inconsistencies and omissions (Seaton 1964).[3]

Such scenes, therefore, provide more than just powerful allegories of the way in which the phenomenological structures instituted by cartographic representation came to dominate the political perception and treatment of geographical terrain during this period. Maps did not simply influence political decisions or facilitate their co-ordination. Rather, in a very practical sense, countries, nations and empires – and, implicitly, their inhabitants – *became* maps, and were read and rewritten as such.

Call for some men of sound direction

If a chart could be drawn showing the relationships between the various figures involved in the dissemination of maps and mapmaking technology in Shakespeare's England, a central place would be occupied by the work of Gerard Mercator as the most famous exponent of those cartographic innovations which were to revolutionise the shapes of world maps for the next few hundred years. Mercator relied upon and reformed the models and principles of Ptolemy's *Cosmographia*, which provided clear applications of Euclid's geometrical propositions to the drawing of map projections. Ptolemy's procedures involved the cartographer envisaging the globe from a single central viewing position, in which the eye was diametrically oppo-site to the chosen prime meridian, what Marlowe refers to as the 'point / That shall begin the perpendicular'. The 'thick rotundity' of the globe could then be 'struck flat', as the latitudes and longi-tudes were stretched out from this spot to produce a two-dimensional representation.

Mercator produced his projection by straightening the meridians – which, on a globe, would meet at either pole – until they extended parallel to one another. Because he was concerned to provide a projection usable by navigators, Mercator also needed to lengthen the meridians, in order to counteract the east–west stretching pro-duced by straightening them. The resulting arrangement – which has been the dominant template for maps of the world until very recently – is remarkable for the increasing distortion of land masses approaching the polar regions, while the Arctic 'circle' itself actually becomes a strip along the top edge. Mercator's map, moreover, required many further adjustments and calculations before it could be used by navigators. For although directions could now be accu-rately charted, distances – especially those further from the equator – were wildly inaccurate, so a series of mathematical scales needed to be provided to remedy this fault. The map was eventually modified by Edward Wright, a Cambridge mathematician, and John Davis, a mariner. Their version was published in 1599, along with an account of the latter's voyage to the New World, in Richard Hakluyt's *Principal Navigations . . . of the English Nation* (Hakluyt 1903, 1: 356; see Figure 2). It is here, perhaps, that Shakespeare saw it.

In *Twelfth Night*, Maria remarks that, having fallen in love with Olivia, Malvolio 'does smile his face into more lines than is in the new map with the augmentation of the Indies' (III.ii.74–5). The three most obvious features of Wright's map are highlighted here: the novelty of the Mercator projection, the additions to the western coastline of the Americas, made during Drake's circumnavigation of 1577, and the peculiarly dense network of rhumb lines drawn all over the map, fanning out from several compass roses placed at strategic positions around the world.

Rhumb lines were drawn on a map in order to facilitate its use by mariners. The navigator, having drawn a line between the ship's position on the map and its intended destination, would find the rhumb parallel to this and, tracing this back to the appropriate compass rose, thereby discover the necessary direction to follow. Wright's 'new map', then, positions the gaze of the reader in several

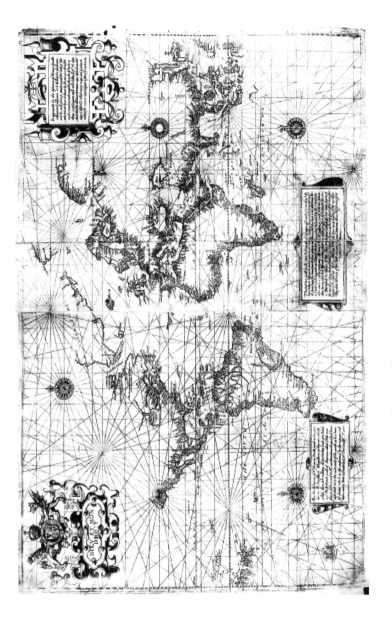

Figure 2. Edward Wright's Map of the World

important ways. First, according to the principles of Ptolemy and Mercator, as outlined above, it demands the fixed viewing point characteristic of Renaissance linear perspective. From this spot, the map flattens the world, stretching it out along a grid of latitudes and longitudes reticulated from the central vanishing point located on the prime meridian. The actual central point of the map, the geometrical locus around which the parallels and perpendiculars are organised, remains a blank, located somewhere (or, in effect, nowhere) in the mid-Atlantic, indicated on Wright's map only negatively, as the spot from which the middle star of compass rays fans out.

Faced by the nothingness of this vanishing point, the eye of the map reader is pushed inexorably outwards, along the rhumb lines – radiating outwards from the central visual field like the crow's feet spreading out from Malvolio's eye – to the edges of the map.[4] It is, of course, toward these areas – northeast and northwest, the West Coast of North America and the Far East, those parts of the map most extravagantly and anamorphically distorted – that the acquisitive eyes of Elizabethan merchants, explorers and colonists were mainly directed at this time, in the search for colonies and trading routes to Cathay and the Spice Islands.[5] As the English cartographer Robert Thorne wrote to Henry VIII:

> out of Spaine they have discovered all the Indies and Seas Occidentall, and out of Portingall all the Indies and Seas Orientall: . . . So that now rest to be discovered the . . . North parts, the which it seemeth to mee, is onely your charge and duety. (Hakluyt 1903, 2: 161)

These hyperbolic margins of the world map had been the target of English voyages of exploration for some time, from Sebastian Cabot's discovery of Newfoundland in 1497, to the quests in search of the Northeast passage by Sir Hugh Willoughby and Anthony Jenkinson in the 1550s and 1560s (Rogers 1916, 179–81). All these efforts were commemorated by maps of their own. Cut by Clement Adams, Cabot's map showed the imagined location of the Northwest Passage and also displayed his North American discoveries. It hung on the wall of the Privy Gallery at Whitehall Palace from 1549 onwards, where it was seen and 'regularly described by visitors for the next century and a half' (Barber 1992, 44). As this was the chamber in which foreign dignitaries awaited their audience with the monarch, it is not difficult to imagine the propagandist power of such a map, which led the gaze naturally and inevitably out from the centre to trace the contours of past English discoveries and projected English possessions. On Wright's map, again, the route followed by Sir Francis Drake – whose voyage of 1577 merits a special descriptive cartouche in the lower left-hand corner – draws the calculating Elizabethan eye to the exaggerated extremities, down through the Straits of Magellan, and northwards to the invitingly unfinished western coastline of North America, culminating there in the suggestive name 'NOVA ALBION'. This point, in turn, becomes the origin for another set of rhumb lines, inviting both eye and navigator to wander further still. The exaggerated land masses produced at the edges of the known world create a centrifugal effect, for which the compass lines radiating out from the centre offer a striking diagram, which cannot but contribute to the desire to conquer, colonise and exploit the new worlds currently being drawn into European maps.

The cartographic developments exemplified by Wright's map also play a crucial part in the dissemination of Euclidean geometrical principles into many areas of early modern knowledge. Samuel Edgerton has traced the influence of Ptolemy's *Cartographia* – with its institution of the central viewing axis, from which the grid of parallels and perpendiculars reticulates – upon the early practitioners of Quattrocento linear perspective (Edgerton 1975). Among these, he focuses upon the architecture of Filippo Brunelleschi and the applications of Euclidean geometry to painting by his friend Leon Battista Alberti in *De pictura* (*c*. 1435). These developments influenced the dominant modes of optical representation throughout the ensuing centuries. In Britain, John Dee's 'Preface' to the English translation of Euclid's *Elements of Geometry* (1570) provides a family tree of the prodigious multiplication of sciences and arts issuing from these geometrical principles, including perspective, astrology, cosmography, hydrography, and chorography, architecture and music, astronomy and navigation, and the measurement of distance, depth and breadth on land or water. Above all, however, Dee emphasises the role of cartography in the mathematical sciences, pointing out that geometry implies '(according to the very etimologie of the word) Land measuring' (Dee 1975, sig. a2v). Dee's promotion of English colonial activity influences much of his mathematical writings, which contain the first extant use of the term 'British Empire'. He also proposed the maintenance of a permanent navy, and in 1580 submitted to Elizabeth a map supporting the legitimacy of her claims in North America (Dee 1986, 47–53).

Unsurprisingly, therefore, this complicity between political and mercantile opportunism, navigation, geometry and cartography pervades many of the metaphors by which Shakespearean characters describe their nation and its relation with the rest of the world. In *King John*, Salisbury's speech performs just such a graphic re-drafting of the map of Europe:

> . . . O nation, that thou couldst remove;
> That Neptune's arms who clippeth thee about
> Would bear thee from the knowledge of thyself
> And gripple thee unto a pagan shore . . .
> (V.ii.33–6)

Salisbury's rhetoric wrestles his nation from its present shameful position and performs a drastic cartographic revision, imagining the British Isles manoeuvered into a new geographical alignment. The underlying nautical metaphor – 'grippled', as a variant of 'grappled' – recalls the expanding maritime activity which in Shakespeare's time was playing such an active role in redrawing political maps: Ralegh's voyage to Virginia, Drake's discoveries, the Spanish Armada. This 'tickling commodity', the 'smooth-faced gentleman' of political and commercial expediency, features earlier in the play in the Bastard's famous speech as 'the bias of the world':

> The world who of itself is peisèd well,
> Made to run even upon even ground,
> Till this advantage, this vile-drawing bias,
> This sway of motion, this Commodity,
> Makes it take head from all indifferency,
> From all direction, purpose, course, intent
> (II.i.574–81)

Two developments in Renaissance cosmography sustain this conceit. A Copernican universe displaces the Ptolemaic centrality of the earth, which can thus 'run' rather than standing still. But at the same time, the relationship between the personified Commodity and a world reduced to a globe the size of the bowling ball, on which 'all direction, purpose, course, intent' have been altered, also reflects the economy of the new cartographic relationship between the reader and the world map, as forged by the likes of Mercator modifying Ptolemy. Simultaneous with the displacement of the medieval religious cosmology, with 'man' at its centre under the gaze of God, comes the installation of the new subject, ruled by commodity, who takes 'his' bearings from an astronomical cosmos centred on the sun, and which places the earth under a powerful gaze of 'his' own.

The Machiavellian Richard III shows an awareness of the need for the sovereign to align himself with this centralised and privileged gaze of the map reader, when he first expresses his desire for the crown:

> ... I do but dream on sovereignty
> Like one that stands upon a promontory
> And spies a far-off shore where he would tread,
> Wishing his foot were equal with his eye,
> And chides the sea that sunders him from thence
> (*3 Henry VI* III.ii.134–8)

The components of this verbal panorama are familiar from our preceding discussion of cartography. The establishment of a direct line of sight between the privileged viewing position – 'one that stands upon a promontory' – and the distant locus of desire matches the organisation of the map around a central vanishing point diametrically opposite the subject's eye. The elision between this optical positioning and the means of its translation into practice – 'wishing his foot were equal with his eye' – evokes the fantasy of an effective power. And the desire for a 'far-off shore' from which the subject is separated by the sea parallels the exhortations of Dee, Drake, Hakluyt and the like to their monarch to acquire possessions abroad. The visual economy utilised by Renaissance tragedy to situate each of the central figures cited so far – Lear, Tamburlaine and Richard – functions as a new-found means for contemporary politicians, merchants, explorers, patriots and cartographers to pursue their acquisitive drives and capacities.[6]

The knowledge of navigation displayed in Shakespearean drama derives from Richard Eden's translation of the Spanish *Art de navigar* (1561; Knobel 1916, 453). The stars by which mariners conventionally fixed their course were those in the constellation of Ursa Minor, particularly the two 'Guards' and the Pole Star. This expert knowledge is displayed by the Second Gentleman in *Othello*, when he describes a tempest of such ferocity that these crucial navigational co-ordinates are eclipsed:

> The wind-shaked surge with high and monstrous mane
> Seems to cast water on the burning Bear
> And quench the guards of th'ever-fixèd Pole.
>
> (II.i.13–15)

The astrolabe (or one of its variants, the quadrant, sextant or octant) was employed by mariners to fix their position *vis-à-vis* these stars, and by Elizabethan cartographers to plot latitude on land, situating their position according to the height of the sun or the Pole Star above the horizon at the place of observation (Brown 1951, 180–5). An accurate point on the map could be plotted only when the eye was lined up, via the optical instrument, with the astronomical referent. The accuracy of such hand-held instruments depended upon, and in turn consolidated, the fixed gaze of the cartographer. Once again, the practices of cartography instal and privilege a monocentric viewpoint.

The insistent invocation by Shakespearean figures of these astronomical bodies attests to the construction of a subject position guaranteed – by means of the infallibility of its optical geometry, its cartographic methods and its instruments – in diametric opposition to the constancy of the sun and the Pole Star. Richard II offers only one example of the many Shakespearean rulers who repeatedly designate their sovereignty through reference to the sun (*Richard II* III.ii.32–49, III.iii.61–6), while Julius Caesar famously defines himself as being

> .. as constant as the Northern Star,
> Of whose true fixed and resting quality
> There is no fellow in the firmament.
> The skies are painted with unnumbered sparks;
> They are all fire, and every one doth shine;
> But there's but one in all doth hold his place.
> So in the world: 'tis furnished well with men,
> And men are flesh and blood, and apprehensive;
> Yet in the number I do know but one
> That unassailable holds on his rank,
> Unshaked of motion...
>
> (*Julius Caesar* III.i.60–70)

'I am he,' Caesar concludes, exemplifying an emergent subjectivity, almost invariably associated in Shakespearean drama with the 'great man', whose reference to the field of geometrical optical space both guarantees and represents his pre-eminent position in the symbolic realm, the world of politics, society and knowledge.

This speech, of course, proves to be Caesar's last. It directly precedes and even provokes his assassination. Richard II similarly is deposed, melting away before 'the sun of Bolingbroke' (IV.i.251). In fact, wherever it appears in Shakespearean drama, this guaranteed stability granted by the privileged central viewing position in the scopic economy will prove to be both illusory and liable to dissolution.

Melted from the smallness of a gnat to air

Lacan has emphasised precisely this instability of the centralised mastery of the post-Renaissance subject in his discussion of the gaze. 'I see only from one point, but in my existence I am looked at from all sides', he remarks. The gaze 'is presented to us only in the form of a strange contingency, symbolic of what we find on the horizon' (1979, 72). What the Elizabethan subject of cartography finds on the horizon, at the edges and the limits of its maps, threatens the organisation of that subject's own position. The distortion on the margins of what we might call this Elizabethan 'world picture' reveals the means of its construction and, implicitly, the 'strange contingency' of the centralised viewing position upon which it depends. This skewed perspective from the frame of the map thereby operates in the same way as Lacan's description of the anamorphosis in Holbein's *Ambassadors*, which decomposes the site of privileged vision by demanding from the spectator an ex-centric viewing position:

> All this shows that at the very heart of the period in which the subject emerged and geometral optics was an object of research, Holbein makes visible for us here something that is simply the subject as annihilated . . .
>
> For us, the geometral dimension enables us to glimpse how the subject who concerns us is caught, manipulated, captured, in the field of vision. (Lacan 1979, 88–92)

Lacan identifies the emergence of anamorphoses in the development of the geometrical optical principles that produce both Albertian perspective painting and those maps based on Mercator's projection. These anamorphoses appear in pictorial art as grotesquely elongated shapes which only become legible from an oblique perspective, an alternative viewing position to that of the centralised spectator. They are thereby symptomatic of the limits of the optical economy being instituted, and of the inherent failure of that system to guarantee the place of the subject within it. Within the 'systematic establishment of the geometrical laws of perspective formulated at the end of the fifteenth and the beginning of the sixteenth centuries,' Lacan remarks, the appearance of anamorphosis represents 'a sensitive spot, a lesion, a locus of pain, a point of reversal of the whole of history' (1992, 140).

Chapter 2 discussed the manifestation of this 'locus of pain' in the Dover cliff scene from *King Lear*; the displacement of the central viewing position emerges by means of the reversed line of sight which Edgar directs upwards from the foot of the cliff, once Gloucester has (supposedly) fallen through the vanishing point of the linear perspective Edgar had previously described from above. The imaginary Dover cliff offers (as elsewhere in Shakespearean drama) a symbolic location to mark the farthest limit, the end of Lear's Britain. This representative function again links this scene to the role played by the distorted edges of the Elizabethan map, in which the enlargement of the northern and southern land masses betrays the means employed in the construction of the map, and the political and commercial interests invested in it. In both cases, from the symbolic limits of a geographic entity (Lear's Britain, Wright's world), an anamorphic perspective returns to displace the pictorial or cartographic economy and the viewing subject's secure place within it.

Shakespeare's stage portrays this disarming gaze returning to trouble not only the composition of the perspective painting, but also that situation of the subject by means of navigational geometry. In *Cymbeline*, Innogen discusses with Pisanio the departure of Posthumus. The verbal picture they create situates the mariner on his ship at the vanishing point of this perfectly modulated perspective, the inverse position of that occupied by the navigator or cartographer when reading the map or plotting the ship's location according to the sun and Pole Star:

PISANIO. For so long
As he could make me with this eye or ear

Distinguish him from others he did keep
The deck, with glove or hat or handkerchief
Still waving, as the fits and stirs of's mind
Could best express how slow his soul sailed on,
How swift his ship.
INNOGEN. Thou shouldst have made him
As little as a crow, or less, ere left
To after-eye him.
PISANIO. Madam, so I did.
INNOGEN. I would have broke mine eye-strings, cracked them, but
To look upon him till the diminution
Of space had pointed him sharp as my needle;
Nay, followed him till he had melted from
The smallness of a gnat to air, and then
Have turned my eye and wept.

(I.iii.8–22)

The mathematical diminution of space here operates in an identical fashion to that of Edgar's speech on Dover cliff. In both, the illusion of distance depends upon a series of metonymic reductions, decreasing the proportions of the visual plane step by step until it reaches vanishing point. In the *Lear* passage, crows and choughs appear the size of beetles, a man no bigger than his head, fishermen like mice, a ship 'Diminished to her cock, her cock a buoy / Almost too small for sight' (F IV.v.13–20). In *Cymbeline*, as the Arden editor observes, 'this diminution is suggested by several subtle devices. Sail contrasts with handkerchief: eye and ear are resolved into eye alone, and they to eyestrings, and the eye image may be implicit in 'needle': similarly the life-size figure of Posthumus yields to crow, crow to gnat, and gnat to thin air' (Nosworthy 1969, 16). As well as indicating the muscles or tendons of the eye, which were thought to crack at death or loss of sight, 'eye-strings' might refer to the line of vision stretched between Innogen's 'eye' and the vanishing point, threaded through the 'eye' of the needle. The point of this needle, at which Posthumus vanishes into the distance, provides a punctilious correlative for what Lacan above calls the 'locus of pain' from which an alternative perspective emerges to reduce the stable place of the subject to nothing.

Innogen, in short, positions herself at the origin of what Ptolemy (and Alberti after him) called the 'centric ray' between the cartographer and the prime meridian, or the spectator and the vanishing point of the painting. According to the cartographic and navigational economies discussed so far, however, that locus of mastery really ought to be occupied by the male adventurer, the mariner on his ship. The text emphasises Posthumus's suitability to occupy this position in its insistence on the power and fixity of his eye, which could 'behold the sun with . . . firm eyes' (I.iv.11), recalling the means by which the eye of the navigator or surveyor plotted a position on the map according to the sun through his astrolabe.[7] This position, however, in the passage quoted, is 'usurped' by a woman, so that Posthumus finds himself caught in the diminishing field of the picture's vanishing point, struggling in vain to remain discernible, trying to 'make' the viewer 'with this eye or ear / Distinguish him from others'. The Folio version of the play actually reads '*his* eye' at this point, which could only mean Posthumus's own eye, so that the text and its editors replay this struggle between the viewer and the viewed to attain the position of visual dominance, to be the maker of the picture rather than to be made by it.

Through Innogen's insistent imagination of the scene, however, the text ultimately instals hers as the central viewpoint from which this perspective picture appears. She composes the picture and Posthumus's place in it, telling Pisanio 'Thou shouldst have made him / As little as a crow, or less'. In fact, her dilemma in the play is precisely that she attempts to position herself too actively, too masterfully, marrying whom she pleases against the will of her parents. In this play, feminine disobedience constitutes the reversed perspective which disrupts the centrality of the viewing subject. Like Posthumus in the passage just quoted, Innogen's father, Cymbeline, also suffers displacement from the site of the sovereign eye, for although he is King, he proves to be subject to domination by his Queen (I.i.104–7). Just as anamorphosis features as an enigmatic stain on the perspective painting, and the exaggeration of the polar regions renders the representation of those areas on Mercator's map wildly unreliable, the woman's perspective appears as an illegible distortion in the masculine optical economy of a play such as this. Tellingly, Cymbeline's discovery at the end of the play of his Queen's designs prompts the remark 'Who is't can read a woman?' (V.vi.48).

We the globe can compass soon

Two-dimensional maps were not the only product of the new cartography. The sixteenth and seventeenth centuries also saw modifications, and a widespread proliferation, in the creation and sale of spherical models of the earth, so that Hakluyt could draw a distinction in 1589 between 'the olde imperfectly composed, and the new lately reformed Mappes, Globes, Spheares, and other instruments of this Art...' (Hakluyt 1903, 1: xviii)

Model globes, unlike two-dimensional maps, were of little practical use for the charting of exploratory or colonial ventures. Even more than the flat maps, however, they did possess a particular iconographic potency, as witnessed by the ubiquity of globes or orbs in contemporary royal portraiture. The 'Armada' portrait of Elizabeth I offers one famous example among many, in which 'a globe is tipped at an angle towards the viewer, and its meaning is derived from the central figure of the Queen, whose imperial hand extends to grasp the whole world' (Harley 1983, 33). Not only monarchs, but politicians of all ranks and nationalities invested in the visual capital of the globe. Returning to Holbein's *Ambassadors*, painted in London in 1533, we might note that both terrestrial and celestial globes lie among the range of objects, symbolic of their mastery over the Renaissance sciences and arts, furnishing the space dominated by the figures of Jean de Dinteville and Georges de Selve (see Figure 1, p. 54). More specifically, the globes denote geometrical knowledge, for between the two figures Holbein displays also sundials, a quadrant, a set square, a German book on arithmetic and a lute: these details, according to Stephen Greenblatt, 'virtually constitute a series of textbook illustrations for a manual on the art of perspective' (1980, 17, 260 n. 8). As an instrument of geometrical practice, therefore, the globe plainly contributes to and participates in the valorisation of the scopic position of the emergent Renaissance subject. This recalls the way in which Ptolemy's methods of flat cartographic projection – which offered a basis for both Mercator-style maps and Albertian pictorial perspective – also began by envisaging the spectator placed before a globe.

However, the augmented emblematic power of the model globe contributes to the iconography of this incipient subjectivity in other ways as well. If the two-dimensional map – along with the astronomical, navigational and geometrical techniques required to produce and use it – situates its viewer in a centralised and exalted locus of optical mastery, a comparable metaphorical effect results from the visual contrast in any picture of the world reduced to the dimensions of a model globe alongside an enlarged human figure. The erect and frozen figures of Elizabeth or the Ambassadors ('stiffened in their showy adornments,' as Lacan describes them) are granted, by these portraits, a representational and spatial dominance inversely proportional to their relationship with a shrunken world (Lacan 1979, 88). The globe thereby appears manipulable, within the reach and grasp of the ego, reduced to the status of an object of learning, a commodity for possession, or a territory inviting political rule.

Shakespeare's *Julius Caesar* has already provided one instance of the exaltation of the ego within a geometrical and cartographic economy. He also exemplifies the appearance, in the metaphorical vocabulary of the plays, of this emblematic contrast between a diminished globe and an augmented human figure. Cassius, complaining to Brutus of the emergence of a new, imperial political idiom represented by the rise of Caesar, remarks,

> Why, man, he doth bestride the narrow world
> Like a Colossus, and we petty men
> Walk under his huge legs and peep about
> To find ourselves dishonourable graves.
>
> (I.ii.136–9)

The attenuated gaze of the 'petty men' who 'peep about' also offers a contrast with the heightened omnivoyance of the giant, surveying a world contracted into a map or globe beneath his feet.[8] This shortsightedness, of course, will indeed bring Cassius to his 'dishonourable grave', for he kills himself after mistaking Titinius' victory for defeat. The text explicitly attributes this error to Cassius' myopia ('my sight was ever thick'), which he fails to redress by urging Pindarus to 'get higher on that hill', a vain attempt to approach the panoramic visual mastery of the Colossus (V.iii.20–1). Increased stature, implementing a perspective from above, brings its own optical advantages, which – as Cassius's death proves – could prove strategically critical. We might recall in this connection Richard III before the Battle of Bosworth, calling for 'some men of sound direction' to 'survey the vantage of the ground' (*Richard III* V.iii.15–16), or the assault on Orleans in *1 Henry VI*, which begins with the same kind of cartographic reconnaissance: the English, from 'yonder tower' in the suburbs, 'overpeer the city,

/ And thence discover how with most advantage / They may vex us with shot or with assault' (I.v.8–13).

The heightened gaze associated with the gigantic figure, capable of casting the net of an all-encompassing vision over the diminutive globe, bears obvious similarities not only to the reader poring over the map, but to the view of the surveyor who drafts it. During his surveys of England and Wales, the cartographer Christopher Saxton was granted by the Privy Council special privileges requiring mayors, justices of the peace and other officials 'to see him conducted unto any towre, castle, high place or hill, to view that country' (Brown 1951, 167). Similarly, in *Cymbeline*, when both Innogen and Cloten follow Pisanio's map to Milford Haven, Cloten expresses the hope that 'Pisanio have mapped it truly' (IV.i.2), while Innogen's remark suggests that he has at least followed the surveyor's practice of taking his bearings from the highest available point: 'Milford, / When from the mountain-top Pisanio showed thee, / Thou wast within a ken' (III.vi.4–6). The visual advantages of such altitudes were attested by another contemporary surveyor, John Norden. Referring to a particularly lofty point, 'whereon standeth the principall beacon in Cornwall as in a place beste deseruing it', Norden wrote:

> vpon that hill a man bendinge his eye to whatsoeuer parte, shall obserue that all the Countrye rounde about it as it were falleth at the feete of this. And from this hill may be seene a parte of *Deuonshire* eastwarde aboue 30 myles, and almoste to the landes ende westewarde aboue 40 myles: The seas north and south, with there dispersed Iles, are likewise playnlye discouered. (cited in Ravenhill 1983, 117–18)

Norden envisages the landscape he surveys as if it were already mapped, inscribed with a set of compass directions, reduced to a configuration of perspectival distances, framed by pre-existent geographical limits: Land's End, the north and south coasts, a border between Cornwall and Devon. The countryside falls prostrate 'at the feet' of the surveyor, offering itself up for dissection by a heightened, omnivoyant gaze representative of the new confidence and prestige which accrued to the cartographic arts at this time.[9] This attitude also infiltrates many of Shakespeare's plays. In *A Midsummer Night's Dream*, Puck can 'put a girdle round the earth / In forty minutes' (II.i.175–6), while Oberon makes the cartographic tenor of this metaphor even more explicit: 'We the globe can compass soon, / Swifter than the wand'ring moon' (IV.i.96–7). Another practitioner of magic, Prospero – identified by one critic with the geometer John Dee (Yates 1979, 159–63) – can envisage with apparent ease the dissolution of 'the great globe itself' (*The Tempest* IV.i.153).

The contrast between a shrunken or 'narrow' world and the figure of the colossus astride it recurs throughout another of the Roman plays. *Antony and Cleopatra* repeatedly figures Caesar's protégé according to an identical conceit. At the beginning of the play Antony shares this exalted position with Octavius and Lepidus, as 'triple pillar of the world' (I.i.12). His first speech makes explicit the contrast between 'the dungy earth', in which 'Kingdoms are clay', and the dimensions of his own body or ego: 'Here is my space.' His self-aggrandisement, according to which he will 'stand up peerless', corresponds with his contraction of the world to a fragile construct: 'Let Rome in Tiber melt, and the wide arch / Of the ranged empire fall' (I.i.35–42). The gradual diminution of the status of Lepidus will reduce the triumvirate to a rivalry between the remaining two, so that a few scenes later Antony can be considered 'the demi-Atlas of this earth' (I.v.23).

This word 'Atlas' was, in Shakespeare's time, increasingly becoming associated with the cartographic representation of the earth. According to Lloyd Brown, the first widely distributed map collection to use the word in its title was Mercator's *Atlas sive Cosmographicae meditationes . . .*, of which the first part was published in 1595.

> A genealogical tree in the introductory text gave the ancestry of Atlas, the mythological character who led the Titans in their war against the god Jupiter, and was therefore condemned to support the heavens on his shoulders. (1951, 165)

José Rabasa, however, offers an alternative explanation for the use of the name in connection with cartography, claiming that 'Mercator first coined the name Atlas after the mythical King of Libya "who was supposed to have made the first celestial sphere"' (1985, 1). Both suggestions are consistent with our discussion so far of the Shakespearean (and more widespread Renaissance) employment of the emblematic relation between world and subject: that of a Titan whose vast dimensions enable him to hold the weight of the celestial dome, and that of a king who reduces the cosmos to a model.

Ultimately, Antony stands alone as a figure of colossal proportions, independent of his rival, in a metaphor which echoes and
develops that used in the earlier play to describe his patron Julius
Caesar. Cleopatra describes her dream of 'an Emperor Antony':

> His face was as the heav'ns, and therein stuck
> A sun and moon, which kept their course and lighted
> The little O o'th'earth . . .
> His legs bestrid the ocean; his reared arm
> Crested the world. His voice was propertied
> As all the tunèd spheres, and that to friends;
> But when he meant to quail and shake the orb,
> He was as rattling thunder. For his bounty,
> There was no winter in't; an autumn 'twas,
> That grew the more by reaping. His delights
> Were dolphin-like; they showed his back above
> The element they lived in. In his livery
> Walked crowns and crownets. Realms and islands were
> As plates dropped from his pocket
>
> (V.ii.78–91)

This passage combines in one extended conceit the metaphorical
usages of all the cartographic optical structures discussed so far.
The world is reduced to a representation, either an orb which shakes
at the mere sound of Antony's voice, or the two-dimensional map
of a 'little O' drawn on paper. Antony, in contrast, has attained the
stature of a giant, straddling the ocean, with his acquisitive grasp
on the world signified by the reduction of its component 'realms
and islands' to 'plates', a word denoting both appetite and silver
coin. His gaze, like that of the cartographer and the navigator, is
fixed in reference to the celestial bodies, 'a sun and moon' shining
in the 'heavens' of his face. At such moments, along with the cartographical shrinking and mastering of the world, there emerges a
corresponding increase in the stature of 'man': the beginning, according to Lacan, of the ego's era, which will facilitate and collude
with the acceleration of imperialism and capitalism.

In the English history plays, various kings claim the same titanic
status as Shakespeare's Roman protagonists. Richard II, as mentioned
earlier, portrays himself as a sun god, whose sovereign gaze radi-
ates from above, reducing the globe to a 'terrestrial ball' (*Richard II*
III.ii.33–49). In the sequel to this play, Prince Hal attributes an

equivalent stature to Hotspur – whose assumption of a commanding and dissecting gaze over the map of Britain has already been
noted – when he remarks, 'When that this body did contain a spirit,
/ A kingdom for it was too small a bound' (*1 Henry IV* V.iv.88–9).
Having defeated his rival and taken the throne, 'King Harry' now
describes his own determination to retain the crown in terms of
gargantuan struggle: 'put the world's whole strength / Into one giant
arm, it shall not force / This lineal honour from me' (*2 Henry IV*
IV.iii.175–7).

These plays, however, also produce another figure of planetary
proportions, a 'globe of sinful continents' (*2 Henry IV* II.iv.288). Falstaff,
as the incarnation of a world of misrule that Hal must renounce in
order to achieve political maturity, appears to repeat the transcription
of the earth into a model or map, albeit one in the shape of a man:
'Banish plump Jack, and banish all the world' (*1 Henry IV* II.v.485).
However, in his exorbitant dimensions and the flamboyance of his
character, Falstaff instead comes to signify what escapes the clinical
and calculating gaze of geometry as represented by Prince Hal's telling
eye for political expediency. 'Why, you are so fat, Sir John, that you
must needs be out of all compass, out of all reasonable compass, Sir
John,' remarks Bardolph (*1 Henry IV* III.iii.20–2). To be 'out of all
compass' is to be beyond the reach of cartographic representation,
for 'compass' could refer to two different instruments familiar in Shakespeare's time: the magnetic device to locate direction, and the geometrical implement for drawing circles. Falstaff, as the representative
of a world Hal distances himself from in his ascent to the throne,
also embodies what cannot be mastered in the illusory relation between
gigantic ego and diminished world.

Indeed, each of the plays mentioned so far provides, along with
the metaphors which elevate its protagonist to the stature of a
colossus, accompanying images of that figure's deflation. Richard
II, for instance, exchanges his 'large kingdom for a little grave'
(*Richard II* III.iii.152), and Hal remarks of Hotspur's death, 'Ill-weaved
ambition, how much art thou shrunk!', adding that 'two paces of
the vilest earth / Is room enough' to contain the body of his defeated rival (*1 Henry IV* V.iv.87–91). Antony repeats this reaction as
he stands over Julius Caesar's corpse:

> O mighty Caesar! Dost thou lie so low?
> Are all thy conquests, glories, triumphs, spoils,
> Shrunk to this little measure?
>
> (*Julius Caesar* III.i.149–51)

Antony's own fall from the political summit figures in more elaborate terms. His status, as 'The triple pillar of the world transformed / Into a strumpet's fool', appears ambiguous from first few lines of the play (*Antony and Cleopatra* I.i.12–13). Not long after the scene related by Octavius, in which Antony and Cleopatra publicly map their empire by listing its dominions (III.vi.3–16), Antony's defeats, rather than his achievements, are seen – from another perspective – in the same colossal terms:

> The greater cantle of the world is lost
> With very ignorance; we have kissed away
> Kingdoms and provinces
>
> (III.x.6–8)

At this point, his mastery of a submissive globe seems so uncertain that 'the land bids me tread no more upon't, / It is ashamed to bear me' (III.xi.1–2).

However, Antony expresses the evanescence of this egomorphic gigantism most explicitly in his dialogue with Eros after the next battle against Octavius, describing his dissolution into nothing from a figure of gigantic visibility, a cynosure. Like a cloud in the shape of 'A towered citadel, or blue promontory', Antony's imperial image, which had seemed to loom over the earth, has evaporated, becoming 'indistinct / As water is in water' (IV.xv.2–14). He declines from an Atlas figure with the entire world in his grasp to one who cannot even contain his own body: 'Here I am Antony, / Yet cannot hold this visible shape' (ll. 13–14). As he makes this speech, in the BBC version of the play, Antony discards his armour, displaying to the audience the dramatic equivalent of a decomposing body, shedding its aspect of armed and statuesque potency.

The same contrast between the contained or self-sufficient ego, and its dissolution, structures the dominant idiom of another Roman play, *Coriolanus*. Caius Martius' political pre-eminence depends upon his capacity to integrate the civic collectivity into his own colossal stature, but his contempt for the public works against this process, nearly provoking the citizens into a dangerous realisation of their individuality, figured once more in explicitly cartographic terms:

SECOND CITIZEN. . . . truly I think if all our wits were to issue out of one skull, they would fly east, west, north, south, and their consent of one direct way should be all at once to all the points o'th' compass. (II.iii.21–4)

Incapable of contracting this 'many-headed multitude' into a single frame, Coriolanus becomes the last of the figures from the Roman plays to attempt the assumption of colossal stature, and to suffer its subsequent disintegration. In his arrogance, he offers a particularly characteristic figure of one elevated (in his own eyes as well as others') to an exaggerated and tenuous mastery over a diminished world – 'The man is noble, and his fame folds in / This orb o'th' earth' (V.vi.124–5) – claiming the right to assert his supremacy over the people, even if they threaten to execute him:

> . . . pile ten hills on the Tarpeian rock,
> That the precipitation might down stretch
> Below the beam of sight, yet will I still
> Be thus to them
>
> (III.ii.3–6)

This passage participates in the same Albertian pictorial principles as Edgar's Dover cliff speech in *Lear,* and the description of Posthumus' departure in *Cymbeline*: a vertiginous perspectivism that once again proves liable to decomposition. Looking down upon the citizenry from his position of self-assured superiority, Coriolanus, like the other figures discussed so far, embodies the exorbitant stature and panoramic vision of the colossus. Here, the prospect of Coriolanus's fall from the extravagantly multiplied altitude of the Tarpeian Rock into a vanishing point 'below the beam of sight' represents the threat of collapse implicit within this structure.

Bid kings come bow

The anthropomorphic projections of the 'ego's era', therefore, result in what Lacan describes as the 'hominisation of the world, its perception in terms of images linked to the structuration of the body' (1988a, 141).[10] Teresa Brennan points out that this perceptual and representational transaction takes as its ideal, specifically, the male body and its conventional association with activity (Brennan 1993, 52–62). This ego produces, as its object, an inert, submissive body. In one sense, psychoanalysis can be read as the exploration of this dialectic, whereby masculinity and femininity respectively affiliate with one of the two poles of this activity–passivity opposition. Cartography collaborates in this version of gender in so far as it subjugates the geographical contours of the land under the rubrics of a two-dimensional projection or a spherical model, 'passifying' the world beneath the geometrical net cast from an erect and masterful gaze (Lacan 1977b, 42). Lacan, moreover, describes this 'symbolic system' as a 'conquest, rape of nature, transformation of nature, hominisation of the planet', again implying the forcing of a passive femininity by an active masculinity (1988a, 265). I have described already the ways in which Elizabethan surveyors like John Norden imagined the countryside offering itself submissively to their view; this recalls also discussions by many recent critics of the feminisation of both Britain and the New World through the mapping of the terrain by a specifically male gaze.[11]

Shakespearean chorography involves the same subjection of both land and female body to a masculine gaze, for example, when conflating the siege of a city, or the invasion of a territory, with the pursuit and rape of a woman. So, in *Henry V*, the King graphically evokes, in a single threat, the imminent 'hot and forcing violation' of both the walls of Harfleur and of its maidens (III.iii.90–126). By the end of that play, Princess Catherine embodies the land of France, forced to submit to Henry's mastery. This metaphorical correlation proves indissociable from the royal and imperialist gaze, for the superimposition of Catherine's body over the French cities can only be perceived from Henry's standpoint and according to his perspective:

> KING HENRY . . . you may, some of you, thank love for my blindness, who cannot see many a fair French city for one fair French maid that stands in my way.
> KING CHARLES. Yes, my lord, you see them perspectively, the cities turned into a maid – for they are all girdled with maiden walls that war hath never entered. (V.ii.313–19)

The Oxford editor points out the reference here to the popular Elizabethan perspective toy 'which showed different images when viewed from different angles' (Taylor 1982, 279). Like the kind of anamorphic painting exemplified by Holbein's *Ambassadors*, such a device betrays an inconsistency in the masterful viewing position of the subject, a contradiction which can be traced in Shakespeare's metaphor. King Henry, emphasising the stability of his viewpoint and the fixity of his gaze, imagines Catherine blocking his line of sight, which would otherwise reach out to encompass the wider territory of France. When King Charles suggests that Henry can see both woman and cities 'perspectively', what seems to be the evocation of an omnivoyant gaze actually undermines the centralised visual location Henry had claimed for himself, for the perception of two different aspects, in either the device referred to by Shakespeare or the anamorphic painting, requires a change of viewpoint, a new perspective, displacing the fixed eye of the subject. In this passage, therefore, the feminisation of the land, or conversely the mapping of the female body, simultaneously solicits and disrupts the mastery of the male gaze.

In *King John*, similarly, the city of Angiers represents another female body to be anatomised, undressed and penetrated. John, in a conceit progressing from the town's 'eyes', which are 'winking', to its 'waist', from which the belt of stones will be 'dishabited', equates the threat posed by the French forces with the ravishment of a female body (II.i.208–34). The subsequent transactions of the play – conducted through a repetitive enumeration of the territories under debate – almost reach resolution in the betrothal of Blanche and Louis, which again occurs in consistently cartographic mode. Blanche – whose name designates her as a blank space, available for inscription – provides the parchment upon which a map may be drawn that redefines the boundaries between France and England. Blanche is a 'treaty', a 'book of beauty', a list of territories ('Anjou and fair Touraine, Maine, Poitiers . . .'), a white page onto which princes copy, narcissistically, their own images, or an empty mirror in which they see their own masterful reflections, just as Louis sees himself 'Drawn in the flattering table of her eye' (II.i.497–503). However, just as 'commodity' makes maps, it also revises them when they are out of date, and in the accelerating cartographic politics out of which the text is written, the lifespan of a particular strategic alignment, as expressed in a given map, can prove brief. When Pandolf appears and demands France's allegiance to Rome against England, the alliance forged by the marriage becomes invalid. Blanche, the map on which the compromise borders were drawn, simply rips apart like a parchment:

> Which is the side that I must go withal?
> I am with both, each army hath a hand,
> And in their rage, I having hold of both,
> They whirl asunder and dismember me.
>
> (III.i.253–6)

Through the power of representation, the female body is transmuted into a chart, a political *carte blanche* or blank cheque, to be torn up when no longer of use.

After the conclusion of peace between France and England, as ratified by the redrafted map of Blanche's betrothal to Louis, Constance establishes her own protest against this cartographic structure. She does so by means of a gesture that refuses to participate in the competition to occupy the spectatorial mastery of the male gaze cast over a passive terrain:

> (*She sits upon the ground*)
> To me and to the state of my great grief
> Let kings assemble, for my grief's so great
> That no supporter but the huge firm earth
> Can hold it up. Here I and sorrows sit;
> Here is my throne; bid kings come bow to it.
> (II.ii.70–4)

The new 'state' founded by Constance establishes a conflicting subject position, an alternative play of gazes, and a different relationship with the earth from that of the two kings. She abolishes the elevated stature from which the land may be cartographically surveyed, and replaces it with a spectatorial position – a 'throne' – closer to the 'huge firm earth', as that which resists diminution to the proportions of a model globe. Her own gaze, from this level, once again offers a reverse perspective that subverts the view from above. Yet it is not submissive, for kings have to 'bow to it', to look down in order to engage with it, thereby becoming implicated in that de-based and lowering gaze which displaces their visual dominance.

Acts commenced on this ball of earth

In another manifestation of the masculine gaze, *Antony and Cleopatra* provides, before the audience sees her for itself, a description of the heroine which superimposes her figure over the contours of the Egypt she rules, translating both into a text or a panorama, supine beneath the traversing eye of the male reader. 'Would I had never seen her!', remarks Antony, to which Enobarbus replies, 'O, sir, you had then left unseen a wonderful piece of work, which not to have been blessed withal would have discredited your travel' (I.ii.144–7).

The mention of 'travel' serves to contextualise the surveying gaze under discussion within a contemporary culture of sightseeing. References to Elizabethan and Jacobean travellers provide evidence that the emergence of the cartographic economy, and the subjectivity it heralds, although modelled upon the privileged view of the sovereign and the explorer, was not confined only to the monarchy and its immediate circle, as the Bastard's satire in *King John* suggests. Having achieved a sudden elevation in social status, Faulconbridge parodies the dinner conversation of the well-travelled Elizabethan gentleman, the 'pickèd man of countries', displaying his familiarity with foreign places, sights, and names:

> . . . talking of the Alps and Appenines,
> The Pyrenean and the River Po,
> It draws toward supper in conclusion so.
> But this is worshipful society,
> And fits the mounting spirit like myself;
> For he is but a bastard to the time
> That doth not smack of observation.
>
> (I.i.193–208)

Yet in a wider context, this passage also suggests that to 'smack of observation' was not even exclusively the prerogative of those who actually ventured beyond England's shores. For Faulconbridge gives his travelogue in the form of the questions and answers of 'an Absey book' (195–200), a primer or introductory language manual, in which such chorographic lists were common (Honigmann 1954, xlvii). These connections demonstrate the popularity, not so much of actual experience in other countries, or even of travel within Britain, but of what might be called 'closet travel', in reference to the words of Gerard Mercator in the Preface to his *Atlas* of 1595, who suggests that the reader of his maps 'by speculation in his closset, may travell through every province of the world' (cited in Rabasa 1985, 7). Many contemporary writers confirm the existence of this evidently substantial readership, consisting of those 'mounting spirits' who enjoyed easy access to maps as stimulants to their imagination of, or their learning, reading, hearing and talking about, foreign lands. R. A. Skelton quotes the editor of a town-atlas published in 1581:

> What could be more agreeable than, in one's home far from danger, to gaze in these books at the universal form of the earth

[and] ... to acquire knowledge which could scarcely be had but by long and difficult journeys? (cited in Skelton 1971, 3)

Similarly, in his 'Mathematicall Preface' to the English translation of Euclid, John Dee writes in 1570 of those who, 'either for their owne iorneyes directing into farre landes: or to vnderstand of other mens trauailes. ... liketh, loueth, getteth, and vseth, Mappes, Chartes, & Geographicall Globes' (Dee 1975, sig. a4r).

The existence of this market for maps suggests the increasing potency of both cartographic representation and its textual equivalent in prose, poetry and drama, to establish and disseminate its characteristic scopic economy across a wide range of readers. Moreover, writing of his visit to London in 1599, Thomas Platter remarks that plays fulfil much the same function as maps for closet travellers:

With these and many more amusements the English pass their time, learning at the play what is happening abroad; indeed men and womenfolk visit such places without scruple, since the English for the most part do not travel much, but prefer to learn foreign matters and take their pleasures at home. (Platter 1937, 170)[12]

Unless Faulconbridge's 'bastards to the time' made up the entire theatregoing public, therefore, a considerable number of Shakespeare's audience must have had some experience, if not of actual touring, then of maps or traveller's descriptions representing various parts of the known world. Shakespearean drama, with its ubiquity of geographical references, confirms its spectators in the positions prescribed for them by the cartographic economy – not only through the rhetorical and theatrical representation of the spatial developments involved, but in the actual encounter that takes place between audience and stage. It does so, however, in a thoroughly conflicted way.

In the first place, the theatre itself offers a manifestation of the reduction of the world to a model for consumption by the spectator. The emblematic figure of Rumour invokes this role of the stage in the prologue to *2 Henry IV*: 'I from the orient to the drooping west, / ... still unfold / The acts commencèd on this ball of earth' (Induction 3–5). The world and its histories can be folded and unfolded like a map, diminished to the size of a ball, the object of (a) play, while 'acts' of global significance become equivalent in scope to those performed on the stage. Like the famous name of the theatre built by Shakespeare's company in 1599, the titles of a number of contemporary atlases and map collections insist on a correlation between stage and cartography, from the *Theatrum Orbis Terrarum* of Abraham Ortelius (1570 and later editions), to Speed's *Theatre of the Empire of Great Britain* (1611).[13]

However, the prologues of the plays often seem less than confident in their ability to contain the world within the frame of the stage. In the Prologue to *Henry V*, the Chorus expresses more obvious reservations about the translation of world into theatre when it wishes for

> A kingdom for a stage, princes to act,
> And monarchs to behold the swelling scene.
>   . . . But pardon, gentles all,
> The flat unraisèd spirits that hath dared
> On this unworthy scaffold to bring forth
> So great an object. Can this cock-pit hold
> The vasty fields of France? Or may we cram
> Within this wooden O the very casques
> That did affright the air at Agincourt?
> O pardon: since a crookèd figure may
> Attest in little place a million,
> And let us, ciphers to this great account,
> On your imaginary forces work.
> Suppose within the girdle of these walls
> Are now confined two mighty monarchies,
> Whose high uprearèd and abutting fronts
> The perilous narrow ocean parts asunder.

>   (ll. 1–22)

This passage opens the play with an overt delineation of the geographical relationship between England and France, reliant – like the other Shakespearean charts discussed so far – on a correlation between the land and a 'girdled' female body, protected by inviolable boundaries, as exemplified by the habitual references to precipitous coastlines and an encircling sea; typically, the demarcation between the nation and its others, sundered by an ocean both 'perilous' and 'narrow', remains precarious.

The evocation of this familiar chorography, and its theatrical efficacy, depend upon the same 'imaginary forces' operating among the audience that contemporary writers describe at work in the 'closet travel' or vicarious sightseeing of Elizabethan readers poring over maps in their studies. But in drama, by contrast, the surveying eye produced by such a cartographic imagination operates communally, not in isolation. For the institution of a single spectatorial eye plainly conflicts with the actual conditions of Elizabethan and Jacobean public theatre, in which the relationship between audience and stage was dispersed, interactive, dialogic, and communal.[14] The 'wooden O' of the Shakespearean theatre could not actually play to a single, fixed or privileged spectatorial position. On the contrary, the round auditorium instituted a circular array of viewpoints which crossed and recrossed the stage, according to the conflicting perspectives elicited by the play. The Prologue hints at this conflict between a single privileged gaze and the multiple eyes of the public theatre when it expresses the desire for 'monarchs to behold the swelling scene'. In order to achieve the perfect illusion of three-dimensional cartographic perspective, so that a 'kingdom' may be equated with a 'stage' and 'princes' with actors, the drama needs to play to the monocentric viewpoint of the sovereign eye, as typified by the seat of the monarch watching a court masque.[15] In its failure to isolate in the audience such a privileged gaze, the stage degenerates into what the Prologue calls a 'flat unraised' representation, with the same two-dimensional limits and anamorphic distortions as a map or painting.

What, we might ask, would the successful establishment of this singular viewing position involve? For one thing, the repression of the vestigial medieval theatrical relationship between audience and stage, and the historical foreclosure of the gaze, in so far as it constitutes a multiplicity of perspectives, or a return of the line of sight upon the spectator from the stage. The elaborate perspectival designs of the Jacobean and Restoration court masque, which would resolve into perfect visibility only from the monarch's central position, aimed at precisely this effect.[16] This movement from the visual kaleidoscope of Elizabethan public theatre to the almost cinematic dramaturgy of optical illusion – which will prove important to my discussion of *Macbeth* in the next and final chapter – reached its apogee in the 'realist' Shakespeare productions of the nineteenth-century stage, which contructed tableaux aiming for a total verisimilitude on a vast stage behind the frame of the proscenium arch.[17] It is no accident that at the same time, cartography was completing its long project of subjugating the entire British Empire beneath a single mapping gaze, culminating in the Ordnance Survey of Ireland, and the triangulation of the Indian subcontinent under the direction of Sir George Everest, after whom the highest point on the globe was subsequently named in implicit acknowledgement of the role played in the colonising drive by the surveyor's omnivoyance.[18] That these two movements coincided should not be surprising if, as my reading suggests, the space of the stage and that of cartography are conterminous, so that identical strategies and perceptual systems play from one to the other. It is the singular eye/I, as representative of an ascendent subjectivity instituted by this reconfigured space, which will find itself increasingly central to the theatre, the painting, the map, and the political sphere of post-sixteenth-century Europe.

6
Macbeth: Mimicry and Masquerade

What does Macbeth want? For one thing, it might be seen that many of his actions and words display the desire to *see*; or rather, the desire for access to an omnipotent and all-encompassing vision – of the witches, for example, or their apparitions; of his subjects, or of the future. In this respect, the play typifies the humanist fascination with lucid and penetrating vision as the primary expression of the sovereignty and agency of the subject. But perhaps more often, Macbeth's most desperate utterances reveal a 'black and deep' desire for *sightlessness*: that is, both invisibility and blindness: 'Let not light see my black and deep desires' (I.iv.51); 'I am afraid to think what I have done, / Look on't again I dare not' (II.ii.49–50); 'Avaunt, and quit my sight! Let the earth hide thee' (III.iv.92); 'Strange things I have in head that will to hand, / Which must be acted ere they may be scanned' (III.iv.138–9); 'But no more sights!' (IV.i.171).

If emergent Renaissance humanism figures the subject's reason and knowledge, and the sovereignty of this 'I' over its 'others' according to the mastery of the eye over the optical field, this representation remains haunted by its unconscious inversion: the fear of being exposed to the gaze of an other. The subject's agency thus rests not only on its ability to see, but also on its capacity to do so without being seen in turn; so that by the time Descartes writes his treatise on optics, the *Dioptrique*, his famous *cogito ergo sum* might be said to accompany or inhabit a kind of *speculor ergo sum*: 'I spy, therefore I am.' Because the action and dialogue of *Macbeth* hinge on the various crises endemic to sovereignty (succession, usurpation, insurrection, tyranny), an exploration of the representation of these reversals and disruptions as they affect the position of the sovereign I/eye within the optical field reveals much about the troubled emergence of the Renaissance humanist subject.

Frame one: supernatural soliciting

At the start of the play – before the play – the witches are there, on stage. Stéphane Mallarmé insists that the three sisters do not enter in the usual manner of actors, but rather they are revealed to be already present, 'as if, in the masterpiece, the curtain had simply risen a minute too soon' (Mallarmé 1945, 348). Certainly their exits are far from conventional: producers have always had difficulty effecting the required vanishment 'Into the air . . . as breath into the wind' (I.iii.79–80). Mallarmé suggests that this first scene offers a glimpse behind the scenes at the preparation of the play itself, into 'the kitchen in which the deed is cooking', a transgressive representation of the dramaturgy doing its work.[1]

Undeniably, during their first brief appearance, the witches do feature as 'producers' of the play, deciding upon the initial location ('Upon the heath'), the timing ('ere the set of sun'), and the context within which the action will take place ('When the battle's lost and won') (I.i.4–6). They next inform the audience of the aim of all this preparation: to allow them 'to meet with Macbeth' (l. 7). Having thereby named both the play and its main character, the witches even script his first lines for him: 'Fair is foul, and foul is fair, / Hover through the fog and filthy air' (ll. 10–11).

The ensuing scenes follow these directions to the letter. A bleeding Captain describes Duncan's forces first in danger of defeat, then triumphant, then at a disadvantage again, and finally victorious (I.ii.1–42). This 'hurly-burly', oscillation of fortunes – described again by Ross (ll. 48–58) – conforms to the witches' prescription of a battle 'lost and won'. The scene also prepares the audience for the treacherous role to be played by Macbeth, consistently portraying him confronting the rebels – first Macdonald, then the Thane of Cawdor – 'with self-comparisons . . .' (l. 55). 'Point against point, rebellious arm 'gainst arm', Macbeth offers a violent mirror-image to both traitors, whose betrayal of Duncan he is about to emulate (l. 56).[2] So far Macbeth's future, like his reputation, precedes him. And when he does enter 'in person', he immediately speaks the lines allocated him by the witches: 'So foul and fair a day I have not seen' (I.iii.36).

In short, the first appearance of the Weird Sisters sets the climate for the play in every respect. Witches were widely believed to command considerable meteorological influence: and these three, having chosen from a range of possibilities – 'In thunder, lightning or in rain?' (I.i.2) – eventually settle on 'fog and filthy air', as providing the atmosphere through which they can most easily 'hover' (l. 11). Darkness, moreover, also facilitates the manipulation and delusion of vision, and throughout the play, the witches will manifest an ominous relationship with the faculty of sight.

In his *Daemonologie* (1597), King James I confirms – or more likely provides the source for – the witches' preference for vaporous darkness. He writes that they enjoy a privileged relationship with the element of air through their collusion with the devil, 'he hauing such affinitie with the aire as being a spirite, and hauing such power of the forming and moouing thereof. . . . For in the Scripture, that stile of *the Prince of the aire* is giuen vnto him' (James I 1966, 46–7). Hence Macbeth's description of the witches' disappearance: 'they made themselves air, into which they vanished' (I.v.4–5). Practitioners of the demonic arts were also thought to be adept manipulators of vision itself, for as James points out, given the devil's facility with atmospheric effects, 'why may he not far easiler thicken & obscure so the air, that is next about them by contracting it strait together, that the beames of any other mans eyes, cannot pearce thorow the same, to see them?' (1966, 39). Darkness can therefore be fabricated by knitting together rays of light into a thick material which the 'beames' of human eyesight cannot pierce. Later in the play, Lady Macbeth will invoke just such an atmospheric screen, requesting 'thick night' to 'Come . . . / And pall thee in the dunnest smoke of hell', in order that heaven may be unable to 'peep through the blanket of the dark . . .' (I.v.49–52). Night itself constitutes a form of camouflage, a secure hiding place for evil and a menacing obscurity for the innocent.

Such a representation of darkness remains of interest to modern psychoanalysis. In his discussion of the relation between mimicry and psychosis, Roger Caillois suggests that darkness also brings about the sensation of a breakdown of any distinction between ego and environment. Citing psychoanalyst Eugène Minkowski, Caillois describes this as an experience of

> *depersonalization by assimilation to space*, i.e., what mimicry achieves morphologically in certain animal species. The magical hold (one can truly call it so without doing violence to the language) of

night and obscurity, the *fear of the dark*, probably also has its roots in the peril in which it puts the opposition between the organism and the milieu. . . . darkness is not the mere absence of light; there is something positive about it. While light space is eliminated by the materiality of objects, darkness is 'filled', it touches the individual directly, envelops him, penetrates him, and even passes through him: hence 'the ego is *permeable* for darkness while it is not so for light'; the feeling of mystery that one experiences at night would not come from anything else. (Caillois 1984, 30)

The failure of vision leaves the subject's position in the spatial field uncertain, unsure of its location, threatened by absorption into surroundings within which it now features as merely a component, rather than as the organising central eye. Like James I in the *Daemonologie*, Caillois envisages darkness as palpable, attaining a 'magical' hold through the coagulation of space into substance.

Macbeth's audience observes this atmospheric matter pervading the play, conjured up first by the witches to cover Macbeth, then by Lady Macbeth to cloak the murder of Duncan, and later by Macbeth himself to envelop Banquo:

> – Come, seeling night,
> Scarf up the tender eye of pitiful day,
> And with thy bloody and invisible hand
> Cancel and tear to pieces that great bond
> Which keeps me pale. Light thickens, and the crow
> Makes wing to th' rooky wood.
> Good things of day begin to droop and drowse,
> Whiles night's black agents to their preys do rouse.

> (III.ii.47–54)

Macbeth instructs his 'agents', the murderers, that both Fleance and his father 'must embrace the fate / Of that dark hour' (III.i.138–9). But in fact this hungry, assimilative darkness comes to dominate the entire social and political environment of the Scotland of the play, threatening the establishment and maintenance of any secure identity, or the maintenance of any social boundaries:

> By th' clock 'tis day,
> And yet dark night strangles the travelling lamp.

Is't night's predominance or the day's shame
That darkness does the face of earth entomb
When living light should kiss it?

(II.iv.6–10)

From the beginning of the play, when Duncan confesses that 'There's no art / To find the mind's construction in the face', until its end, suspicion, distrust and misrecognition colour all visual transactions, even between those who should know each other (I.iv.11–12). Once Macbeth has called upon the stars to hide their fires (I.iv.50), Banquo can no longer identify him, even in his own castle (II.i.9–10). Even Macbeth's enemies repeatedly deceive and mistake each other. Malcolm mistrusts Macduff, telling him a succession of lies (IV.iii.11–140); and on the arrival of another supposed ally among the Scots exiles, he remarks 'My countryman, but yet I know him not... Good God betimes remove / The means that make us strangers!' Ross in turn describes a Scotland 'Almost afraid to know itself' (IV.iii.161–6).

Lady Macbeth best characterises this strategy of mimetic camouflage, in the famous injunction to her partner to 'look like the innocent flower, / But be the serpent under't' (I.v.64–5). Macbeth accedes to this suggestion, realising that in the dissimulating atmosphere they have propagated, 'False face must hide what the false heart doth know' (I.vii.82). The serpent looking like a flower derives from a conventional emblem, as editors of the play have noted (Muir 1972, 32), but it also looks remarkably like an instance of the morphological mimicry so common in nature, according to which many species of animal come to resemble their environment.

Caillois, again, proposes a similarity between such camouflage and sympathetic magic. He bases this comparison on the shared principle of '*like produces like*', resulting in an 'overwhelming tendency to imitate, combined with a belief in the efficacy of this imitation...'. According to this analogy, 'Mimicry would thus be accurately defined as *an incantation fixed at its culminating point* and having caught the sorcerer in his own trap', the end result of which would be the organism's (or the sorcerer's) '*assimilation to the surroundings*' (1984, 25–7). The Macbeths' mimetic incantations suffuse the play with an atmosphere of treacherous masquerade which becomes, in the end, involuntary. Like the darkness with which it is associated, this dissimulative ambience scrambles the co-ordinates of secure identity: 'To know my deed 'twere best not know myself' (II.ii.71).

Macbeth and Lady Macbeth have created an environment which will subsequently consume them.

Returning to Macbeth's initial appearance in the play, it becomes apparent that the blanket of 'filthy air' smothering the stage also masks the appearance of the witches from their observers:

> – What are these,
> So withered, and so wild in their attire,
> That look not like th'inhabitants o'th' earth
> And yet are on't?

(I.iii.37–40)

Banquo's baffled concentration on the clothing of the Weird Sisters already betrays the strategy of masquerade that will come to dominate the scopic field of the play. 'I'th' name of truth, / Are ye fantastical or that indeed / Which outwardly ye show?' (I.iii.50–2). He cannot tell whether the witches' outward show – their symbolic representation 'I'th' name of truth' – will prove consistent with their true substance.

Dress, as the external signifier of identity, manifests a disconcerting equivocality throughout the play. When Macbeth expresses discomfort at being (ad)dressed in the 'borrowed robes' of the rebel Thane of Cawdor, Banquo reassures him that 'strange garments, cleave not to their mould / But with the aid of use' (I.iii.107, 144–5). However, both *Macbeth* and the contemporary controversy surrounding theatrical transgression of the social codes governing dress would seem to suggest the reverse: that garments can create the role and the identity they represent. Stephen Gosson, writing against the stage in both *The Schoole of Abuse* (1579) and *Playes Confuted in Fiue Actions* (1582), repeatedly criticises actors' wearing of inappropriate garments – those of a higher rank, or those of women – comparing the effect of such disguise to 'the wreathinges, and windinge of a snake', which will 'binde vppe cordes when they haue possession' (Gosson 1974, 96 and 175). Apparel, and the social role it symbolises, here assumes a sinuous capacity to grasp and distort the *persona* of the wearer to its own form.[3] Similarly, Macbeth will indeed 'cleave ... to [the] mould' of his newly 'borrowed robes', putting on the dangerous aspirations of the rebel Thane of Cawdor against his king, wreathing into the form of the serpent while looking as innocent as the flower. Just as he spoke his first lines prompted by the witches, Macbeth now performs a role already scripted, and puts on the costume which will possess him.

Frame two: the air-drawn dagger

With the initial appearances of the witches, then, the audience have seen what they should not: the representational system working behind the scenes to inscribe the subject within its optical milieu. In contrast, the play's next apparition appears invisible to them. On his way to perform the murder of Duncan, the overwrought Macbeth stops and gazes in horror before him:

> Is this a dagger which I see before me,
> The handle toward my hand? Come, let me clutch thee.
> I have thee not, and yet I see thee still.
> Art thou not, fatal vision, sensible
> To feeling as to sight?
>
> (II.i.33–7)

The audience cannot help but trace the trajectory of Macbeth's gaze at this point and, through the mere projection of sight itself, form 'insubstantial air' into something almost palpable, 'sensible / To feeling as to sight'. And surely what proves most 'alarming' about the 'shape of such a weapon' is precisely the extent to which it appears capable of 'embodying' that line of vision which precedes and informs that of the spectator.

The dagger does not merely occur as an object of sight. Rather, it represents sight itself. Its form, nature and origin incorporate the very physiology of visual illusion or hallucination, according to both the theatre and the medical science of Shakespeare's age:

> Or art thou but
> A dagger of the mind, a false creation
> Proceeding from the heat-oppressèd brain?
> I see thee yet, in form as palpable
> As this which now I draw.
> Thou marshall'st me the way that I was going,
> And such an instrument I was to use.
> Mine eyes are made the fools o'th' other senses,
> Or else worth all the rest. I see thee still,
> And on thy blade and dudgeon gouts of blood,
> Which was not so before. There's no such thing.
> It is the bloody business which informs
> Thus to mine eyes.
>
> (ll. 37–49)

In the early seventeenth century, dreams, daydreams, fantasies and various other visual effects were considered to arise from an imbalance of humours. An overabundance of melancholy – of which Macbeth, like so many Shakespearean tragic heroes, shows every sign – was particularly apt to produce hallucinatory visions. The excess humour sent vapours to the head which, subsequently 'proceeding from the heat-oppressèd brain', issued forth as invisible streams from the eyes. These would 'inform' – Macbeth's use of this word relies on the contemporary meaning, 'to give shape to' – 'false creation[s]' or images imprinted upon the air.[4]

'This is the air-drawn dagger,' as Lady Macbeth later describes it, 'which you said / Led you to Duncan' (III.iv.61–2). Her words suggest a vision both delineated upon the air and moving through the air. An audience might also hear the phrase as 'air-drawing', denoting a visual faculty capable of inscription in space, or of pulling the air along with it. This 'drawing' incites Macbeth to action, leads him to the employment of the more substantial knife 'which now I draw': 'Thou marshall'st me the way that I was going, / And such an instrument I was to use.' Here Macbeth's hallucinatory rapture matches Lacan's description of the scopic structure of the dream, in which 'our position . . . is profoundly that of someone who does not see. The subject does not see where it is leading, he [*sic*] follows' (1979, 75). Macbeth does not 'see' in the sense that he has complete agency over the visual field: rather, it shows him. Vision, as a path of light or a gleaming blade, 'grasps [him], solicits [him] at every moment' (Lacan 1979, 96).

Here Lacan displays the influence of Merleau-Ponty, for whom this prompting or pre-empting by the gaze characterises the scopic field in general. Light constructs a theatrical apparatus in which both vision and visibility become possible:

> The lighting directs my gaze and causes me to see an object, so that in a sense it *knows* and *sees* the object. If I imagine a theatre with no audience in which the curtain rises upon illuminated scenery, I have the impression that the spectacle *is in itself visible* or ready to be seen, and that the light which probes the back and foreground, accentuating the shadows and permeating the scene through and through, in a way anticipates our vision. Conversely our own vision merely takes up on its own account and carries through the encompassing of the scene by those paths traced out for it by the lighting, just as, when we hear a sen-

tence, we are surprised to discover the track of an alien thought. We perceive in conformity with the light, as we think in conformity with other people in verbal communication. (Merleau-Ponty 1962, 310)

Macbeth's situation anticipates this dramaturgy of the future, this post-Shakespearean theatre of light in which the subject cannot choose but to act. The evolution of European theatre towards the kind of staging implied by Merleau-Ponty – which of course finds its apotheosis in the cinema – represents the emergence of a visual regime which is implicit in Macbeth's hallucination, according to which light, the substance of vision, both shows him a scene and shows him seen.

I have observed that, at the beginning of the play, the witches prescribed the role Macbeth was to play. They located him in a setting, interpellated him according to the various roles he was to assume – 'Hail to thee, Thane of Glamis . . . Thane of Cawdor . . . that shall be king hereafter' (I.iii.46–8) – and even prompted his first line. This 'supernatural soliciting', furthermore, was already associated with visual illusion, with a 'horrid image' capable of causing violent physiological effects in the beholder: unfixing Macbeth's hair, making his 'seated heart knock' at his ribs. But the power of this hallucinatory reality did not stop there:

> Present fears
> Are less than horrible imaginings.
> My thought, whose murder yet is but fantastical,
> Shakes so my single state of man that function
> Is smothered in surmise, and nothing is
> But what is not.

> (I.iii.136–41)

Lacan asks a question appropriate to these lines of Macbeth's: 'In the end, doesn't the feeling of the real reach its high point in the pressing manifestation of an unreal, hallucinatory reality?' (1988a, 66–7). Macbeth's first imaginary vision of the dead Duncan, a 'thought, whose murder yet is but fantastical', comes to usurp the place of 'reality'. If 'nothing is / But what is not', the 'fantastical' vision dictates and delineates reality, so that the very thought of murder takes on the power to execute what 'is'. Now, immediately preceding the deed, just as the bell 'invites' him, Macbeth's hallucinated dagger embodies that 'fatal vision' which precedes his eye, leading him on according to the image of an action already completed: 'I go, and it is done' (II.i.62).

Nor did the early modern physiology of vision confine its effects to the production of delusions and dreams. Experts agreed on the capacity of the eye actually to inflict harm. The visual beams issuing from the ill-humoured eye were believed to produce various emotional disturbances, diseases or even death, in any person upon whom they were cast. A ubiquitous belief in this 'evil eye' firmly associated optical power once more with magic and sorcery. Even the sceptical Reginald Scot, author of the *Discoverie of Witchcraft* (1584), concedes the likely existence of 'fascination', and describes its mode of operation 'as an extermination or expulsion of the spirits through the eies, approching to the hart of the bewitched, and infecting the same . . .' (Scot 1930, 281). Scot goes on to expound a visual theory identical to Macbeth's, according to which the distempered humours,

> ascending into the highest parts of the head, doo fall into the eies, and so are from thence sent foorth, as being of all other parts of the bodie the most clear, and fullest of veines and pores, and with the verie spirit or vapor proceeding thence, is conveied out as it were bye beames and streames a certeine fierie force; whereof he that beholdeth sore eies shall have good experience. For the poison and disease in the eie infecteth the aire next unto it, and the same proceedeth further, carrieng with it the vapor and infection of the corrupted bloud: with the contagion whereof, the eies of the beholders are most apt to be infected. By the same meanes it is thought that the cockatrice depriveth the life, and a woolfe taketh awaie the voice of such as they suddenlie meete withall and behold. (281–2)

Macbeth also invokes the wolf as the sentinel of 'withered murder', participant in the same movement towards the 'design' of Duncan's assassination (II.i.52–6). Other references confirm Shakespeare's familiarity with this theory of vision. The French queen in *Henry V* compares Henry's eyes to 'The fatal balls of murdering basilisks' (V.ii.17), a punning reference to a type of large cannon, the shot from which follows the same trajectory, and produces the same effect, as the projection of venomous light from the eyes of the cockatrice. Again, the king in *2 Henry VI* says to the Duke of Suffolk: 'Look not upon me, for thine eyes are wounding – / Yet do not go away. Come, basilisk, / And kill the innocent gazer with thy sight' (III.ii.51–3). And Juliet also refers to the 'poison' in the 'the death-darting eye of cockatrice' (*Romeo and Juliet* III.ii.46–7).

Relating such allusions to the phantom knife that incites Macbeth to murder Duncan makes apparent the extent to which visual power was imagined as an active, penetrative force, capable of inflicting disease, wounds, and death. It is in this light that Lady Macbeth's oddly phrased request that her 'keen knife see not the wound it makes' should be understood (I.v.51). Vision penetrates, stabs out from the eye like a knife from the hand, leaving its lethal effects in the form of gashes, scars and infections.

This model of vision was already old in Shakespeare's time. Among the ancient Greeks and their medieval successors, all philosophical, physiological and mathematical debates about the operation of sight tended to coalesce around two points of view, following two opposing trajectories. The Atomists insisted that perception arises when *eidola* enter the senses from outside. They attributed sight to those images streaming off objects which impinged upon the eye. The Platonists, on the other hand, postulated a visual fire with the capacity to flash out from the eyes. As Plato describes it in the *Timaeus*,

> whenever there is daylight round about, the visual current issues forth, like to like, and coalesces with it and is formed into a single homogeneous body in a direct line with the eyes, in whatever quarter the stream issuing from within strikes upon any object it encounters outside. (cited in Lindberg 1976, 2–3)

Subsequent debates invariably returned to these two opposing views: light either streaming from the eye (extramission), or entering the eye from outside (intromission). Thus the Stoics described how the optical *pneuma* flows from the seat of consciousness to the eye, and then excites the air adjacent to it, which, combining with the illumination of the sun, renders the object visible. Similarly Pliny, Galen, Euclid and Ptolemy all favoured variants of the extramission hypothesis. Islamic scholars such as Al-Kindi followed this line of thought, dismissing the intromission thesis, until Avicenna attacked the Euclidean version of extramission in the eleventh century. His contemporary Alhazen then produced a new theory of intromission which, in a modified form, would gain ground in the West through its adoption by medieval writers such as Witelo, John Pecham, Roger Bacon and Robert Grosseteste. This model – that of light rays entering the eye from the object and creating within it an image passed to the brain – would receive its early modern formulation in Johannes Kepler's theory of the retinal image, upon which Descartes based his *Dioptrique* (Lindberg 1976).

However, even in Descartes a lingering trace of the extramission hypothesis can be discerned. For instance, he admits that

> the objects of sight can be perceived not only by means of the action in them which is directed towards our eyes, but also by the action in our eyes which is directed towards them. Nevertheless, because the latter action is nothing other than light, we must note that it is found only in the eyes of those creatures which can see in the dark, such as cats, whereas a man normally sees only through the action which comes from objects. (Descartes 1985, 1: 154)

Having strayed back into an extramission model – 'the action in our eyes which is directed towards' objects – the text hastens to limit this power to animals and re-associate human sight with intromission alone. Nevertheless, the guiding metaphor in the *Dioptrique* – that of the blind man who 'sees' by means of two sticks, which are held and manipulated in each of his hands – recalls once more the model of rays proceeding from the eyes, rather than light originating from the object. Extramission, which keeps the agency of sight firmly in the 'hands' of the subject, appears irresistibly attractive to Descartes, returning in the form of a metaphor that conflicts with his overt endorsement of the intromission theory.

In fact, despite the gradual ascendancy of the intromission model among Western philosophers, the evidence already adduced from *Macbeth* would suggest that extramission retained a strong hold into Shakespeare's time, in popular culture as well as the sciences and arts. Early modern beliefs in the evil eye, the basilisk and the fiery sight of nocturnal creatures attest to this. Indeed all these instances had for centuries featured in optical treatises as proofs of the extramission theory (Lindberg 1976, 106 and 160). Pliny's *Natural History* – which, in the translation by Holland, offers one likely source for Shakespeare's basilisks – also attests to the existence of fascination, to the harmful vision of wolves, and (like Descartes) to the fiery eyes of night-roaming animals such as cats (Pliny 1940, 2: 517–19; 3: 59 and 527). The physiological and medical theories of Shakespeare's contemporaries, moreover, were based upon Galen, who also subscribed to the extramission theory.

But, as I have argued throughout the preceding chapters, it was Euclidean and Ptolemaic geometry that exerted the most powerful influence upon the optical theory of early modern artists, architects and writers. Although both Euclid and Ptolemy concentrated upon the mathematical aspects of vision, and were little concerned with either its physical nature or its physiological origin, their insistence upon the model of a cone or pyramid of visual rays, with its apex in the eye of the beholder and its base forming the picture seen, undoubtedly replicates the structure of extramission. Euclid describes how the visual beams 'proceeding from the eye diverge indefinitely', so that 'those things are seen upon which visual rays fall' (cited in Lindberg 1976, 12). Clearly the eye here operates as the agent and origin of sight. Ptolemy's extrapolation of this Euclidean optical geometry, moreover, exerted a decisive influence not only on perspective painting via Alberti, but also on cartography and Shakespearean theatre as well.[5]

It is upon this extramission/intromission dialectic that the modern psychoanalytic discussion of the scopic drive superimposes its theory of projection and introjection, the subject's imaginary identification with, and assimilation of, an image. For example, Christian Metz's description of the spectator in the cinema sounds like an updated version of Plato's optical fire: 'All of us have experienced our own look . . . as a kind of searchlight turning on the axis of our own necks.' But Metz follows the Lacanian account of the subject's location in the optical field, which would perceive any sense of mastery granted by this active or extramissive visual agency to be entirely illusory and misleading. He therefore sees this 'cone of light' emanating from the eye as only half of the scopic structure:

All vision consists of a double movement: projective (the 'sweeping' searchlight) and introjective: consciousness as a sensitive recording surface (as a screen). I have the impression at once that, to use a common expression, I am 'casting' my eyes on things, and that the latter, thus illuminated, come to be deposited within me (we then declare that it is these things that have been 'projected', on to my retina, say). A sort of stream called the look, and explaining all the myths of magnetism, must be sent out over the world, so that objects can come back up this stream in the opposite direction (but using it to find their way), arriving at last at our perception, which is now soft wax and no longer an emitting source. (Metz 1982, 49–50)

The sensation of extramissive vision confirms the subject in its omnivoyant mastery, an illusion giving rise to 'all the myths of magnetism' including the evil eye, witchcraft and fascination.

To expose this illusion, Lacan insistently emphasises the return of light upon the subject, an intromissive visuality which precedes and exceeds the eye's imaginary linear control over a geometrical field. Thus, in a passage quoted earlier, he asserts that

Light may travel in a straight line, but it is refracted, diffused, it floods, it fills – the eye is a sort of bowl – it flows over, too, it necessitates, around the ocular bowl, a whole series of organs, mechanisms, defenses. The iris reacts not only to distance, but also to light, and it has to protect what takes place at the bottom of the bowl, which might, in certain circumstances, be damaged by it. The eyelid, too, when confronted with too bright a light, first blinks, that is, it screws itself up in a well-known grimace. (1979, 94)

Here Lacan echoes precisely the terms of the debate between intromission and extramission theorists. Al-Kindi, for instance, argues that the morphology of each organ implies its mode of functioning: the hollowness of the ear indicates its capacity to collect sound, while by contrast, the eye's spherical form and mobility suggests an ability to seek out and select the object to which it will send its ray (Lindberg 1976, 22). Lacan, on the other hand, by imagining the eye as 'a sort of bowl', reverses the trajectory of what Al-Kindi proposes in support of an extramission hypothesis. Moreover, what Lacan calls the 'well-known grimace' of the eye in response to the glare is cited by Alhazen as evidence of intromission, proof 'that light produces some effect in the eye' (Lindberg 1976, 62). Finally – if we trace the intromission theory as far back as the Atomists – Lucretius compares the *simulacra* emanating from visible objects to wood throwing off smoke, fire radiating heat, and snakes shedding their used skins (Lindberg 1976, 2–3). Lacan, associating animal mimicry with the pre-existence of an intromissive visual light, asks whether 'If a bird were to paint would it not not be by letting fall its feathers, a snake by casting off its scales, a tree by letting fall its leaves? What it amounts to is the first act in the laying down of the gaze' (1979, 72). Intromission, then, like mimicry, implies the surrender or laying down of the illusory mastery offered by an extramissive, active and agentive gaze in the face of a pre-emptive visuality prior and external to the subject's eye, a 'dependence of the visible on that which places us under the eye of the seer' (Lacan 1979, 72). Macbeth, captivated by his 'fatal vision', will relinquish agency and follow wherever it leads. Embodying and executing his intentions and desires, the 'air-drawn dagger' draws him into a pre-existing scopic field, a picture already painted. 'In this matter of the visible, everything is a trap . . .' (Lacan 1979, 93).

Macbeth himself describes the intromissive light which then returns to inscribe and frame him within the 'horrid image' (in)to which he is drawn:

> heaven's cherubin, horsed
> Upon the sightless couriers of the air,
> Shall blow the horrid deed in every eye
> That tears shall drown the wind.

> (I.vii.22–5)

The picture's impact upon the eye – as opposed to the eye's impact upon the world – results in blindness, a defeat of the scopic power claimed by the subject. In so far as Macbeth here equates vision with a movement of the air, blowing into the eye, the resulting 'tears' that 'drown the wind' represent the eye's failure in the face of a disabling visual excess. Sight itself becomes 'sightless', both blind and invisible. Again, the witches, who were commonly believed to ride 'horsed / Upon . . . the air', hover behind this metaphor, and are thereby associated with the visual excess that blinds the extramissive eye – just as, in the passage quoted earlier, James attributed to them the power to 'thicken & obscure so the air . . . by contracting it strait together, that the beames of any other mans eyes, cannot pearce thorow the same'.[6]

From the illusion pictured by Macbeth, then, an excessive visibility blows back into the eye. Elsewhere, this intromissive sight will be associated with a reversal of the dangerous penetrative power attributed to extramission. Thus Alhazen likens the propagation of light to an arrow from a bow (Lindberg 1976, 80), and Michel de

Certeau repeats the same comparison in his discussion of the preface to Nicholas of Cusa's optical treatise *De Visione Dei sive De icona* (1453):

> the problematics of the gaze grow out of a geometric perspective. The gaze is a vector – a line and an action in space. Like an arrow, it implants itself in each of the spectators.... This mathematics of the point is in concordance moreover with the anthropological conception which, in the tradition of Euclidian optics, from Guillaume of Conches up to Ficino or even Bramante, considers the gaze as the effect of 'natural spirits' emitted by the eye and 'going out' toward things – a conception which is maintained, in an increasingly hesitant and ambiguous way, up to Descartes' *Dioptrique*. But in the Cusan preface, if the traditional movement remains, its terms are reversed: the supposed object (the painting) looks, and the subjects (the spectators) make up the tableau. (de Certeau 1987, 15–16)

Michael Kubovy has suggested that for Italian artists of this time, the figure of an arrow offers a metaphor for the linear perspective, emanating from the eye of the beholder (1986, 1, 11, 14). For de Certeau, this arrow also returns upon the spectator, so that, as my discussion so far has suggested, the 'traditional movement' of natural spirits emitted by the eye has from antiquity always been accompanied by its diametrical reversal, in the form of the intromission theory.

In *Macbeth*, certainly, the incisive and potentially lethal force of extramissive vision – like the arrow or the 'air-drawn dagger' – does prove a dangerously two-edged sword. Macbeth relies upon a penetrative and violent vision to 'Carv[e] out his passage' through the play (I.i.20), cutting his way through the rebel armies, then through Duncan, Banquo and Macduff's family. Until the very end, he associates sight with violence: 'Whiles I see lives, the gashes / Do better upon them.' Yet at this point he also mentions – while denying it – the possibility of this incisive vision returning upon himself, in the temptation to 'play the Roman fool, / And die on mine own sword' (V.x.1–3). Although he wards it off, this intromissive threat soon returns to locate Macbeth at the wrong end of another blade. Macduff too has been led on by this sword:

> But gentle heavens
> Cut short all intermission. Front to front

Bring thou this fiend of Scotland and myself.
Within my sword's length set him.

(IV.iii.233–6)

The 'sword's length' measures out the range of a gaze eager to 'cut short all intermission'. This time the searching, penetrative and lethal vision executes an action against Macbeth, rather than by him. By this stage, moreover, Macbeth himself appears to be no more than another hallucination, like the 'fatal vision' which was once the object of his gaze. He tells Macduff, 'Thou losest labour. / As easy mayst thou the intrenchant air / With thy keen sword impress as make me bleed' (V.x.8–10). As another figure drawn in the air, like the dagger, Banquo's ghost, and all the other apparitions of the play, Macbeth becomes the ephemeral product or object of a gaze, and no longer the agent of extramissive vision.

Throne of Blood, Akira Kurasawa's Samurai film of the play, portrays this aspect of its main character's situation better than any other cinema version. Like Macbeth, Washizu has been guaranteed, by a woodland spirit, immunity from defeat until the forest moves against his castle. Near the end of his career, as the enemy forces advance, Washizu repeats the oracle to his army, who are thereby persuaded into a renewed trust in him. But once he and his troops see the forest sweeping up to the castle and realise the delusion upon which Washizu has based his power, he loses command both of himself and of them. He staggers back and forth, gazing with stupefaction at the impossible landscape bearing down upon the fortress. This horrifying panorama produces its own fatal effects. He orders his men back to their posts, but no one moves, until finally, a long death sequence shows Washizu fighting his way in vain through a forest of arrows shot at him by his own troops.

Frame three: death's masterpiece

The gaze of the audience, which has previously focused upon the vector of Macbeth's look, taking the form of a blade penetrating the air, should now move to focus on its apparent object: the murdered Duncan. But although the next scenes circle obsessively around that 'horrid image', the play continues to deny its spectators any sight of it.

Instead, it displays once more the characters' compulsive fascination with a spectacle invisible to the audience. In fact even the rhetoric and gestures provoked by the image function as a screen – or a canvas – to further obscure it. Macbeth, although a soldier and therefore accustomed to 'Strange images of death' (I.iii.95), will not expose his eyes again to the picture he has created: 'I am afraid to think what I have done, / Look on't again I dare not' (II.ii.49–50). Lady Macbeth, however, attempts to domesticate the sight by reducing it to a mere representation:

> The sleeping and the dead
> Are but as pictures. 'Tis the eye of childhood
> That fears a painted devil. If he do bleed
> I'll gild the faces of the grooms withal,
> For it must seem their guilt.

> (II.ii.51–5)

The infamous pun here signals this tactic of aestheticisation. Lady Macbeth transforms Macbeth's knife into a paintbrush, daubing the faces of the grooms with blood, surrounding them with a 'gilt' that frames them in every sense. Macbeth soon adopts the same strategy to establish his innocence and outrage, gaining distance and control over the image of the murdered Duncan by touching it up with an even more elaborate gloss: 'Here lay Duncan, / His silver skin laced with his golden blood . . .' (II.iii.111–12). Critics have puzzled over the extravagance of this speech, but it undoubtedly contributes to the baroque frame within which the Macbeths seek to contain and delimit the spectacle of the assassinated king.[7]

Something escapes, of course. The picture will not be confined by the frame or the gaze of the spectator. The bloody paint leaks out of canvas, staining the hands of the murderers, threatening to tint even the 'multitudinous seas' bright red (II.ii.59–61). Stories of corpses bleeding anew when brought into the presence of their murderers were often recounted by contemporary authors (James I 1966, 80; Thomas 1971, 691), and Macbeth soon begins to realise that, as 'they say', 'Blood will have blood' (III.iv.121). Duncan's gore overflows and drenches the play with a sanguinary visual excess, until the protagonists have to wade through it like a river (III.iv.135–7): 'who would have thought the old man to have had so much blood in him?' (V.i.36–8). The very hands with which Macbeth produced this 'most bloody piece of work' become unrecognisable to him (II.iii.127), their 'filthy witness' threatening to destroy his own scopic agency: 'What hands are here! Ha, they pluck out mine eyes' (II.ii.45, 57).

Macduff's reaction to the image of Duncan's corpse also attests to its startling power over the viewer: 'Confusion now hath made his masterpiece . . .', he remarks, and continues,

> Approach the chamber and destroy your sight
> With a new Gorgon. Do not bid me speak.
> See, and then speak yourselves.
> . . . .
> Shake off this downy sleep, death's counterfeit,
> And look on death itself. Up, up, and see
> The great doom's image. Malcolm, Banquo,
> As from your graves rise up, and walk like sprites
> To countenance this horror.

> (II.iii.65–80)

The 'masterpiece' of confusion destroys the visual mastery of those who witness it, like a 'new Gorgon' turning all spectators to stone. This lethal power – recalling that manifested by the basilisk or evil eye – represents another blinding return of vision upon the eye.[8] The face of 'death itself' transforms Malcolm and Banquo into its mimetic counterfeits, rising from their beds as though from the grave. More than any of the others, however, Duncan's sons are wary of the fatal effects of this sight which, once again, take the form of penetrative weapons:

> DONALBAIN.   Where we are
> There's daggers in men's smiles. The nea'er in blood,
> The nearer bloody.
> MALCOLM. This murderous shaft that's shot
> Hath not yet lighted, and our safest way
> Is to avoid the aim.
> (II.iii.138–42)

One by one, each of the apparitions in *Macbeth* sends out its own visual emanation upon the spectator, giving the play a basilisk stare with dire effects of its own.

Stephen Gosson attributes a lethal visual power to plays in general, comparing the fate of those who 'so looke, so gaze, so gape vpon plaies' to 'men that stare on the head of *Maedusa* & are turned to stones' (1974, 180). A similar response can be found in Freud's discussion of the character of Lady Macbeth. Writing of the play's peculiar ability to stun the critical faculties of its viewers, Freud writes that

> The dramatist can indeed, during the representation, overwhelm us by his art and paralyse our powers of reflection; but he cannot prevent us from attempting subsequently to grasp its effect by studying its psychological mechanism. (1985b, 306–7)

It is only after the play has ended, once we have escaped from the Medusa-like face presented by the tragedy, that the paralysis leaves us, and we regain our 'grasp' upon our 'powers of reflection'.

Lacan, in turn, explicitly compares this 'hypnotic value of painting' to the emanation from within the frame of a gaze 'filled with voracity, the evil eye' (1979, 115). Macbeth, too, has been rendered immobile. Of course the witches – with whom Shakespeare's audience would immediately associate the evil eye – first conjured up in Macbeth's mind this picture of the murdered Duncan, a 'horrid image' which 'shakes so [his] single state of man' that he stands in a state of paralysis, to which Banquo's remark immediately draws the audience's attention: 'Look how our partner's rapt (I.iii.129–41). This phrase echoes his previous description of Macbeth's reaction to the witches – 'My noble partner... seems rapt withal' (I.iii.52–5) – and Macbeth cannot resist the fascination of the word itself, for he reiterates it in his letter to his wife: 'I stood rapt in the wonder of it...' (I.v.5–6). Deriving from the Latin for 'carried away', the term 'rapture' suggests a Macbeth beside himself, deprived of any stable position from which to survey the spectacle that fascinates him. He is both paralysed and carried away by this rapture. On one hand, the gaze emanating from this spectacle turns Macbeth to stone, fixing him to the spot and producing him as its object, and on the other it removes him from his position of privileged spectatorship.

Each of the apparitions so far – the witches, the dagger, the dead king – casts its own spell on Macbeth. But following Duncan's murder, he will attempt with increasing desperation to assert his control over the visual field. He has already shown the first signs of this, in the strategy of framing by which he and Lady Macbeth translated Duncan's corpse into its own aestheticised double. This optical struggle for mastery will become still more critical after the next murder and its corresponding apparition.

Frame four: the gap in the feast

Macbeth and Lady Macbeth inaugurate their reign with a banquet, which they stage according to the order and hierarchy proper to a royal assembly. Here, as elsewhere, the dramatic technique displays the influence of the court masques which at the time were becoming both increasingly popular with the monarch, and increasingly elaborate in their choreography of the optical field.

As Stephen Orgel points out, the use of perspective settings for court performances after 1605 established in the audience only one privileged point of view,

> one perfect place in the hall from which the illusion achieves its fullest effect. At court performances this is where the king sat, and the audience around him at once became a living emblem of the structure of the court. The closer one sat to the monarch the 'better' one's place was, an index to one's status, and more directly, to the degree of favour one enjoyed. (1975, 10–11)

'You know your own degrees; sit down,' Macbeth orders his thanes, confirming the place of each within a harmonious spectacle in which 'Both sides are even', like a well-composed canvas or one of Inigo Jones's masques (III.iv.1, 9). By the end of the banquet scene, however, the ordered composition will be irreparably torn apart – 'displaced' with a 'most admired disorder' – leaving Lady Macbeth to dissolve the hierarchy invoked at the start: 'Stand not upon the order of your going, / But go at once' (III.iv.108–9, 118–19).

The cause of this disruption will be Macbeth's violent attempt to assert his own scopic mastery in the face of a gaze that returns upon him from the spectacle of Banquo's ghost, and from his audience, the thanes. This tension once again recalls the court masque, in which the privileged view from the throne relies upon a range of looks directed at the monarch, confirming his or her place in the visual field:

> At these performances what the rest of the spectators watched was not the play but the queen at a play, and their response

would have been not simply to the drama, but to the relationship between the drama and its primary audience, the spectator.
(Orgel 1975, 9)

The presence of Banquo's ghost would in itself have no power if
Macbeth were to ignore it. Only the disjunction between his sight
– represented by his extreme reaction – and the view of the rest of
the company (who do not see the ghost) destroys the scene. As
with the image of the murdered Duncan, as with the ghostly dagger, what the theatre audience will focus on is not the apparition
itself but the gazes produced by it; in particular, the accusing gaze
of the Ghost, which replicates in its effect on Macbeth the impact
of Hamlet's 'Mousetrap' on Claudius.

Certainly, Banquo's ghost functions primarily as an absence:

> MACBETH. Here's our chief guest.
> LADY MACBETH. If he had been forgotten
> It had been as a gap in our great feast,
> And all-thing unbecoming.
>
> (III.i.11–13)

In so far as the feast shares some of the aspects of that visual regime which structures a pictorial composition or a masque, Banquo
appears as the 'gap', the vanishing point, around which Macbeth's
viewpoint, and all the others' following it, will come to organise
themselves. Macbeth describes Banquo to the murderers as a recalcitrant threat to the otherwise omnipotent gaze of his reign:

> every minute of his being thrusts
> Against my near'st of life; and though I could
> With barefaced power sweep him from my sight
> And bid my will avouch it, yet I must not,
> For certain friends that are both his and mine,
> Whose loves I may not drop . . .
>
> (III.i.118–23)

Banquo represents all those gazes that keep Macbeth subject even
in his position as king, thereby undermining his regime of 'bare-
faced power'. For his continued dependence upon the regard of
these others necessitates the continuation of the thoroughgoing

masquerade discussed earlier, 'Masking the business from the common eye', making 'our faces visors to our hearts, / Disguising what
they are' (III.i.126, III.ii.35–6).

Macbeth reacts most strongly, therefore, not to the ghost as a
sight, but to the ghost's sight; not to what it looks like to him, but
to how it looks at him: to 'those eyes / Which thou dost glare
with' (III.iv.94–5). For in that look he perceives all the accusing
eyes around the table pointed at him, an array of perspectives framing
him into the very picture of guilt: 'Thou canst not say I did it.
Never shake / Thy gory locks at me' (ll. 49–50). Once again, the
power of this gaze, like that returning from the perspective painting, lies in its capacity to render the spectator's stable and central
position untenable. The ghost actually takes Macbeth's place at the
table, prompting Lennox to ask 'What is't that moves your high-
ness?' (l. 47). It thereby comes to represent the capacity to 'push
us from our stools', to displace the privileged position of the monarch in the visual field (l. 81).

Paradoxically, however, the chaotic disarray pervading the scene
only arises as a result of Macbeth's assertion of his sovereign position in this scopic arena. This prosecuting gaze emerges as the result
of the pursuit of visual mastery itself, for the ghost actually comes
and goes at the spectator's own bidding. The Macbeths have invited Banquo to the feast in the most compelling terms, and he
arrives at the start, therefore, in the form of a bloodstain on the
face of the first murderer:

MACBETH. (*To First Murderer*) There's blood upon thy face.
FIRST MURDERER. (*aside to Macbeth*) 'Tis Banquo's then.
MACBETH. 'Tis better thee without than he within.
                                                    (III.iv.11–13)

Like the 'filthy witness' seeping from the murdered Duncan, Banquo's
blood will not stay put: 'he within' ironically hints towards the
imminent irruption of Banquo's ghost within the scene Macbeth is
attempting to compose. And the apparition itself obeys his summons promptly. No sooner has he wished 'the graced person of
our Banquo present', than he sees it sitting in his place (III.iv.39–
50). He dismisses it – 'Never shake / Thy gory locks at me' – and it
departs, only to enter once more as soon as he calls for it: 'I drink
to . . . our dear friend Banquo, whom we miss. / Would he were
here' (ll. 88–90). Finally, he bids it

> Hence, horrible shadow,
> Unreal mock'ry, hence!   *Exit Ghost*
>   Why so, being gone
> I am a man again. Pray you sit still.

> (III.iv.105–7)

The visual mastery which Macbeth here struggles to reassert depends, again, upon a fixed position – 'If I stand here, I saw him' (l. 73) – from which he can summon the ghost, dismiss it, summon it, and dismiss it. And 'so, being gone', its obedience makes him a 'man again', reassured of his position within the scopic field. His 'firm nerves' are thereby restored, along with his capacity to confirm the places of the others: 'Pray you sit still.'

However, the collective astonishment of the thanes now takes over the accusing, anamorphic role of the ghost, so that Macbeth finds his supremacy finally dependent upon the gaze from the Other. Their gazes 'make me strange / Even to the disposition that I owe', alienating him even from his own estimate and 'ownership' of himself, disrupting the security and familiarity of the self-possessed position from which he sees himself (ll. 111–12). Lady Macbeth attempts to disarm these glances – 'If much you note him / You shall offend him, and extend his passion. / Feed, and regard him not' (III.iv.55–7) – but her plea fails, for it contradicts the entire visual rubric of the court occasion, which aims to focus all eyes upon the monarch.

In psychoanalytic terms, Macbeth's behaviour in this scene recalls Freud's description of the *'fort/da'* game played by his grandson Ernst. Freud asserts that the child, by repeatedly throwing a cotton reel away and subsequently drawing it back to him by its string, was symbolically seeking to master – by a ritual of dismissal and summoning – his relation with his mother. Freud compares this game with the 'artistic play and artistic imitation carried out by adults, which, unlike children's, are aimed at an audience . . .'. Such re-enactments

> do not spare the spectators (for instance, in tragedy), the most painful experiences and can yet be felt by them as highly enjoyable. This is convincing proof that, even under the dominance of the pleasure principle, there are ways and means enough of making what is in itself unpleasurable into a subject to be recollected and worked over in the mind. (Freud 1984, 287)

At this point in his discussion, Freud suggests that the transaction between spectator and 'artistic imitation' reasserts the subject's mastery by means of the same tactic of repetition. The remainder of *Beyond the Pleasure Principle*, however, will undermine this hypothesis of a 'working over' taking place under the agency of the subject, interpreting such activity instead as a 'compulsion to repeat'. This quite involuntary impulse creates in those who witness it the impression of a person 'being pursued by a malignant fate or possessed by some "daemonic" power' (Freud 1984, 292). Similarly, Macbeth oscillates between mastery of the scopic field and slavery to the gaze of an Other; between moments of apparent control – dismissal and recall – and others in which he obeys the command of diabolical forces, 'the common enemy of man' to whom he has sold his 'eternal jewel' (III.i.69–70).

From now on, Macbeth's demand for optical sovereignty will become more and more extravagant, as will his enslavement to the dictates of a diabolical vision. His promise to acquaint Banquo's murderers with 'the perfect spy o'th' time' signals the establishment of a paranoid regime of surveillance, in which agents keep watch on his own hirelings as well as his enemies: 'There's not a one of them but in his house / I keep a servant fee'd' (III.i.131, III.iv.130–1). He pursues this ambition for panoptic omnipotence by supernatural means as well, demanding prophetic visions from the Weird Sisters: 'for now I am bent to know / By the worst means the worst' (III.iv.133–4).

Frame four: magic sleights and artificial sprites

From a reversed viewpoint, signalled by a drastic change of tone, the next scene offers a different perspective on Macbeth's performance as sovereign. Hecate, the witches' 'mistress', enters to provide both a parody of the royal banquet and a commentary on Macbeth's illusory mastery of the optical field: 'you all know security / Is mortals' chiefest enemy' (III.v.32–3). She also predicts Macbeth's captivation by what he will see in the following scene:

> Upon the corner of the moon
> There hangs a vap'rous drop profound.
> I'll catch it ere it come to ground,
> And that, distilled by magic sleights,
> Shall raise such artificial sprites

> As by the strength of their illusion
> Shall draw him on to his confusion.

> (III.v.23–9)

Hecate herself functions as the playwright's collaborator here, complaining meanwhile of the witches' failure to invite her help in showing 'the glory of our art' (ll. 6–9). Her interpolated scene displays an influx of dramaturgical techniques deriving from the court masque, as typified by an emphasis on spectacular illusion – 'magic sleights' and 'artificial sprites' – and a reliance upon the optical economy of pictorial perspective to achieve this.

Court spectacles of the time usually contained an embedded antimasque, over which the characters and settings of the masque proper could triumph, in order to establish that panoramic harmony which was supposed to reflect the regime of its royal spectator. Ben Jonson's *Masque of Queens*, for instance, opens with an elaborate witches' coven, subsequently (and effortlessly) routed by the royal company, led by a thinly disguised Queen Anne (Orgel 1975, 60–1). Of course there could be no more appropriate material for the anti-masque, since according to contemporary accounts, the liturgy of the typical witches' sabbat mirrored – in reverse – the visual pageantry of the court itself (Clark 1980, 121). Accordingly, when Hecate holds court with her witches and observes the dances and songs of her spirits, their mimicry colours and dominates retrospectively the audience's perception of the banquet held by the 'hellhound' Macbeth and his 'fiend-like queen' (V.x.3; V.xi.35).

Hecate's mention of 'the glory of our art', therefore, refers both to magic and to visual illusion, to the practices of the occult as well as those of pictorial and dramatic representation. Use of the Italian *quattrocento* principles of linear perspective in painting and in theatre arrived late in England, where the Puritan suspicion of papist idolatry resisted optical wizardry with the same vehemence as witchcraft itself.[9] For the anti-theatrical writers of Shakespeare's time, there was no question that theatrical fantasies derived from the same source, and exercised the same powers, as those perpetrated by sorcery. Anthony Munday asks in 1580, 'Do wee not vse in these discourses [plays] to counterfet witchcraft, charmed drinkes, and amorous potions, thereby to drawe the affections of men, & stir them vp vnto to lust . . .' (1972, 100–1). Stephen Gosson considers plays a 'doctrine and inuention of the Deuill', perpetrated 'the better thereby to enlarge his dominion and pull vs from God' (1974, 151). As a diabolical artifice, plays draw their spectators into lust and away from God. In the same way, just as the phantom dagger led Macbeth to the murder of Duncan, Hecate now constructs a spectacle to 'draw him on to his confusion'. King James, his own enthusiasm for the theatre notwithstanding, recognises the devil's power to delude the sight with 'faire armies of horse-men and foote-men in appearance, castles and fortes: Which all are but impressiones in the aire' (James I 1966, 22), and Macbeth builds an entire regime upon a series of such 'air-drawings', each of which participates in the optical economy common to contemporary artistic illusionism.

Furthermore, the actual techniques by which visual fantasies were evoked in the theatre – techniques developed to the full in the court masque – were often thought to produce the same effects, and generally aroused the same antipathy, as the rituals of witch-craft itself. John Dee describes the practice of 'Thaumaturgike', as 'that Art Mathematicall, which giueth certaine order to make strange workes, of the sense to be perceiued, and of men greatly to be wondered at' (1975, sig. A1r). Dee's instances of this art correspond to the special effects mechanisms of the Jacobean stage, 'Some by waight. . . . Some, by Stringes strayned, or Springs, therwith Imitating liuely Motions' (sig. A1v). So also do the other wonders which he ascribes to 'Perspective' itself – by which in this case he means use of a conjuring mirror – which can cause 'a man to be curstly affrayed of his owne shadow' (sig. b1v), by producing 'an Image, appearing in the ayre, betwene you & the glasse, with like hand, sword or dagger, & with like quicknes, foyning at your very eye, likewise as you do at the Glasse' (sig. b1v). Elsewhere he describes how the spectator can be made 'to see the liuely shew of Gold, Siluer or precious stones: and commyng to take them in your hand, to finde nought but Ayre' (sig. A1v).

It was of course 'for these, and such like marueilous Actes and Feates, Naturally, Mathematically, and Mechanically, wrought and contriued', that Dr Dee found himself 'condemned, as a Companion of the Helhoundes, and a Caller, and Coniurer of wicked and damned Spirites', and consequently lost the high social and political status he had enjoyed under Elizabeth (Dee 1975, sig. A1v–A2r; Yates 1979). Dee's error lay in underestimating the extent to which, for a con-temporary audience, the visual marvels wrought by mathematics and optical geometry appeared indistinguishable from those produced by the occult.

Reginald Scot also attests to this association, describing 'the woonderous devises, and miraculous sights and conceipts made and conteined in glasse . . . whereto the art perspective is verie necessarie', and adding that 'it is most true, that some for these feats have been accounted saints, some other witches' (1930, 179). The details given in Scot's account of necromancy repeat the essential elements of the final apparitions in *Macbeth*. The witches in the play produce a parade of *'eight kings, the last with a glass in his hand'*, which 'shows [Macbeth] many more' (IV.i.128–36), while Scot confirms that spirits may be conjured to appear in 'anie christall stone, glasse, or other mirror . . .' (1930, 246). He also asserts that such spirits will usually take the 'fair forme of a childe of twelve yeares of age', which – like the *'child crowned, with a tree in his hand'* seen by Macbeth (l. 102) – 'will shew manie delusions, to drive you from your worke' (232).

James's *Daemonologie* insists that the mastery which the conjuror holds over the summoned spirits remains highly unstable:

> when the conjured Spirit appeares, which will not be while after manie circumstances, long praiers, and much muttring and murmuring of the conjurers . . . if they have missed one iote of all their rites; or if any of their feete once slyd ouer the circle through terror of his feareful apparition . . . hee carries them with him bodie and soule. (James I 1966, 18)

Control over the apparition is conditional upon its conjuror's remaining within the circle, just as the illusionism perpetrated by either the court masque or the perspective painting depends upon the spectator's occupation of a singular, central and immobile position. The precarious relationship with the diabolical 'master' holds the conjurer between the two threats of entrapment within the bounds set by the spell, or being carried off 'bodie and soule'. This parallels the dialectic implicit in Macbeth's 'rapture' in response to the earlier apparitions, which saw him caught – again, like the observer in relation to the geometrical perspective – between the threat of fixation, as the object of the Other's gaze, and that of removal from visual mastery.

King James, in fact, might have found himself rather too close to these two menacing possibilities if *Macbeth* was initially composed for a court performance. Adherents to this idea have often imagined that the 'glass' held by the last of Banquo's heirs was in this context a mirror, turned to capture the image of James himself, seated in the banqueting room at Whitehall as the play's primary spectator.[10] The Arden editor, however, insists that the 'glass' was 'not an ordinary mirror in which King James could see himself . . . but a prospective, or magic, glass' (Muir 1972, 114). In fact, this makes little difference to the optical economy in operation, since both the 'prospective glass' and the mirror would confirm the scene's participation in the occult and artistic visual experiments described so far. The passages from Scot and Dee quoted above demonstrate that the association between perspectivism, Euclidean geometry, mirror optics and conjuration in glasses would have been powerfully established in the minds of Shakespeare's audience. Even the words 'prospective' and 'perspective' were at the time interchangeable.[11] Macbeth himself, in response to the witches' initial apparition, relies upon this etymological link between prophetic vision and the optical sciences when he remarks that 'to be king / Stands not within the prospect of belief . . .' (I.iii.71–2). Subsequent events prove that in fact Macbeth's sovereign optical position operates only in so far as he does 'stand' within a 'prospect', or perspectival visual field. And as a sequel to the witches' initial display, the show of kings will demonstrate his increasing entrapment by this structure.

Whereas at the start of the play Macbeth seemed to be hailed by the witches, whose 'supernatural soliciting' invited him to follow their suggestions, in Act IV he enters as the master of ceremonies. Nevertheless the control he exercises throughout this scene, like that granted by both geometrical and occult illusionism, ultimately appears to be delusory. For although Macbeth seeks out the witches, they are already expecting him; when he does command the spirits to appear, the audience recalls hearing Hecate prepare them in advance; and even as he seems to interrogate them, they pre-empt his questions.

Nevertheless, his opening words are certainly those of a conjuror or producer of illusions rather than their passive spectator:

> I conjure you by that which you profess,
> Howe'er you come to know it, answer me.
> Though you untie the winds and let them fight
> Against the churches, though the yeasty waves
> Confound and swallow navigation up,
> Though bladed corn be lodged and trees blown down,
> Though castles topple on their warders' heads,

> Though palaces and pyramids do slope
> Their heads to their foundations, though the treasure
> Of nature's germens tumble all together
> Even till destruction sicken, answer me
> To what I ask you.
>
> (IV.i.66–77)

Macbeth employs a spell which confirms the extravagant supremacy of his situation, invoking various powers typically attributed to the magician, all of which appear in Scot's *Discoverie of Witchcraft*: the ability to raise tempests, ruin the harvest, even to unmake and remake the world (Scot 1930, 6). Although the witches appear to recognise his power –

> FIRST WITCH. Speak.
> SECOND WITCH. Demand.
> THIRD WITCH. We'll answer.
> FIRST WITCH. Say if thou'dst rather hear it from our mouths
> Or from our masters.
>
> (ll. 77-9)

– their mention of 'masters' evokes the continual ambiguity characteristic of the magician's relationship with the 'familiar'.

According to contemporary theories of the occult, witches and warlocks maintained a pact with the devil, who accompanied them as an attendant demon, usually in the form of an animal. This familiar – also referred to as a 'master' – would perform the conjuror's bidding, but nevertheless retained a prior and dominant power over her or him. The witches in *Macbeth*, therefore, although they can summon their 'masters', are at the same time ultimately answerable to them. Although, as seen earlier, the sisters appear to stage-manage the play in the first scene, they in turn obey the summons of their familiars: 'I come, Grimalkin', 'Paddock calls' (I.i.8–9). Even Hecate exits at the prompting of her 'little spirit': 'Hark, I am called!' (III.v.36).

In fact, experts attempted to differentiate between the witch and the necromancer according to this relation to the forces invoked. Epistamon, James's interlocutor in the *Daemonologie*, asserts that 'the Witches ar servantes onelie, and slaues to the Devil; but the Necromanciers are his maisters and commanders'. When asked by

Philamon how it can be said 'that any men being specially adicted to his service, can be his commanders?', he replies,

> Yea, they may be: but it is onelie *secundum quid*: For it is not by anie power that they can haue over him, but *ex pacto* allanerlie: whereby he oblices himself in some trifles to them, that he may on the other part obteine the fruition of their body & soule, which is the onlie thing he huntes for. (James I 1966, 9)

In this dialogue, the difference initially proposed between witch and necromancer rapidly disintegrates, as the latter's command over the diabolical 'master' turns out to be nothing more than a disguised and postponed slavery. Insofar as Macbeth plays the role of a necromancer, his subsequent obedience to the spirits invoked conforms to the ambiguous terms of this transaction:

> *Thunder. First Apparition: an armed head*
> MACBETH. Tell me, thou unknown power –
> FIRST WITCH. He knows thy thought.
> Hear his speech, but say thou naught.
> FIRST APPARITION. Macbeth, Macbeth, Macbeth, beware Macduff,
> Beware the Thane of Fife. Dismiss me. Enough.
>
> *Apparition descends*
> MACBETH. Whate'er thou art, for thy good caution thanks.
> Thou hast harped my fear aright. But one word more –
> FIRST WITCH. He will not be commanded. Here's another,
> More potent than the first.
> (IV.i.85–92)

His hold over the apparitions appears tenuous. Although they come at his request, their replies pre-empt his 'thought'. Moreover they leave suddenly, and 'will not be commanded'. On the other hand, Macbeth will demand further answers, and he will get them:

> MACBETH. Tell me, if your art
> Can tell so much, shall Banquo's issue ever
> Reign in this kingdom?
> ALL THE WITCHES. Seek to know no more.
> MACBETH. I will be satisfied. Deny me this,
> And an eternal curse fall on you! Let me know.

The cauldron sinks. Hautboys
MACBETH. Why sinks that cauldron? And what noise is this?
FIRST WITCH. Show.
SECOND WITCH. Show.
THIRD WITCH. Show.
ALL THE WITCHES. Show his eyes and grieve his heart,
Come like shadows, so depart.

(IV.i.117–27)

Threatening them with their own occult curse, Macbeth forces the witches' illusionism to the limit – 'if your art / Can tell so much' – and remains confident of his optical mastery over it: 'I will be satisfied'.

What he sees next, however, does not satisfy him at all, but only captivates him further:

A show of eight kings, the last with a glass in his hand; and Banquo
MACBETH. Thou art too like the spirit of Banquo. Down!
Thy crown does sear mine eyeballs. And thy hair,
Thou other gold-bound brow, is like the first.
A third is like the former. Filthy hags,
Why do you show me this? – A fourth? Start, eyes!
What, will the line stretch out to th' crack of doom?
Another yet? A seventh? I'll see no more –
And yet the eighth appears, who bears a glass
Which shows me many more; and some I see
That twofold balls and treble sceptres carry.
Horrible sight! Now I see 'tis true,
For the blood-baltered Banquo smiles upon me,
And points at them for his.

(IV.i.128–40)

The 'horrible sight' of the 'blood-baltered Banquo' – like the 'horrid image' of Duncan's incontinently bleeding corpse – threatens to make Macbeth's eyes 'start' out of his head. He falls back, blinded by that searing glare, which returns along the 'line' that will 'stretch out' from the spectator to the picture's vanishing point, its 'crack of doom'. He has completely lost the scopic mastery he had previously claimed, for in spite of his vowing to 'see no more', 'yet the eighth appears'. Fascinated by this picture, Macbeth no longer sees, but instead passively registers what is shown him, helplessly following a sight that captivates him, directed by the pointing finger of Banquo's ghost. He attempts once more to dismiss the optical economy he has summoned – 'But no more sights!' (IV.i.171) – but his subsequent persecution of the Macduffs, his belief that he possesses a charmed life, and his disabling fear of the moving forest, all betray a continuing dependence upon these visions shown him by the witches. The next scene set at Dunsinane also demonstrates to the audience this captivation, in the form of Lady Macbeth's hypnotic rehearsal of every previous phantasmal image haunting the play: the bell that demands the murder, the old man's blood, Banquo's return from the grave, the Thane of Fife's wife (V.i.1–65).

The final cut

As in the psychoanalytic account of vision, the intromissive beam of light 'photo-graphs' the subject, inscribing it within a scene or picture preceding its sight. In doing so, it embodies that gaze which returns upon the spectator and 'changes all perspectives, the lines of force, of my world, orders it, from the point of nothingness where I am' (Lacan 1979, 84). Lacan calls this the 'pre-existence to the seen of a given-to-be-seen' (1979, 77), a condition comparable with Ulysses's image, in *Troilus and Cressida*, of the actor who depends for his knowledge of himself upon the applause which 'like a gate of steel / Fronting the sun, receives and renders back / His figure and his heat' (III.iii.116–18).

Macbeth's final speeches manifest an overwhelming subjection to this blinding gaze, and an increasing awareness that he functions not as the author, but as a character – 'a poor player / That struts and frets his hour upon the stage...' (V.v.23–4) – within 'a tale / Told by an idiot' (25–6) – or rather, told by the predictions of the apparitions and the witches. In the pact typical of such occult 'masters', they have granted him an imaginary security which will ultimately be revealed as a slavery in disguise:

MACBETH. I bear a charmèd life, which must not yield
To one of woman born.
MACDUFF. Despair thy charm,
And let the angel whom thou still hast served
Tell thee Macduff was from his mother's womb
Untimely ripped...

(V.x.12–16)

The answers given by 'these juggling fiends' to Macbeth's questions 'palter with [him] in a double sense' and thereby script his
downfall (V.x.19–20). Each time he enters, during the final scenes
of the play, Macbeth's rhetoric betrays his increasing entrapment
within a plot and spectacle that precedes him, and his exposure to
the mocking gaze of a dismissive audience. He imagines himself
captured as the prime exhibit in the bear-baiting arena which stood
in such close proximity to the Globe – 'They have tied me to a
stake. I cannot fly, / But bear-like I must fight the course' (V.vii.1–2)
– or as an actor in one of the Roman plays so frequently performed
by Shakespeare's company: 'Why should I play the Roman fool . . .?'
(V.x.1).

As suggested earlier, Macduff's vengeful search for Macbeth represents a return of the fatal vision that has characterised the optical
energy of the play. Now that gaze seeks him out and pins him
down – 'That way the noise is. Tyrant, show thy face!' (V.viii.1) –
positioning him within the spectacle that he has become:

> MACDUFF. Then yield thee, coward,
> And live to be the show and gaze o'th' time.
> We'll have thee as our rarer monsters are,
> Painted upon a pole, and underwrit
> 'Here you may see the tyrant'.
>
> (V.x.23–7)

The entire play in fact offers this portrait of optical tyranny, represented by the figure of Macbeth – as both 'painted' image and as
theatrical 'show' – taken captive by the 'gaze o'th' time'. This perspective – like its correlative, his own earlier desire to attain the
'perfect spy o'th' time – represents the geometrical optical economy
increasingly dominating the pictorial arts and illusionistic theatre
of the court.

If Macbeth becomes a spectacle, so too does any spectator too
closely involved with the play. King James, of course, must be the
figure most often and most closely identified with the play as its
'original' spectator, the one 'for whom' it was written, the one whose
gaze preceded and produced the play. Considering the suggestion
that James's reflection was captured in a mirror held by one of the
actors in the show of kings, I have observed how the glass – whether
mirror or crystal, 'perspective', or 'prospective' – like the reflected
light from the crown that sears Macbeth's eyeballs, makes the ob-

server into the object of a gaze. At the same time, whether he is mirrored explicitly or only gestured towards implicitly, as the heir to Banquo's line, King James also becomes the 'subject' of the drama, depicted in it as a structuring absence, just as his ancestor provided the 'gap' in the Macbeths' 'great feast'. Shakespeare here comes as close as possible to infringing the contemporary ban on portraying a reigning monarch in drama.

Such readings, however, seem to repeat the tactic – which has now become all but inevitable in cultural materialist or new historicist interpretations of Shakespeare – of tracing the theatrical gaze insistently back to the sovereign. Criticism's endless rehearsal of the central place and power of the monarchy, while playing an important role in defining the political agenda of the Shakespearean play, does not circumscribe the limit of its possible readings. For a discussion of the optical structure of the plays, I would suggest, it is necessary to rethink this connection with the monarchy, perceiving it as a more unstable metaphorical complex, increasingly available for the identifications and appropriations of later audiences, rather than as an irresistible gravitational field around which all the cultural and signifying practices of Elizabethan and Jacobean England were compelled to orbit. Such a reading would therefore emphasise the ascendancy of a sovereign subjectivity for which Shakespeare's tragedies, pre-eminently, will come to provide a set of models or paradigms, optical and otherwise.

The scopic mastery enjoyed by the monarch at a court masque, therefore, may influence the visual dynamics of a play like *Macbeth*, but this position will increasingly become occupied by or identifiable with the emergent early modern individual. Thus Catherine Belsey points out that the hierarchy of optical sovereignty established by the theatre of the Jacobean court – according to which only the king had a perfect view of the elaborately constructed stage perspective, while the viewpoints of the courtiers were proportionate to their rank – would be, after the civil war,

> offered at a price, or a range of prices, to those, including increasing numbers of the bourgeoisie . . . who were willing to pay between one and four shillings for seats and who, we may assume, generally possessed property sufficient to guarantee their representation in the House of Commons. The scenic stage of the Restoration period addressed a unified and unifying spectacle to a series of unified spectator-subjects who, as guardians

of the liberties of the people of England, each possessed a degree of sovereignty in the new regime. (Belsey 1985, 25–6)

As a figure of identification for the historical development of the bourgeois ego, *Macbeth* foreshadows both the character of this ascendant subjectivity and its usurpation of the optical place formerly monopolised by the monarch. Moreover, in so far as modern subjectivity continues to participate in this ambition for sovereignty over the scopic drive, my reading of *Macbeth* suggests that, to expropriate a phrase of Michel Foucault's, 'we still have not cut off the head of the king'.[12]

Retrospectively, therefore, we may imagine that Macbeth's conjuring scene might have offered King James another prophecy, to which he no doubt remained blind. For the mirror brought on stage during the show of kings, in showing to Macbeth the figure of Banquo's ultimate descendant and heir, would in turn have operated as a 'prospective' glass displaying to James the face of *his* future successor: the upstart (early) modern subject, the actor, Macbeth.

In so far as the spectator of the play identifies with Macbeth, therefore, she or he identifies with a subject who usurps, and strenuously struggles to maintain, a position of scopic mastery. This ocular regime, however, proves vulnerable to the accusing eyes of its enemies, represented by the intromissive glare stabbing out from the apparitions.[13] Macbeth seeks to adapt to this gaze from the Other by means of a desperate masquerade. In its increasingly deluded megalomania, his reign anticipates, as I have suggested, to the Lacanian description of the subject's situation in the scopic field, split between an eye struggling for sovereignty, and a gaze to which it seeks to conform. A primary symptom of this split is the subject's inability to apprehend the totality of its own body, except through the mediation of the other's gaze or the other's image. 'The image of his body is the principle of every unity he perceives in objects. Now, he only perceives the unity of this specific image from the outside, and in an anticipated manner' (Lacan 1988b, 166). Through the imaginary dominance of the optical field granted by the mirror, the subject seems to see itself steadily and whole. 'But in the dream, because of an alleviation of the imaginary relations . . .', according to Lacan,

the subject encounters the experience of his being torn apart. . . . If there is an image which could represent for us the Freudian notion of the unconscious, it is indeed that of the acephalic subject, of a subject who no longer has an *ego*, who doesn't belong to the *ego*. (Lacan 1988b, 167)

Macbeth fluctuates between the mirror of totality and the nightmare of dismemberment, and it leaves us with the split between eye and gaze, in the form of the severed head and body of the main character, which are brought on-stage to provide a paradoxical but continued focus for the audience. Having identified with Macbeth so consistently throughout the play, the spectator – at least the modern spectator – cannot help but continue to do so. Inviting us both to *look at* and to *see from* the perspective of its decapitated anti-hero, *Macbeth* enacts the dilemma of the subject in the optical field at its most radically disconcerting.

Ultimately, it is to the cinema – as a descendant of the illusionistic and perspectival visual economy under discussion – that I turn once more for representation of this final perspective. In the closing scenes of Roman Polanski's version of the play, the camera first graphically shows the removal of Macbeth's head and, a moment after it falls, the hands of the remaining body spasmodically thrown upwards in an involuntary gesture of protection. Following this, however, comes a long, jerky and disturbing sequence, shot as though from the viewpoint of the severed head, carried by Macduff through the jeering crowd of its enemies. The soundtrack remains silent throughout this sequence, furthering the impression of a disembodied eye helplessly subject to and carried away by the gaze of the Other. Finally, the film shows the head, raised on a spear above the battlements of Dunsinane, seen once more from the point of view of the celebrating army outside. Macbeth as spectator, the spectator as Macbeth, end up 'painted upon on a pole', subject to 'the show and gaze o'th' time', having occupied that place from the beginning.

Conclusion

In the end, what is perspective? Shakespeare's twenty-fourth sonnet offers some possible answers:

> Mine eye hath played the painter, and hath steeled
> Thy beauty's form in table of my heart.
> My body is the frame wherein 'tis held,
> And perspective it is best painter's art;
> For through the painter must you see his skill
> To find where your true image pictured lies,
> Which in my bosom's shop is hanging still,
> That hath his windows glazèd with thine eyes.

(Sonnet 24.1–8)

Depending upon where the superlative rests in line four, 'perspective' might be understood either as the painter's best art, that is, the technique most vital to the production of the picture, or alternatively as that process which itself produces the best painter. Of course, for my purposes both interpretations are important: throughout this study the art of perspective has exemplified an optical regime which simultaneously composes both the scene and the seer.

Moreover, Shakespearean usage would extend the connotations of the term to include a whole range of optical toys and anamorphic effects other than the geometrical illusionism of Brunelleschi and Alberti. In *Richard II*, for example, Bushy refers to more than one type of perspective in a single conceit:

> For sorrow's eye, glazèd with blinding tears,
> Divides one thing entire to many objects –

Like perspectives, which, rightly gazed upon,
Show nothing but confusion; eyed awry,
Distinguish form.

(II.ii.16–20)[1]

The first lines of this passage describe the kaleidoscopic effects of cut glass, producing multiple images of whatever is seen through it; but then Bushy changes his metaphor and seems to have in mind the type of anamorphic device shown in the foreground of Holbein's *The Ambassadors*.

To come back to sonnet 24: most editors suggest that the word be read as an adverb, 'perspective[ly]' – that is, from the viewpoint of the speaker, seen 'through the painter', according to 'his skill' – the image on the table of the heart is perfectly in proportion, 'it is best painter's art', a 'true image'.[2] But because the techniques of both perspective art and anamorphic trickery are represented by the same word, the lifelikeness of the picture, when looked at through the eyes of the painter and according to the rules of central projection, becomes inextricably associated with optical illusionism, and with kinds of the artificial perversion of natural vision or right gaze that Bushy describes. The polyvalence of the term therefore reflects the competing dynamics at work in the visual field, and the conflict between its different senses illustrates the extent to which any given 'perspective' is biased, reliant on the fixation of the eye of the beholder in a certain location, and on the imposition of strict perceptual rubrics. Anamorphosis, as the introduction of a skewed alternative viewpoint, proves disconcerting because it shows the apparently central or natural perspective to be in its turn contingent and arbitrary, to be no less potentially anamorphic.

Of course, the early modern notion of perspective multiplies even more prolifically, for it also includes the construction and use of 'prospective glasses', both magical and scientific: crystal balls and conjuror's stones, as well as mirrors, telescopes, and all reflecting or refracting lenses. 'Perspective', the art of commanding a 'prospect', thereby reaches out to embrace many fields of visual transaction: astronomy, dramaturgy, necromancy, optics, painting, architecture, cartography, navigation, poetry. As such, it exemplifies the scopic economy influencing the emergence of nation and empire, and indeed, the formation of the early modern European subject 'itself'.

In the establishment of this scopic regime, one function or image pervades the various contributing fields more insistently than any other: that of the mirror. And of course each of the 'arts perspective' tends to owe its techniques, first and foremost, to catoptrics. Early modern cartographers frequently acknowledged this. Mercator did so explicitly in the preface to his Atlas, which he claimed '(as in a mirror) will set before your eyes, the whole world' and 'by this meanes leade the Reader to higher speculation' (cited in Rabasa 1985, 3), and others did so implicitly in their titles: for example William Cunigham's *Cosmographical Glasse* of 1559 (Harley 1983, 27), John Norden's *Speculum Britanniae*, published in instalments during the late 1590s (Helgerson 1992, 125) and Lucas Janszoon Waghaener's sea atlas, *Spieghel der Zeevaerdt*, published 1584–5 in Dutch, and 1588 in English (Barber 1992, 65; Skelton 1971, 26). In acknowledging the specular nature of cartographic representation, early modern map-makers evoke both the realism and the illusionism of their worlds. And the same genealogy pertains to the development of perspective painting, in so far as the *Quattrocento* development of linear perspective painting by innovators such as Brunelleschi, Alberti, Giotto and Van Eyck depended upon the application of principles extrapolated, in the first place, from experiments with mirror geometry (Edgerton 1975, 134–5). At the same time, however, the more consciously illusionistic artifices practised in the name of perspective also made use of specular mechanisms, from the radically decentred anamorphoses of the sixteenth century, which required the interpolation of a cylindrical mirror in order for the viewer to recompose a legible picture (Baltrusaitis 1977, 131–58), to the conjuration within a looking glass practised to such dangerous effect by John Dee (Dee 1975, sig. b1v).

No wonder, then, that in early modern texts as well as recent psychoanalytic theory, the visual relation between the body and its mirrored double provides a pervasive paradigm for the intersubjective relation between the eye of the subject and the gaze of the other, or between a sovereign vision and its environment; between actor and audience, representation and referent, male and female. And no wonder that the mirror – as an idiom and a structuring image, but also, at key moments, as an actual prop – has never been far from Shakespeare's dramatic stage either.

As Lacan remarks, 'it is the subjective possibility of the mirror projection of such a field into the field of the other that gives human space its originally "geometrical" structure' (1977b, 27). While the phrase 'human space' represents the kind of universalism of which psychoanalysis is often justly accused, Lacan's formulation does describe accurately the emergence of what might be called *humanist* space, that is, the modern European visual regime. Moreover, the history of the function of the mirror in the establishment of this geometrical regime, and of the subject's place within it, allows an analogy to be drawn between Lacan's remarks about the evolution of the individual ego and the emergence from the Renaissance of the co-ordinates of the modern humanist ego as a cultural function. He insists that according to his theory of the mirror stage, 'the sight alone of the whole form of the human body gives the subject an imaginary mastery over his body, one which is premature in relation to a real mastery' (1988a, 79). Just as the formation of the ideal image of the individual ego is 'premature', in an analogous way the visual apprehension represented by the geometrically organised painting, stage or map anticipates and inaugurates the 'actual' attainment of that subjectivity, nationality or empire which it apparently reflects.[3]

In Lacanian theory, therefore, the mirror identification always appears fraught with 'aggressivity'. The pre-emptive attitude of the supposed 'original' towards its reflection will always produce a violent rivalry: an insatiable drive to take the place of, and a voracious desire to incorporate, the other in the mirror, along with an implacable fear of being replaced or devoured by that other. *Troilus and Cressida*, for example, stages these tendencies in the confrontations between Aeneas and Diomedes, Achilles and Ajax, Achilles and Hector, even between Achilles and the 'glass' of his own pride; but in fact such specular conflict occurs wherever rivalry appears in other plays as well – between Hamlet and Laertes, Macbeth and Macdonald, Antony and Octavius – accompanied in each case by the vocabulary of reflection, emulation and appetite.

These twin desires – to consume the other, or to take its place – embody the paradoxes not only of the mirror relation, but also of the rational and empiricist regime of observation which it founds and represents. As the paradigmatic object of geometry, the mirror exemplifies the perfect mapping of one object or field onto another. The relation between the 'original' and its 'reflection' purports to be one of equivalence; but the scopic regime based on this Euclidean fantasy produces altogether different effects from those which might be expected of such a harmonious arrangement. The antagonism between the ego and its double – which may manifest as a person, an object or a territory – introduces an entirely destructive element into the mirror relation. The privileged eye of the incipient humanist subject, while claiming for itself a position of objective detachment – a non-position, in effect – proves on the contrary to be inextricably implicated in its transactions with its objects and environments, and often lethally aggressive towards them.

In order to legitimate its dominance of the optical field the eye of the ascendant humanist ego can only repress the other upon whom its identity depends, and upon whom it projects all the fraudulent attributes of the mimetic process: producing for example the faithless woman, with her painted face; or the untrustworthy Moor, whose liability to sudden and lethal passion belies his 'noble' countenance. The female or the racially other features as the object of a dominant gaze, to be either tamed or demonised: Cleopatra becomes a country to be visited, Blanche a map to be ripped apart, Othello a book of traveller's tales. Eroticised or exoticised, the other features as an object of conquest, domestication and consumption, like a landscape offering itself up to the surveyor, sightseer or colonist. Nevertheless, Shakespearean drama cannot foreclose altogether the trace of a reverse gaze which might return to interrupt this triumph of the eye. Cordelia's excessive vision returns from banishment, transgressing her father's visual sovereignty. Innogen reverses the expected trajectory of the maritime gaze in *Cymbeline*. The cases of Constance in *King John* and Catherine in *Henry V*, in very different ways, exemplify the limits and contradictions implicit in the conquest of the female body by the male gaze. And from the repressed of racial difference, another gaze emerges. In the postcolonial world Caliban, Othello and even Aaron from *Titus Andronicus* cease to operate as objects of a Eurocentric analysis and become the loci from which new perspectives may return to change the face of Shakespearean drama.[4]

So the imaginary rapture of the specular relation remains haunted by the (im)possibility of identity and the spectre of reversal. The desire for incorporation betrays the disjunction between the subject's imagined unity and its specular duality, the paradox of two rival images seeking to occupy the same location, or two perspectives competing for the same object. The stage, as it appears to Troilus, and to the audience watching him, cannot accommodate two Cressidas within a single frame: 'If there be rule in unity itself, / This is not she.' Yet there it/they is/are: 'This is and is not Cressid' (*Troilus and Cressida* V.ii.144–9). Such moments cannot be accommodated by the Euclidean fantasy out of which the visual regime is constructed. Shakespeare's stage, like the mirror, appears two-faced: while purporting to offer a passive, limpid and faithful reflection, the representation can also appear menacing, uncanny and double dealing; the symbolic equivalencies and imaginary symmetries of the visual regime are inhabited by the threat of a skewed perspective, an alien gaze, a disobedient image.

The current movement of theory in the direction of the postmodern looks forward to the return of these threats, and as it also looks back, traces their presence in the optical field of early modernity, and their foreclosure by the subsequent history of the subject. Postmodernity mistrusts the realism of which the mirror, like perspective painting or naturalist drama, has become the emblem, seeking instead those speculative histories that have been forgotten in the service of the dominant visual regime. It seems appropriate, therefore, to end with a fantastic history of the mirror relation faked by Borges:

> In those days the world of mirrors and the world of men were not, as they are now, cut off from each other. They were, besides, quite different; neither beings nor colours nor shapes were the same. Both kingdoms, the specular and the human, lived in harmony; you could come and go through mirrors. One night the mirror people invaded the earth. Their power was great, but at the end of bloody warfare the magic arts of the Yellow Emperor prevailed. He repulsed the invaders, imprisoned them in their mirrors, and forced on them the task of repeating, as though in a kind of dream, all the actions of men. He stripped them of their power and of their forms and reduced them to mere slavish reflections. Nonetheless, the day will come when the magic spell will be shaken off.... Deep in the mirror we will perceive a very faint line and the colour of this line will be like no other colour. Later on, other shapes will begin to stir. Little by little they will differ from us; little by little they will not imitate us. They will break through the barriers of glass or metal and this time will not be defeated. (Borges 1974, 67–8)

Readers of English literature have gazed at Shakespeare's plays, longer and with more intensity than at any other textual corpus in the English language, as if they held a limpid mirror up to nature, and for centuries they have given us back ourselves, looking our best. Now, as the sheen of modernity wears thin, we begin to make out in them such black and grained spots as will not leave their tinct. Other shapes begin to stir. Little by little, they will not imitate us.

Notes

Introduction

1 Although I confine my discussion for the most part of Shakespeare's tragedies and histories, obviously there are numerous features of the comedies relevant to the visual phenomenology with which I am concerned. The obsessive thematisation of cross-gender masquerade in *As You Like It*, for example, or the repeated optical duplicity of the twins appearing in *A Comedy of Errors* and *Twelfth Night*, would allow plenty of scope for readings consistent with mine. Critical approaches dealing with these issues in the comedies are not hard to find. Barbara Freedman's *Staging the Gaze* is the text most obviously concerned with these issues (1991); Marjorie Garber discusses twins in *Shakespeare's Ghost Writers* (1987, 1–27), and cross-dressing in *Vested Interests* (1992) and *Staging the Renaissance* (Kastan and Stallybrass 1991, 221–34); Lisa Jardine also considers transvestism in *Still Harping on Daughters* (1983).

1. *Hamlet*: The Stage Mirror

1 Laura Levine provides an excellent discussion of this conviction, ubiquitous among anti-theatrical pamphleteers, that the theatre has power to incite the spectator to replicate what she or he sees performed there (1986).

2 All quotations from Shakespeare are from the Oxford *Complete Works* unless otherwise stated (Wells and Taylor 1988).

3 The source for Hamlet's lines here, according to the Arden Shakespeare, is Donatus, *Commentum Terenti*, ed Wessner, 1, 22 (Jenkins 1982, 288).

4 The OED gives all the above meanings for the word 'strike' (senses 6, 7, 11, 12; 28a, b, and c).

5 This citation is taken from Frances Yates's *Theatre of the World* (1969, 143). It accompanies one of the illustrations given in Fludd's treatise of a type of stage construction appropriate to the mnemonic art, which Yates argues was actually based on the design of either the first or the second Globe Theatre. 'In short,' she suggests,

> it is possible that Shakespeare throughout his life as a playwright may have had in his mind's eye when constructing his scenes, an arrangement of entrances, chamber and terrace roughly as we see it on the stage wall in the Fludd engraving. (1969, 161)

Of course, this construction of a scene in what both Hamlet and Yates refer to as the 'mind's eye' illustrates precisely the kind of psychical transaction I am describing.

6   Houston Diehl describes another common version of the same concept when he suggests that

> memory was seen in the Renaissance as the storehouse of visual images, 'the Gallery of the soul', as John Donne calls it, 'Hang'd with so many, and so lively pictures of the goodness and mercies of thy God to thee . . .' (1983, 192)

The remainder of this citation from Donne, though Diehl does not give it, proves even more interesting for my discussion: 'And as a well made, and a well plac'd picture, looks always upon him that looks upon it; so shall thy God look upon thee, whose memory is thus contemplating him' (Donne 1955, 2, 237). Donne's internal 'picture gallery' of memory repeats the dialectic that concerns me here, in relation to the stage and the mirror, between the eye of the spectator and the gaze which returns upon it from the image of the super-egoic father.

7   Rorty uses the phrase 'glassy essence' to describe the Cartesian subject's capacity to reflect – a phrase taken from *Measure for Measure* (II.ii.123). In fact, many of the related conceits from this and later dialogues between Isabella and Angelo – 'form', 'coin', 'stamps', 'moulds', 'glasses', 'complexions', 'prints', 'frames' (II.iv.1–138) – are entirely relevant to my discussion here.

8   Freud's development of the Oedipus Complex in *The Interpretation of Dreams*, for example, relies upon two plays: Sophocles's *Oedipus Rex*, and *Hamlet* (Freud 1976, 366–8). Jones pursues this interpretation in *Hamlet and Oedipus* (1949).

9   The Oxford *Complete Works* gives these lines as part of an additional passage following on, in the second Quarto, from V.ii.107 (Wells and Taylor 1988, 690).

10   The exchanges between some of the more prominent Shakespearean critics of the twentieth century in relation to the dumb-show are discussed by Terence Hawkes in his essay 'Telmah' (1986, 92–119).

11   For example, James Halliwell-Phillipps and John Dover Wilson (Jenkins 1982, 502–3).

12   Teresa Brennan offers a concise discussion, along with an incisive critique, of the Lacanian relationship between the law of the father, the phallus, the sexual differentiation of the subject and its entry into the symbolic order (Brennan 1989, 3–5).

13   See, for example, Freud's essay on 'Some Psychical Consequences of the Anatomical Distinction between the Sexes' (1986b).

14   Probably the most famous of Lacan's extended jokes on sexual difference occurs in his essay on 'The Agency of the Letter', where he replaces Saussure's model of signification – the tree and the word 'tree' – with one of gender signification: the 'male' and 'female' toilet doors. I am grateful to Anna Hirsbrunner for pointing out – during our discussion of her paper on Lacan's generic strategies – the ambiguous status of many such 'jokes' in Lacanian discourse.

15   The nearest Lacan comes to a hypothesis of this sort occurs in his last seminars, where he suggests that 'the woman' may have access to a

jouissance (an enjoyment or orgasmic pleasure) which is beyond the phallic; which can be experienced by her but not understood, spoken or known; which, in other words, remains outside the phallic economy of the symbolic order. 'There is a *jouissance* proper to her and of which she herself may know nothing, except that she experiences it – that much she does know' (Lacan 1982, 145). Ultimately, however, this seems to offer yet another instance of the 'real', as that which can be encountered only as a trauma in language itself, as the moment where the symbolic stutters, or the imaginary falters. Lacan thus links *jouissance* to *significance*, which is the name he gives to that which shifts within language (1982, 142). The identification in this case would once more be not with the 'real itself', but with its symptom: the traumatic and compulsive signification it produces in language.

16 Homi Bhabha has discussed this process, which he calls 'narrating the nation' (1990b, 1–7), in terms of the performance of an identity which is by definition other than itself, like the Lacanian ego:

> The performative intervenes in the sovereignty of the nation's *self-generation* by casting a shadow between the people as 'image' and its signification as a differentiating sign of Self, distinct from the Others or the Outside.... The barred nation *It/Self*, alienated from its eternal self-generation, becomes a liminal form of social representation, a space that is *internally* marked by cultural difference and the heterogeneous histories of contending peoples, antagonistic authorities, and tense cultural locations. (Bhabha 1990b, 299)

17 If, therefore, through the colonial enterprise, the position of the central 'geometrical point' of the Cartesian ego corresponds to the viewing and mapping subject, then the radically anamorphic gaze which destabilises its complacent location must eventually derive from postcolonial theory, from beyond the Eurocentric academic institution. Postcoloniality provides positions from which to deconstruct not only the hegemony of various 'centres', but the dominance of the concept of centrality itself:

> Directly and indirectly, in Salman Rushdie's phrase, the 'Empire writes back' to the imperial 'centre', not only through nationalist assertion, proclaiming itself central and self-determining, but even more radically by questioning the bases of European and British metaphysics, challenging the world-view that can polarize centre and periphery in the first place. In this way, concepts of polarity ... are challenged as an essential way of ordering reality. (Ashcroft et al. 1989, 33)

What 'Shakespeare' might look like as the object of such criticism proves impossible to define, for it (re)produces multiple gazes constituting a diversity of 'Shakespearean objects'.

2. *King Lear*: Uncanny Spectacles

1   All references to the play(s) are from this Oxford edition; the two texts are distinguished by reference to the Quarto (Q) and the Folio (F). Although I give no critical priority to either, and aim to foreground their points of difference, where the texts agree I will refer to the Folio, as only this version employs the now conventional division into acts and scenes.

2   As Terence Hawkes argues,

> The notion of a self-present, 'unified subject' Shakespeare, the originator of transparently 'true' texts, is deeply suspect: in no instance more so than that presented by the case of *King Lear*. There are after all *two* 'organically distinct' texts of the play, the Quarto and the Folio versions, not one: a situation now recognized by the editors of the Oxford edition of the plays, who have scandalously published both. If we allow for modern 'conflations' of these, it means that in our time there have always been at least *three* extant texts of the play. In short, Shakespeare himself can be said, Lear-like, to have divided his own kingdom. (1992, 137–8)

Referring to the Oxford editors' determination to present both versions as 'authoritative', moreover, Jonathan Goldberg remarks that 'The kingdom has been divided, but Shakespeare reigns supreme, author now of two sovereign texts' (1986, 214). For further discussion of the doubling of the playtexts, see also Cope (1988) and Urkowitz (1980).

3   Derrida will discuss this disseminal, supplementary function in relation to the psychoanalytic death drive when he conducts his close reading of Freud's 'Beyond the Pleasure Principle', in *The Post Card*: see especially the subsection entitled 'Couriers of Death' (1987b, 353–68).

4   Michel de Certeau, writing on Renaissance texts of possession, describes the effect of the demonic voice as a 'text-*off*', a term coined in reference to the theatrical device of the 'voice-off' (1988, 247). See Lukacher (1994) for an account of the Shakespearean 'daemonic' as a figure for conscience.

5   This association between the repetition compulsion – and its most typical manifestation, that of the transference which takes place during analysis – and the 'daemonic' can be found in a number of other texts written by Freud at about the same time as his essay on the uncanny, for example, 'Beyond the Pleasure Principle' (Freud 1986, 243–4), and 'A Seventeenth-Century Demonological Neurosis' (Freud 1985b, 399).

6   Lacan describes Lear himself in precisely these terms, as one entering what he calls the 'zone between-two-deaths' (1992, 320). Slavoj Žižek offers the following gloss on this concept, which describes Lear's situation precisely: 'Lacan conceives this difference between the two deaths as the difference between real (biological) death and its symbolisation, the "setting of accounts", the accomplishment of symbolic destiny' (1989, 135). In *The Post Card*, similarly, Derrida hints at a parallel relation between the Heideggerian 'being-for-death' and the Freudian death drive

(1987b, 357–60). See Lupton and Reinhard (1993) for an extended discussion of Lacan's reading of *King Lear* in these terms.

7   Freud includes a description of just such a disturbing double in a footnote to 'The "Uncanny"':

> I was sitting alone in my *wagon-lit* compartment when a more than usually violent jolt of the train swung back the door to the adjoining washing-cabinet, and an elderly gentleman in a dressing-gown and travelling cap came in: I assumed that in leaving the washing-cabinet, which lay between the two compartments, he had taken the wrong direction and come into my compartment by mistake. Jumping up with the intention of putting him right, I at once realized to my dismay that the intruder was nothing but my own reflection in the looking-glass on the open door. I can still recollect that I thoroughly disliked his appearance. Instead, therefore, of being *frightened* by our 'doubles', both Mach and I simply failed to recognize them as such. Is it not possible, though, that our dislike of them was a vestigial trace of the archaic reaction which feels the 'double' to be something uncanny? (1985b, 371 n. 1).

Freud imagines this double as emerging from the other side of the mirror, the compartment beyond the washroom. What he finds uncanny in his mirror image is what becomes added to it to make it a double: its look, its 'appearance', that is, both the fact that it appears at all where it should not, and that it casts its look upon what should remain private (Freud in his 'dressing-gown and travelling cap').

8   Both Freud and Lacan mention *Lear* in the context of this irremediable loss of the object in desire. Freud, in 'The Theme of the Three Caskets', attributes Cordelia's 'characteristics that border on the uncanny' to her representing for Lear 'the silent Goddess of Death' who, in a strange reversal of the final scene, 'will take him in her arms' (1985b, 245, 247). Lacan echoes this when he comments that Lear 'appears in the end as still not having understood a thing and holding dead in his arms the object of his love, who is, of course, misrecognized by him' (1992, 310). The operation of the gaze of the Other as death of *memento mori* will recur in Lacan's discussion in *The Four Fundamental Concepts* (1979, 88, 92, 118).

9   Mladen Dolar describes this uncanny mirror relation as follows:

> the double is that mirror image in which the object *a* is included. So the imaginary starts to coincide with the real, provoking a shattering anxiety. The double is the same as me plus the object *a*, that invisible part of being added to my image. In order for the mirror image to contain the object *a*, a wink or a nod is enough. Lacan uses the gaze as the best presentation of that missing object; in the mirror, one can see one's eyes, but not the gaze which is the part that is lost. But imagine that one could see one's mirror image close its eyes: that would make the object as gaze appear in the mirror. This is what happens with the double, and the anxiety that the

double produces is the surest sign of the appearance of the object. (It can also be brought about in the opposite way, by the disappearance of one's mirror image, technically dubbed 'the negative autoscopia' ...) (1991, 13)

10 The whole of this scene is omitted from the Folio text, which again seems to repress many of the uncannier elements in the play. In this case, the scene insists that the forces accompanying Cordelia on her return to Britain are much more explicitly a French invasion force: they are said to be under the command of the 'Marshall of France, Monsieur La Far' (Q. 17.8). The Folio, then, by this exclusion, palliates somewhat the radical alterity of the force invading Britain at this point in support of its king. As Leonard Tennenhouse remarks of this play, 'the seventeenth-century theatre-goer would have been disturbed for the very reason that the political meaning of dramatic events was sharply apparent' (1986, 132).

11 Christopher Pye has discussed this function of the jewel as gaze in relation to both Shakespeare and the Elizabethan portrait: 'The gem's power to scorn the eye inheres in the doubleness of its "mockery". ... Like the sovereign's eye, the gem reflects the gaze in its very opacity and emptiness' (1990, 80).

12 For example, an editor such as G. K. Hunter can simply take this interpretation for granted in his introduction to the Penguin Shakespeare edition (1972, 24–5, 38).

13 Ned Lukacher goes so far as to suggest that Hoffmann's story actually constitutes a 'reading' of *King Lear* (Lukacher 1984, 26 n. 34).

14 Kofman emphasises the supplementary character of the spyglass, and the way in which this reverses the trajectory of castration suggested by Freud:

> Thus eyes, in Hoffmann's tale, are the life principle – but the principle of an artificial life: the hero can only create narcissistically through his eyes, not procreate through his genitals. ... If, in the story, the eye is a substitute for the sex, this must be understood literally and not symbolically. Nathaniel can only create by artificial means, by mimesis, by mimicking or doubling life: a power of representation, of vision, of division which belongs to the death instinct, not to Eros. The eye is a diabolical source of life: a demonic power of doubling. (1991, 143–4)

Thus Nathanael can only perceive the face of Olympian, the 'woman' (actually an automaton) with whom he falls in love from afar, through the spyglass he purchases from the optician Coppola, for which he reaches 'automatically' (Hoffmann 1969, 166). As another double of the Sandman, then, the optician grants Nathanael access to an illusory mastery of the visual field, which however involves the selective blindness necessary for the ordering of space within the geometrical symbolic field.

15 The formation of a spectacle-makers' company in London in 1629 suggests the increasing sophistication of optical instruments at this time,

symptomatic of the historical emergence of a visual regime characterised by a simultaneous precision and selectivity (Turner 1983; 96).

16 Although Goldberg, at this point, does indeed go on to discuss
anamorphosis, he does so by leaving 'King Lear' behind altogether and
turning instead to Richard II, Henry V, and Twelfth Night (1988, 253–4).

3. Othello: Black and White Writing

1 In the OED, the two meanings for 'complexion' most relevant here are:
'3. Constitution or habit of mind, disposition, temperament', and '4.
Natural colour, texture, and appearance of the skin, esp. of the face.'
Shakespearean examples are supplied for each of these connotations,
in both cases from The Merchant of Venice. Using the word in the sense
of 'disposition', Solanio comments of Shylock's loss of his daughter
that 'it is the complexion of them all to leave the dam' (III.i.28); while
the 'tawny Moor' from Morocco who comes to woo Portia offers an
instance of the second usage: 'Mislike me not for complexion, / The
shadowed livery of the burnished sun . . .' (II.i.1–2). In the context of
my argument, it is interesting that these two citations associate the
word complexion with, respectively, femininity and racial difference.

2 A number of critics have summarised the history of this debate. Those
most relevant to my discussion are Jones (1965), Cowhig (1985), Orkin
(1987), and Loomba:

> It had been a major problem for critics of the play to reconcile
> Othello's blackness with his central position in the play. Therefore
> either his colour was ignored, or much critical effort was expended
> in trying to prove that Shakespeare did not intend him to be black
> at all. (Loomba 1989, 42)

3 Throughout this chapter I use the term 'race', not because I respect its
validity, but on the contrary, because I take it to be a fundamentally
'racist' notion; for this reason it constitutes the best shorthand approxi-
mation of the way Othello's difference is articulated on the Shakespearean
stage. Our modern notion of race remains inseparable from nineteenth-
century theories of eugenics, Social Darwinism, racial superiority, and
so on; according to the OED, in Shakespeare's time the term could
refer to 'a tribe, nation, or people, regarded as common stock'; to a
breed of animals; or to the 'natural or inherited disposition' of a particular person. Both modern and early modern notions of race, however,
rely on a fundamental correlation between appearance (anatomical traits)
and essence (internal disposition as degeneracy, either in the modern
biological sense, or the early modern theological sense).

4 Martin Orkin has discussed the role played by this edition of the play
in teaching English in the Republic of South Africa (1987, 184).

5 The citation is attributed to 'Miss Preston', identified by Ridley only as
'a lady writing from Maryland' (1958, li). For a sustained and sensitive
reading of the play that examines this assertion, and the Shakespearean

representation of Othello's 'race', in ways compatible with my own approach, see Dympna Callaghan (1996).

6 Jones cites Leo's *History and Description of Africa*, ed. Robert Brown (1896, 2: 233).

7 In using the word 'alibi' here I am drawing on Roland Barthes's discussion of 'Myth Today', where he comments that

> in the alibi too, there is a place which is full and one which is empty.... Myth is a *value*, truth is no guarantee for it; nothing prevents it from being a perpetual alibi: it is enough that its signifier has two sides for it always to have an 'elsewhere' at its disposal. The meaning is always there to *present* the form; the form is always there to *outdistance* the meaning. (1973, 133)

8 My etymology for 'stereotype' comes from the OED, which also gives the following definitions of the word: '1. The methods or process of printing in which a solid plate or type-metal, cast from a papier-mâché or plaster mould taken from the surface of a forme of type, is used for printing from instead of the forme itself'; '3.b. A preconceived and oversimplified idea of the characteristics which typify a person, situation etc; an attitude based on such a preconception'.

9 The citations in this extract are given according to Raffoul and Pettigrew's translation of Lacan; the equivalent passages can be found in Lacan 1977b, 148 and 147.

10 I am grateful to Catherine Belsey for pointing out to me a comparison between the function of Iago here and that of Vindice, introducing the protagonists in the opening moments of *The Revenger's Tragedy*:

> *Enter VINDICE [holding a skill; he watches as] the DUKE, DUCHESS, LUSSURIOSO his son, SPURIO the bastard, with a train, pass over the stage with torch light.*
>
> Vindice. Duke, royal lecher; go, grey hair'd adultery;
> And thou his son, as impious steep'd as he;
> And thou his bastard, true-begot in evil;
> And thou his duchess, that will do with devil;
> Four excellent characters ...
>
> (I.i.1–5)

The editor of the Methuen edition, R. A. Foakes, remarks that in using the world 'characters', Vindice is 'ironically commenting on their moral qualities as shown in their appearance ...; the world was not used until the 18th century to signify "dramatic personage" (Tourneur 1966, 3). This earlier concept of 'character', as an accepted connection between the visual signifier and an implied but invisible referent, is of course entirely consistent with my discussion here.

Moreover, this overture has much in common with the second scene of *Troilus and Cressida*, in which the Trojan heroes pass over the stage and are each labelled with their conventional attributes by Pandarus: a scene which will be discussed in more detail in the following chapter.

11 Lacan defines a signifier as 'that which represents a subject. For whom? – not for another subject, but for another signifier' (1979, 198). Jean-Luc Nancy and Philippe Lacoue-Labarthe discuss this formulation in terms of the scission between the subject of the statement and that of the enunciation:

> ... 'I' does not achieve its meaning in the code without referring to the message where it can appear as the subject of the statement. But as the subject of the statement it does not signify the subject of enunciation, it designates it without signifying it. When I say 'I', this 'I' does not signify *me*.
> Thus the subject staged in Lacan's text – on one level – as subject of enunciation, must be referred in fact to this other subject: the one which, caught in the separation between the subject of the statement and of enunciation, posits or imposes itself as a pure signifier – or as what a signifier 'represents', a 'representation' which is thus not a reference. (1992, 69–70)

12 The 'dram' which Brabanzio here accuses Othello of using on his daughter's eyes might be compared with the flower Oberon commands Puck to acquire:

> The juice of it on sleeping eyelids laid
> Will make or man or woman madly dote
> Upon the next live creature that it sees
>
> (*A Midsummer Night's Dream* II.i.170–2)

As a 'stage-manager' figure, moreover, who directs and contrives much of the action in the play, Oberon's visual magic becomes a metaphor for the transaction of the theatre, in its ability to conjure up 'shaping fantasies' before the gaze of the spectator. Thus Theseus compares the lover's eye with that of the poet, which 'an imagination bodies forth / The forms of things unknown' (V.i.5–15). Similarly, just as the tears which Othello's tales beguile from Desdemona represent her response to his visual soliciting, Bottom measures his own success as an actor according to his ability to make the audience weep: 'That will ask some tears in the true performing of it. If I do it, let the audience look to their eyes' (I.ii.21–2).

13 The phrase *en abyme* derives originally from heraldry, where it indicates the depiction of a shield within a shield. Punning on *abîme*, Derrida uses the expression to signify an abyssal regression of reflections, echoes, or frames within frames (1987b, 304 n. 9, 511 n. 10).

14 Cornel West emphasises the importance of such aesthetic ideals, derived from Greek antiquity, for the establishment of what he calls the 'normative gaze' (1982, 47–65). By this he means the empirical, scientific and colonising European eye that will categorise the various races it encounters and, by measuring them against this mythical Grecian

ideal, organize them into a hierarchy, thereby facilitating the formulation of a culture of white supremacy. The correlations I am making
here between the psychoanalytic models of Lacan and Fanon, and the
racial transactions of the Shakespearean stage, are thus possible not
because of any universal validity inherent to either of these 'scenes' of
identity-formation, but rather because both participate in the histori-
cally-specific construction of an imperialistic, Eurocentric, narcissistic,
scopic structure – that which West calls the normative gaze, and I call
the visual regime.

15 Fanon suggests that a specular aggressivity permeates the rivalry between white and black, coloured and skewed by racial inequality:

> When one has grasped the mechanism described by Lacan, one can
> have no further doubt that the read Other for the white man is
> and will continue to be the black man. And conversely. Only for
> the white man the Other is perceived on the level of the body im-
> age, absolutely as the not-self – that is, the unidentifiable, the
> unassimilable. For the black man, as we have shown, historical and
> economic realities come into the picture.... I contend that for the
> Antillean the mirror image is always neutral. When Antilleans tell
> me that they have experienced it, I always ask the same question:
> 'What colour were you?' Invariably they reply: 'I had no colour' ...
> in the Antilles perception always occurs on the level of the imagi-
> nary. It is in white terms that one perceives one's fellows. (1970,
> 114–16)

16 Perhaps the most extreme version of this mimesis is to be found in *As
You Like It*, where Rosalind, a male actor disguised as a woman, dis-
guises 'her'self as the boy Ganymede, who in turn pretends 'he' is a
girl in order for Orlando to practise the art of courtship (III.ii).

17 Michel Foucault comments on the tactical importance of silence within
the discursive power relation:

> Silence itself – the things one declines to say, or is forbidden to
> name, the discretion that is required between different speakers – is
> less the absolute limit of discourse, the other side from which it is
> separated by a strict boundary, than an element that function alongside
> the things said, with them and in relation to them within over-all
> strategies.... There is not one but many silences, and they are an
> integral part of the strategies that underlie and permeate discourses.
> (1984, 27)

18 The play repeatedly characterises this 'secret' as a 'monster'. Othello
calls it 'some monster in thy thought / Too hideous to be shown'
(III.iii.111–12), while earlier Iago remarks that 'Hell and night / Must
bring this monstrous birth to the world's light' (I.iii.395–6). Etymologically
and colloquially, the concept of the monstrous appears closely associated with both concealment and revelation, since as Karen Newman
points out. '*monstrum*, the word itself, figures both the creature and its

movement into representation, for it meant as well a showing or demonstration, a *representation'* (1987, 153).

19 John Dover Wilson, famously, goes so far as to posit the operation of a
'double time scheme', whereby short-term events gain their dramatic
impetus from being set against a larger temporal backdrop of events
implied but not staged (Ridley 1958, lxvii–lxx).

20 See also Derrida's discussion of Freud's analysis of dreams of nudity, in
which 'Nakedness gives rise to substitutes. The lack of clothing, or
undress... is displaced onto other attributes... Already a certain chain is
indicated: truth-inveiled-woman-castration-shame' (Derrida 1987b, 415–16).

21 In the same article, Parker treats the handkerchief as a crucial manifestation of this extended trope, remarking that

> the Ensign Iago's 'dilations' open up a sense of something much
> larger than can be unfolded or shown, a disproportion finally fig-
> ured in the 'trifle' of the handkerchief (*Desdemona*: 'What's the matter?'
> / *Othello*: 'That handkerchief' [V.ii.50]), a matter or *materia* both
> enlarged and itself the visual evidence of Desdemona's crime; a showing
> forth or exposure to the eye of something which cannot in itself be
> seen. (1985, 64)

22 Roger Manvell describes how at this point in Welles's film

> Othello, in close shot, pinches out the candle, the contours of his
> face revealed in highlights against the blackout, his eyes concen-
> trated. It is a play of darkness rather than light. When Desdemona
> dies, her face is seen faintly outlined beneath the veils of the fine
> cloth that suffocates her. (1971, 64)

Cinema, of course, is a form of representation that thoroughly fetishises
the kinds of play between showing and hiding with which this discussion has been concerned: hence the double valency of the word 'screen'
(or indeed 'film') in film theory.

23 For further contextualisation and discussion of the psychoanalytic attempt to define masculinity and femininity, see Belsey (1994, 62–4).

24 As emphasised by Stephen Heath (1986, 55–6).

25 Frantz Fanon describes the more conventional interpretation of this
tendency:

> Still on the genital level, when a white man hates black men, is he
> not yielding to a feeling of impotence or of sexual inferiority? Since
> his ideal is an infinite virility, is there not a phenomenon of dimi-
> nution in relation to the Negro, who is viewed as a penis symbol?
> Is the lynching of the Negro not a sexual revenge? (1970, 113)

This view of the black man as a 'penis symbol' reinforces my reading
as well, in so far as the phallus, in Lacanian terms, as 'the privileged
signifier of that mark where the share of the logos is wedded to the
advent of desire... can only play its role as veiled...' (Lacan 1982, 82).

4. *Troilus and Cressida*: Space Wars

1 I am thinking here of the 'author's drift' in terms similar to Roland Barthes's notion of 'floating' (*dérive*) – which he calls 'the very form of the signifier' – as opposed to a pinning or buttoning down of language, guaranteeing a singular and fixed meaning (1977, 215).

2 See Gary Taylor's *Reinventing Shakespeare* for a brief performance history of the play (1991, 244–5, 302–3).

3 For example, when Malcolm Evans suggests that Troilus's 'bifold authority' speech 'could be as essential to a poststructuralist Shakespeare criticism as Ulysses' disquisition on "degree" was to the conservative Shakespeare of the "Elizabethan world picture"', it appears that Shakespeare still simply offers his eternal authoritative stamp to whichever theory appropriates him best (1986, 139). In other accounts, the play seems to have certain inherent qualities which have been lying in wait to be revealed and emphasised by the poststructuralist reader, as Elizabeth Freund comments: 'To the many reasons on account of which *Troilus and Cressida* has been claimed for modernity one could add its self-reflecting wit, its heightened language consciousness' (1985, 21). This latter phrase seems like a contradiction in terms according to a psychoanalytic theory for which language provides nothing other than the paradigm for the unconscious. Surprisingly, even as they write about self-referential discursive practices in the play, many critics display little awareness or self-consciousness of the textual status of their own theories of reading. Thus, when Carol Cook conducts her otherwise incisive psychoanalytic account of the construction of identity in the play as 'a fiction created by mirrors and easily shattered', she does so by invoking Lacan's theory of an 'aggressivity' arising from the 'alienating ego', an 'impulse' unproblematically located within the play's characters and 'most persistently voiced in the play by Thersites' (1986, 46). This psychodynamic paradigm – the authoritative status of which is taken as read – thereby dictates the terms of the fictional construction of identity from a position beyond the reach of, and invulnerable to, the analysis it carries out. Again, Shakespeare and Lacan easily assimilate each other and, standing in a relation of mutually reinforcing authority, guarantee the articulation of psychoanalytic 'truth'. Finally, Linda Charnes's reading of the play in terms of the 'neurosis' of nostalgia engages in this problematic more thoughtfully than most. Her historicist and psychoanalytic methodology – for which she suggests the label 'New Hystericism' (1993, 18) – recognises the potential overfamiliarity of psychoanalytic terminology, without always avoiding it in spite of the generous use of scare-quotes. Nevertheless Charnes's notion of 'notorious identity' seems to me a highly productive way of thinking about the play's conceptualisation of historicity, and her reading thus influences my own approach more than any other (Charnes 1993, 70–102).

4 There are, of course, critics who do theorise this transaction between analysis and literature productively, perhaps the best instance being Sarah Kofman's *Freud and Fiction* (1991). Shoshana Felman's influential discussion of the 'co-implication' of these two 'fields', although useful,

seems to exclude or tame the aggressivity and violence that characterise the relation between the texts at issue (1987).

5 Elizabeth Freund discusses these tropes in some detail (1985, 21–2).
Although – as both the *Arden* and the *Oxford* editors emphasise (Palmer
1982, 99; Muir 1982, 52) – 'digested' was the usual Elizabethan term
for the reduction of material into dramatic form, it seems unlikely that
the term could remain unassimilated by the play's overdetermining
culinary and gastronomic preoccupations.

6 Gary Taylor has discussed the textual status of each of these various
frames (the Prologue, Epilogue and Epistle), and the history of their
respective exclusions and reinclusions (1982b).

7 It could be said that Shakespeare's Pandarus contracts his symbolic disease from a prior post-Homeric Cressida, who, according to medieval
tradition, ended her days as a leprous beggar (Palmer 1982, 303).

8 Weimann points out that occasional acting in the pit (for example, by
the Porter in *Henry VIII*) typifies the liability of the relationship in
Shakespearean theatre between players and spectators. He elsewhere takes
Troilus and Cressida as exemplary of the instability of any barrier between the two (1978, 212, 227–8).

9 See, for example, Derrida's deconstruction of the boundary supposedly
separating Poe's story. 'The Purloined Letter' from Lacan's analysis of
it, in spite of the latter's attempt to keep the literary text in its place
as an 'illustration' of psychoanalytic 'truth' (Derrida 1987b, 411–96).

10 Commenting on Lacan's use of this anecdote, Elisabeth Roudinesco
remarks that Jung

> appears to have reserved for Lacan alone the revelation of the se-
> cret. In his memoirs, he makes no mention of a plague. For his
> part, Freud never uses the word.... Freud simply said, 'They'll be
> surprised when they find out what we have to tell them'.
> ... Today in France everyone uses the world 'plague' to designate
> the Viennese discovery. Abroad, on the contrary, only the partisans
> of Lacan employ that term. (1990, 177)

11 A consideration of the concept of 'homosociality' provides a parallel
reading to the one suggested here (see Charnes 1993, 92–3). Eve Kosofsky
Sedgewick describes this feature in Renaissance texts, according to which
men mediate sexual desire between themselves via the discursive 'exchange' of women (1985). The only women in the play who stand
outside this structure are characters such as Andromache and Cassandra,
whose interventions are, famously, ignored.

12 The essay on the 'Mirror Stage' explicitly conflates the two drives in its
description of contemporary philosophy as providing a 'voyeuristic-sadistic
idealization of the sexual relation...' (Lacan 1977b, 6).

13 Linda Charnes describes this process as follows:

> The characters' names instantly convey the roles they are required
> to play – by Shakespeare, by the audience, and, as we shall see, by
> each other.... Consequently, to attempt to avoid or subvert their

'official' functions is to deconstruct their own origins, to somehow 'undo' their own conditions of existence and of meaning. It is to engage in a politics of rebellion against a culturally mandated 'self'. (1993, 74–5)

For Charnes, however, this rebellion marks the play with an essentialist nostalgia for the return of an inherent identity not dependent on textual predetermination (85–6), which she equates with a fantasised return from the Lacanian symbolic to the imaginary (92). According to my reading, however, the play foregrounds precisely the breakdown of imaginary identity and co-ordination through the staging of a fragmenting aggressivity.

14 Dryden remarks the play starts promisingly enough, but that the author seems to grow 'weary of his task', so that 'the later part of the Tragedy is nothing but a confusion of Drums and Trumpets, Excursions and Alarms' (1984, 13: 226). In his rewriting, he divides the play into acts and scenes, provides stage directions, and drops many of the brief scenes. He also attempts to introduce what critics life d'Aubignac and Corneille referred to as the 'fourth unity' of *liaison des scènes*, by making at least one character remain on stage from the end of one scene to the beginning of the next (517).

15 Gary Taylor chronicles the various critical debates about the play's performance history (1982b). One commentator has described *Troilus and Cressida* in terms of a 'war of genres' (Defaye 1992).

16 In his introduction to the *Signet Classic* edition, Daniel Seltzer remarks that in many scenes of the play,

> if the director plans the moves of his actors to emphasise the apparent climax of the episode, he will find that the real interest of the scene has shifted elsewhere, that the point of the action is not what he thought it was. (Seltzer 1963, xxix)

Gary Taylor also speculates on the reaction of the audience to the play's staging of contemporaneous and competing pockets of activity. For example, he asks, 'Could an audience he expected to attend properly to Ulysses' long description of Troilus, if . . . preparations [for combat] were going on behind him?' (1982b, 114). He then discusses the play's predilection for characters who enter and then exist very soon afterwards, as well as for characters who remain on the verge of entry, are hindered from entering, or who remain offstage but are gestured towards by those on-stage (111–16). For the *Oxford* editor, the play 'is unique even among Shakespeare's works in its changes of viewpoint from scene to scene'. He goes on to describe the identification of the audience with the gaze of each character in turn: in the first scene with that of Troilus, with Cressida's in the second, Ulysses's in the third. Thersites's in the fourth, and Hector's in the fifth (Muir 1982, 20).

17 Freud's description of the assimilation of the superego into the ego at this point incorporates a quote from *Hamlet*: 'Thus conscience does make cowards of us all . . .' (III.i.85).

18 Lacan refers to this circuit with the pun '*la pulsion en fait le tour*', which means both 'the drive moves around the object', and 'the drive tricks the object' (1979, 168, 168 n. 1). He wants to emphasise that the aim of the drive is displaced from the object to the continuation the circuit itself. Attainment of the object, though it orients the drive, cannot satisfy it.

19 Derrida pursues the spatial impossibilities of a number of psychoanalytic topologies in 'Freud and the Scene of Writing'. The article follows Freud's pervasive and sustained use of various writing metaphors to describe the psychical trace. But just as his deployment of the image of the 'Eternal City' calls into question the limits of visual and spatial representation, Freud's use of the metaphor of inscription renders problematic the conventional comprehension of writing itself; hence the 'mystic writing pad', as the culmination of Freud's various scriptorial 'metaphors', would need to be added to a catalogue of psychoanalytic impossible spaces, for it offers

> simultaneously a depth without bottom, an infinite allusion, and a perfectly superficial exteriority: a stratification of surfaces each of whose relation to itself, each of whose interior, is but the implication of another similarly exposed surface. It joins the two empirical certainties by which we are constituted: infinite depth in the implication of meaning, in the unlimited envelopment of the present, and, simultaneously, the pellicular essence of being, the absolute absence of any foundation. (224)

As Derrida's title suggests, 'Freud and the Scene of Writing', like my own discussion, gestures towards the spatial co-ordinates of the stage to provide the exemplary location for these paradoxes. For the oxymoronic junction between 'infinite depth' and 'pellicular essence' can be associated with the paradoxical situation of the theatre, in which the performance is both palpably present and, by definition, a mimetic allusion to what is absent. So in the voluminous emptiness of the writing on the page, 'we find neither the continuity of a line nor the homogeneity of a volume; only the differentiated duration and depth of a stage, and its spacing' (225).

20 As discussed by both Miller (1976, 66) and Freud (1985).

21 Lacan's diagram of the circuit followed by the drive, for instance, constitutes two interlaced loops. The aim of the drive enters and exits from the rim represented by the erogenous zone in order to encircle the internal void that provides its object, a trajectory which represents the relation between inside and outside as a dynamic of mutual interpenetration (1979, 178–9). Similarly, the image of the 'hoop net' inverts the 'traditional' opposition, so that the subject is caught 'within' the enveloping unconscious, instead of the latter constituting a space or gap 'kept in reserve, closed up inside' (144). Finally, the 'mitre' made out of the Moebius strip or 'interior 8', as a 'self-intersecting surface projected into three-dimensional space', demonstrates many of the spatial paradoxes characteristic of Lacan's redrafting of psychical topology: the

continuity of surface between inside and outside, the intersection or meeting which is also a void, the transposition from two dimensions into three, and the disruption of the relation between container and contained (147, 155–6). In a footnote to the 'Seminar of 21 January 1975', Mitchell and Rose suggest that Lacan's theoretical use of patterns of convoluted knots in his representation of the unconscious signals 'his rejection of geometrical optics in favour of topology' (Lacan 1982, 171 n. 6).

22 Lacan hints at a similar emphasis, and also echoes Freud's use of the Roman metaphor, when he insists that 'we must read ... very attentively', because the value of Freud's writings on the instincts, 'in which he is breaking new ground', lies in the way in which 'like a good archaeologist, he leaves the work of the dig in place – so that, even if it is incomplete, we are able to discover what the excavated objects mean' (Lacan 1979, 182). 'Instincts and Their Vicissitudes', again, compares the preservation of the earlier phases of the drive to the layering of geological strata after successive waves of lava have erupted and congealed (Freud 1986, 209).

23 As Robert Weimann argues:

> Unlike the theatre of the subsequent three hundred years, the actor-audience relationship was not subordinate, but a dynamic and essential element of dramaturgy.... The traditional readiness and ability of the audience to be drawn into the play which is indicated here is as noteworthy as the willingness of author and actor to speak directly to the audience and to acknowledge basic agreement with its tastes and ideas. (1978, 213–14)

As I have suggested earlier, moreover, this interactive mode of theatre is most clearly indicated by the abundance of parergonal elements surrounding and infiltrating the Shakespearean play: as Weimann goes on to comment. These links between the world of the play and the audience's world of experience are further extended in prologue, chorus, and song'.

5. Mapping Histories

1 My interpretation of the historical context of Lacan's theory of the ego and the gaze owes much to Teresa Brennan's convincing refutation of the common objection to Lacan's 'ahistoricity' (Brennan 1993, 7–8, 39–40) and *passim*). In those parts of his work that address these topics, at least, Lacan provides more than enough historical references – dates, authors, summaries of contemporary contexts – to make any allegations of 'universalising' or 'totalising' seem premature.

2 See also Terence Hawkes's discussion of Lear's division in terms of cartographic 'reduction' in *Meaning by Shakespeare* (1992, 121–40).

3 Michael Neill has pointed out to me that Marlowe reproduces the same effect when Faustus imagines ordering his familiar spirits to 'wall all

Germany with brass / And make swift Rhine circle fair Wittenberg' (Marlowe 1976, I.i.87–8).

4 See also John Gillies's fascinating *Shakespeare and the Geography of Difference*, which discusses a number of the instances of cartographic transaction I have mentioned above, including Wright's map (Gillies 1994). Gillies's historicist and semiological approach parallels my own in some areas, and provides an interesting contrast in others, although for the most part he is not concerned with the relationship between the phenomenology of the gaze and the construction of an emergent subjectivity in the way that interests me here.

5 For further discussion of the political ramifications of the Eurocentric bias organising the Mercator projection, see Harley (1988, 290).

6 It is worth noting in this connection the many maps collected by Lord Burghley, Elizabeth's long-serving Secretary of State. Along with Ptolemaic maps, the world atlases of Ortelius (1570 and 1595), and Mercator (1589), Waghenaer's sea-atlas (1588), a large number of maps of the British Isles (constantly updated and annotated), and charts relating to the search for the Northeast Passage, Burghley also kept a number of architectural and perspectival urban plans of cities and ports of strategic importance, both English and foreign: Plymouth, Portsmouth, Dover, Calais, Ambleteuse and Boulonnais (Skelton 1971).

7 Lloyd Brown describes how one of the primary difficulties of Elizabethan surveying and navigation lay in the inaccuracy of readings taken from the sun due to the glare faced by the observer looking into it (1951, 184–5).

8 Again, a famous painting of Elizabeth I offers a pictorial comparison: in this case, the 'Ditchley' portrait, in which the queen 'towers over an England drawn after the Saxton model' (Helgerson 1992, 112).

9 In the development of mapping 'technology', however, this growth in the confidence and stature of the gaze is more complicated and conflicted. In survey maps of this period (for instance, those of Christopher Saxton and John Speed), the persistence of 'sugarloaf' icons to show hills, and silhouette or isometric representations of buildings and towns, suggest a residual ground-level perspective combined with the bird's (or giant's) eye view (Harley 1983, 25).

10 Brennan, relying wholly on Lacan's reference to Pascal in the *Écrits* (Lacan 1977b, 71), locates the 'dawn of the ego's era' – with rather too much precision – in 1670, the date of the publication of the *Pensées* (Brennan 1993, 39). However, considering Lacan's persistent recourse to the discussion of Renaissance optics, it would be no less arbitrary, though perhaps no more accurate, to choose 1533, the date of Holbein's *The Ambassadors*.

11 Louis Montrose's 'Work of Gender in the Discourse of Discovery' is one of the most important contributions here (1991). Peter Hulme conducts a similarly compelling analysis of the feminisation of the Americas in early colonial encounters (1985), while Richard Helgerson discusses at length the institution of a 'cult of Britain', producing the nation as a female figure to be anatomised, for example in Drayton's *Poly-Olbion* (1992, 118–20). Finally, Michael Neill describes a similar tactic at work

in the gaze directed from England towards Ireland, 'stripping naked the prostrate body ... and laying her open to the conqueror's gaze' (1994, 23–4).

12 I am grateful to Michael Neill for bringing this passage from Platter to my attention, and for his various other observations on the links between cartography and imperialism.

13 For a more extended extrapolation of the associations between the Shakespearean playhouse and cartography see Gillies (1994, 70–98).

14 Robert Weimann's *Shakespeare and the Popular Tradition* provides an unsurpassed account of the communal and dialogic nature of Shakespearean drama (1978). Weimann does emphasise, however, that this medieval tradition of interactive theatre inherited by the Elizabethans was in transition. My discussion here is concerned to suggest some of the perceptual paradigms involved in this evolution.

15 Stephen Orgel describes how, in the masque, 'Through the use of perspective the monarch, always the ethical centre of court productions, became in a physical and emblematic way the centre as well ... only the King's seat was perfect' (Orgel and Strong 1973, 1: 7).

16 In this connection, it is worth noting that Ptolemy, whose application of geometrical principles to cartographic projection influenced the development of Renaissance linear perspective to such a great extent, most likely developed his facility with Euclidean optics in designing stage sets for Greek theatre (Edgerton 1987, 37).

17 For example, *King John*, one of the most cartographically influenced of the plays discussed in this chapter, was a favourite subject for the extravagantly 'realistic' and historically authentic performances of the nineteenth century, best exemplified by Planché's 'antiquarian' production at Covent Garden in 1823–4, and Kean's 1852 version which, according to the *Arden* editor, 'brought theatrical pedantry to its high-point' (Honigmann 1954, lxxv).

18 Mary Hamer discusses the political and representational stakes in the Ordinance Survey of Ireland, which took place between 1824 and 1846 (1989). Sir George Everest joined the Trigonometrical Survey of India in 1818, becoming Surveyor-General in 1830, and retired in 1843, shortly after completing the survey of the Himalayas.

6. *Macbeth*: Mimicry and Masquerade

1 The translation given here of these comments from Mallarmé's 'La fausse entrée des sorcières dans *Macbeth*' is Barbara Johnson's, taken from Garber (1987, 92).

2 David Willbern discusses at greater length Macbeth's 'alter-ego' or mimetic relationship with the various rebels in the play (1986, 529–30).

3 Laura Levine has discussed the tendency among Puritan pamphleteers to suggest that the theatrical use of improper garments, gestures and manners exerts a transformative power over both actor and spectator: 'Anti-theatrical tracts,' she asserts, 'are dominated by both explicit and implicit claims about magic' (1986, 123), according to which the 'external'

mimesis of femininity – or of any alternative social and political role – can produce a change 'within' the person, contaminating what would otherwise be considered the innate attributes of gender, class or obedience to convention. Other relevant recent discussions of the relationship between the stage and sumptuary laws include Orgel (1975, 5–6), Jardine (1985), and Garber (Kastan and Stallybrass 1991, 221–34).

4 The first meaning given for 'inform' in the *OED* is 'To put into (material) form or shape; to form, shape, frame, mould, fashion'.

5 Once again, John Dee provides a fascinating example of the influence of the geometrical visual regime over a diverse range of fields of inquiry and representation: his tacit adherence to an extramission theory of vision can be observed in the frequent references to optical rays throughout his Preface to the English translation of Euclid (Dee 1975).

6 On the question of occult aviation, the *Daemonologie* describes the Devil like 'a mighty winde' transporting his servants 'from one place to an other' (James I 1966, 38). Reginald Scot also attests to the common belief – deriving from the classic treatise on witchcraft, the *Malleus Maleficarum* of Jakob Sprenger and Heinrich Kramer (1487) – in the power of witches to 'flie in the aire' and to 'passe from place to place in the aire invisible' (Scot 1930, 6).

7 W. A. Murray's 'Why Was Duncan's Blood Golden?' best documents the critical distaste provoked by Macbeth's metaphor (1978).

8 The Medusa's head was a popular subject among artists of the time: Cellini, Rubens, Leonardo and Caravaggio all painted versions. Marjorie Garber gives a provocative reading of the play in terms of the Medusa legend, and in relation to Freud's reading of it as a scopic equivalent of castration (Garber 1987, 87–123; Freud 1940).

9 Keith Thomas confirms the association between the two, reporting that 'In 1657 it was reported to be the recreation of Oxford students of optics to practise "delusions of the sight" of a kind which former generation would have regarded as magical' (1971, 269). Ernest Gilman also attests to a connection between 'the Christian association of optics with magic, pagan soothsaying, and the vanity of appearances on the one hand, and the pictorial illusionism of the artist's perspective on the other . . .' (1978, 95).

10 For the first formulation of these ideas about the play's performance at court, see Paul (1978); for discussion of the implications of this theory for poststructuralist and psychoanalytic readings of the plays, see Garber (1987, 116), Pye (1990, 142–72) and Goldberg (1987, 247–60).

11 According to Ernest Gilman, the meaning of the English 'perspective' expanded 'to accommodate the new connection between optics and the visual arts':

> By the seventeenth century it could refer to the theory of linear perspective; to a telescope (perspective glass) in particular, but also to a microscope or other refracting lens; to an expansive view in nature or to the representation of such a view in a painting that made conspicuous use of the linear perspective; or to a perspective device . . . (1978, 16–17)

My discussion would suggest that the word would also embrace prophetic instruments such as Muir's 'prospective glass'.

12 The full sentence – from *The History of Sexuality Volume One* – reads as follows: 'In political thought and analysis, we still have not cut off the head of the king' (1984, 88–9). Foucault's point here – that 'the representation of power has remained under the spell of the monarchy' – is of course not incompatible with the suggestion that the optical power and position of the modern subject have also consistently worn the 'borrowed robes' of kingship.

13 Notably, modern productions of the play often seem preoccupied with the plot's potential for repetition, for another usurpation: the final sequence of Roman Polanski's film shows Malcolm's brother Donalbain visiting the witches, while the BBC version focuses at the end upon the calculating gaze of Fleance, turning towards the new king Malcolm, recalling the promise made to his father.

Conclusion

1 This passage has been extensively discussed by critics: see especially Žižek (1991a, 11–12), Lukacher (1989, 866–75), and Pye (1990).

2 For a concise (but far from exhaustive) breakdown of the possible meanings for this line, see Kerrigan's commentary in his *Penguin Shakespeare* edition of *The Sonnets* (1986, 204–5).

3 Helgerson, for example, emphasises the premature nature of the Elizabethan 'British Empire', observing that 'in 1580 England did not control a square inch of territory outside the British Isles'. A writer like Hakluyt, therefore, attempts to show the world

> as a field of uncertain and potentially unsettling enterprise. Odd bits of land are to be taken, colonies planted, populations moved, passages explored, trades opened . . . In his *Voyages*, historical narrative is proleptic. It anticipates by enabling future accomplishment. (Helgerson 1992, 164–5)

4 I am thinking here of studies which begin with the history of the racially different character and work back into the Shakespearean text: examples included Brown (1985), Hulme (1985, 88–137), Orkin (1987), Newman (1987), Soyinka (1988, 204–20), Loomba (1989), Gillies (1994, 99–155) and those represented in the volume *Post-Colonial Shakespeares*, edited by Loomba and Orkin (1998).

Bibliography

Adelman, Janet. 1985. '"This Is and Is Not Cressid": The Characterization of Cressida'. *The (M)other Tongue: Essays in Feminist Psychoanalytic Interpretation.* Ed. Shirley Nelson Garner, Claire Kahane and Madelon Sprengnether. Ithaca: Cornell University Press, 119–41.

Althusser, Louis. 1971. *Lenin and Philosophy.* Trans. Ben Brewster. London: Monthly Review Press.

Ashcroft, Bill, Gareth Griffiths and Helen Tiffin. 1989. *The Empire Writes Back: Theory and Practice in Post-Colonial Literatures.* London: Routledge.

Baltrusaitis, Jurgis. 1977. *Anamorphic Art.* Cambridge: Chadwyck-Healey.

Barber, Peter. 1992. 'England II: Monarchs, Ministers and Maps, 1550–1625'. *Monarchs, Ministers and Maps: The Emergence of Cartography as a Tool of Government in Early Modern Europe.* Ed. David Buisseret. London: University of Chicago Press, 57–98.

Barker, Francis. 1984. *The Tremulous Private Body: Essays on Subjection.* London: Methuen.

Barthes, Roland. 1973. *Mythologies.* Trans. Annette Lavers. London: Paladin.

——. 1977. *Image Music Text.* Trans. Stephen Heath. London: Fontana.

Bate, Jonathan. 1989. *Shakespearean Constitutions: Politics, Theatre, Criticism, 1730–1830.* Oxford: Clarendon.

Belsey, Catherine. 1985. *The Subject of Tragedy: Identity and Difference in Renaissance Drama.* New York: Methuen.

——. 1992. 'Desire's Excess and the English Renaissance Theatre: *Edward II, Troilus and Cressida, Othello*'. *Erotic Politics.* Ed. Susan Zimmerman. London: Routledge, 84–102.

——. 1994. *Desire: Love Stories in Western Culture.* Oxford: Blackwell.

Bentley, G. E. 1968. *The Jacobean and Caroline Stage.* Vol. 6. Oxford: Clarendon.

Bergeron, David, ed. 1985. *Pageantry in the Shakespearean Theater.* Athens: University of Georgia Press.

Bethell, S. L. 1944. *Shakespeare and the Popular Dramatic Tradition.* London: Staples.

Bhabha, Homi K. 1984. 'Of Mimicry and Man: The Ambivalence of Colonial Discourse'. *October* 28 (Spring): 125–33.

——. 1990a. 'Articulating the Archaic: Notes on Colonial Nonsense'. *Literary Theory Today.* Ed. Peter Collier and Helga Geyer-Ryan. Cambridge: Polity Press, 203–18.

——, ed. 1990b. *Nation and Narration.* London: Routledge.

Borges, Jorge Luis. 1973. *Dreamtigers.* Trans. Mildred Boyer and Harold Morland. London: Souvenir Press.

——. 1974. *The Book of Imaginary Beings.* Trans. Norman Thomas di Giovanni. Harmondsworth: Penguin.

Bradley, A. C. 1991. *Shakespearean Tragedy: Lectures on Hamlet, Othello, King Lear, and Macbeth.* London: Penguin.

Brennan, Teresa, ed. 1989. *Between Feminism and Psychoanalysis.* London and New York: Routledge.

——. 1993. *History after Lacan*. London: Routledge.

Briggs, K. M. 1962. *Pale Hecate's Team: An Examination of the Beliefs on Witchcraft and Magic Among Shakespeare's Contemporaries and His Immediate Successors*. London: Routledge and Kegan Paul.

Brockbank, Philip, ed. 1976. *Coriolanus*. London: Routledge. *The Arden Shakespeare*. Gen. ed. Richard Proudfoot.

Brooke, Nicholas, ed. 1990. *The Tragedy of Macbeth*. Oxford: Oxford University Press. *The Oxford Shakespeare*. Gen. ed. Stanley Wells.

Brown, Lloyd A. 1951. *The Story of Maps*. London: Cresset.

Brown, Paul. 1985. '"This Thing of Darkness I Acknowledge Mine": *The Tempest* and the Discourse of Colonialism'. *Political Shakespeare*. Ed. Jonathan Dollimore and Alan Sinfield. Manchester: Manchester University Press, 48–71.

Bryson, Norman. 1983. *Vision and Painting: the Logic of the Gaze*. London: Macmillan.

Burgin, Victor, James Donald and Cora Kaplan, eds. 1986. *Formations of Fantasy*. London and New York: Methuen.

Butler, Judith. 1990. *Gender Trouble: Feminism and the Search for Identity*. London: Routledge.

Caillois, Roger. 1984. 'Mimicry and Legendary Psychaesthenia'. Trans. John Shepley. *October* 31 (Winter): 17–32.

Callaghan, Dympna. 1996. 'Othello Was a White Man'. *Alternative Shakespeares 2*. Ed. Terence Hawkes. London and New York: Routledge, 192–215.

Cartwright, Kent. 1991. *Shakespearean Tragedy and its Double: The Rhythms of Audience Response*. Pennsylvania: Pennsylvania State University Press.

Certeau, Michel de. 1987. 'The Gaze of Nicholas of Cusa'. Trans. Catherine Porter. *Diacritics* 17.3 (Fall): 2–38.

——. 1988. *The Writing of History*. Trans. Tom Conley. New York: Columbia.

Chambers, E. K. 1974. *The Elizabethan Stage*. Vol. 4. Oxford: Clarendon.

Charnes, Linda. 1993. *Notorious Identity: Materializing the Subject in Shakespeare*. Cambridge, Mass.: Harvard University Press.

Cixous, Hélène. 1976. 'Fiction and its Phantoms: A Reading of Freud's *Das Unheimliche* (The "Uncanny")'. Trans. Robert Dennommé. *New Literary History* 7.3: 525–48.

Clark, Stuart. 1980. 'Inversion, Misrule and the Meaning of Witchcraft'. *Past and Present* 87: 98–127.

Coleridge, S. T. 1969. *Coleridge on Shakespeare*. Ed. Terence Hawkes. Harmondsworth: Penguin.

Cook, Carol. 1986. 'Unbodied Figures of Desire'. *Theatre Journal* 38: 34–52.

Cope, Jackson I. 1988. 'Shakespeare, Derrida, and the End of Language in *Lear*'. *Shakespeare and Deconstruction*. Ed. G. Douglas Atkins and David M. Bergeron. New York: Peter Lang, 266–80.

Copjec, Joan. 1991. 'Vampires, Breast-Feeding, and Anxiety'. *October* 58 (Fall): 24–43.

Cowhig, Ruth. 1985. 'Blacks in English Renaissance Drama and the Role of Shakespeare's Othello'. *The Black Presence in English Literature*. Ed. David Dabydeen. Manchester: Manchester University Press, 1–25.

Dee, John. 1975. *The Mathematicall Preface to the Elements of Geometrie of Euclid of Megara, 1570*. New York: Science History Publications.

——. 1986. *Essential Readings*. Ed. Gerald Suster. Great Britain: Crucible.

Defaye, Claudine. 1992. '*Troilus and Cressida* ou la guerre des genres'. *La Licorne* 22: 191–206.

Derrida, Jacques. 1976. *Of Grammatology*. Trans. Gayatri Spivak. Baltimore: John Hopkins University Press.

——. 1978. *Writing and Difference*. Trans. Alan Bass. London: Routledge and Kegan Paul.

——. 1981. *Dissemination*. Trans. Barbara Johnson. Chicago: University of Chicago Press.

——. 1987a. *Positions*. Trans. Alan Bass. London: Athlone.

——. 1987b. *The Post Card: From Socrates to Freud and Beyond*. Trans. Alan Bass. Chicago: University of Chicago Press.

——. 1987c. *The Truth in Painting*. Trans. Geoff Bennington and Ian McLeod. Chicago and London: University of Chicago Press.

——. 1993. *Aporias*. Trans. Thomas Dutoit. Stanford, California: Stanford University Press.

Descartes, Réné. 1985. *The Philosophical Writings of Descartes*. Vol. 1. Trans. John Cottingham, Robert Stoothoff, and Dugald Murdoch. Cambridge: Cambridge University Press.

Dessen, Alan. 1975. 'Two Falls and a Trap: Shakespeare and the Spectacles of Realism'. *English Literary Renaissance* 5 (Autumn): 291–307.

Diehl, Huston. 1983. 'Horrid Image, Sorry Sight, Fatal Vision: The Visual Rhetoric of *Macbeth*'. *Shakespeare Studies* 16: 191–203.

Doane, Mary-Anne. 1982. 'Film and the Masquerade: Theorising the Female Spectator'. *Screen* 23.3–4: 74–87.

Doesschate, G. ten. 1964. *Perspective: Fundamentals, Controversials, History*. Nieuwkoop, Netherlands: B. de Graaf.

Dolar, Mladen. 1991. '"I Shall Be With You On Your Wedding-Night": Lacan and the Uncanny'. *October* 58 (Fall): 5–23.

Dollimore, Jonathan. 1989. *Radical Tragedy: Religion, Ideology and Power in the Drama of Shakespeare and his Contemporaries*. 2nd edn. New York: Harvester Wheatsheaf.

——. 1990a. 'Critical Developments: Cultural Materialism, Feminism and Gender Critique, and New Historicism'. *Shakespeare: A Bibliographical Guide*. Ed. Stanley Wells. Oxford: Clarendon, 405–28.

——. 1990b. 'Shakespeare, Cultural Materialism, Feminism and Marxist Humanism'. *New Literary History* 21: 471–93.

——. 1991. *Sexual Dissidence: Augustine to Wilde, Freud to Foucault*. Oxford: Clarendon.

Dollimore, Jonathan, and Alan Sinfield, eds. 1985. *Political Shakespeare*. Manchester: Manchester University Press.

Donne, John. 1955. *The Sermons of John Donne*. Vol. 2. Berkeley: University of California Press. Gen. eds. George R. Potter and Evelyn M. Simpson.

Drakakis, John, ed. 1985. *Alternative Shakespeares*. London: Methuen.

Dryden, John. 1984. *Plays*. Ed. Maximillian E. Novak, George R. Guffey, and Alan Roper. Berkeley: University of California Press. Vol. 13 of *The Works of John Dryden*. Gen. eds. Alan Roper and Vinton A. Dearing.

Eastwood, Bruce S. 1989. *Astronomy and Optics from Pliny to Descartes: Texts, Diagrams and Conceptual Structures*. London: Variorum Reprints.

Edgerton, Samuel Y. 1975. *The Renaissance Rediscovery of Linear Perspective*. New York: Basic Books.

——. 1987. 'From Mental Matrix to Mappamundi to Christian Empire: The Heritage of Ptolemaic Cartography in the Renaissance'. *Art and Cartography*. Ed. David Woodward. Chicago: Chicago University Press, 10–50.

——. 1991. *The Heritage of Giotto's Geometry: Art and Science on the Eve of the Scientific Revolution*. Ithaca: Cornell University Press.

Edwards, Philip. 1979. *Threshold of a Nation: A Study in English and Irish Drama*. Cambridge: Cambridge University Press.

Evans, Malcolm. 1986. *Signifying Nothing: Truth's True Contents in Shakespeare's Texts*. London: Harvester.

Fanon, Frantz. 1970. *Black Skin, White Masks*. Trans. Charles Lam Markmann. London: Paladin.

Felman, Shoshana. 1987. *Jacques Lacan and the Adventure of Insight: Psychoanalysis in Contemporary Culture*. Cambridge, Massachusetts: Harvard University Press.

Ferguson, Margaret W., Maureen Quilligan, and Nancy J. Vickers, eds. 1986. *Rewriting the Renaissance: The Discourses of Sexual Difference in Early Modern Europe*. Chicago: University of Chicago Press.

Fineman, Joel. 1986. *Shakespeare's Perjured Eye: The Invention of Poetic Subjectivity in the Sonnets*. Berkeley: University of California Press.

Foucault, Michel. 1970. *The Order of Things: An Archaeology of the Human Sciences*. London: Tavistock.

——. 1977. *Discipline and Punish: the Birth of the Prison*. Trans. Alan Sheridan. Pantheon: New York.

——. 1984. *The History of Sexuality, Volume One: An Introduction*. Trans. Robert Hurley. London: Penguin.

Freedman, Barbara. 1991. *Staging the Gaze: Postmodernism, Psychoanalysis and Shakespearian Comedy*. Ithaca: Cornell University Press.

Freud, Sigmund. 1910a. 'The Psycho-Analytic View of Psychogenic Disturbance of Vision'. *The Standard Edition of the Complete Psychological Works of Sigmund Freud*. Ed. and trans. James Strachey. Vol. 11. London: Hogarth, 211–18.

——. 1917. 'A Metapsychological Supplement to the Theory of Dreams'. *The Standard Edition of the Complete Psychological Works of Sigmund Freud*. Ed. and trans. James Strachey. Vol. 14. London: Hogarth, 222–35.

——. 1940. 'Medusa's Head'. *The Standard Edition of the Complete Psychological Works of Sigmund Freud*. Ed. and trans. James Strachey. Vol. 18. London: Hogarth, 273–4.

——. 1976. *The Interpretation of Dreams*. Trans. James Strachey. London and New York: Penguin. Vol. 4 of *The Penguin Freud Library*. Gen. eds. Angela Richards and Albert Dickson.

——. 1979. *Case Histories II*. Trans. James Strachey. London and New York: Penguin. Vol. 9 of *The Penguin Freud Library*. Gen. eds. Angela Richards and Albert Dickson.

——. 1984. *On Metapsychology*. Trans. James Strachey. London and New York: Penguin. Vol. 11 of *The Penguin Freud Library*. Gen. eds. Angela Richards and Albert Dickson.

——. 1985a. *Civilization, Society and Religion*. Trans. James Strachey. London and New York: Penguin. Vol. 12 of *The Penguin Freud Library*. Gen. eds. Angela Richards and Albert Dickson.

——. 1985b. *Art and Literature*. Trans. James Strachey. London and New York: Penguin. Vol. 14 of *The Penguin Freud Library*. Gen. eds. Angela Richards and Albert Dickson.

——. 1986. *The Essentials of Psycho-Analysis*. Ed. Anna Freud, trans. James Strachey. London and New York: Penguin.

Freund, Elizabeth. 1985. '"Ariachne's Broken Woof": the Rhetoric of Citation in Troilus and Cressida'. *Shakespeare and the Question of Theory*. Ed. Patricia Parker and Geoffrey Hartman. New York: Methuen, 19–36.

Frye, Roland Mushat. 1980. 'Ways of Seeing in Shakespearean Drama and Elizabethan Painting'. *Shakespeare Quarterly* 31: 323–42.

Garber, Marjorie. 1987. *Shakespeare's Ghost Writers: Literature as Uncanny Causality*. New York: Methuen.

——. 1992. *Vested Interests: Cross-Dressing and Cultural Anxiety*. New York: Routledge.

Gentleman, Francis. 1770. *The Dramatic Censor*. Vol. 1. London: J. Bell.

Gillies, John. 1994. *Shakespeare and the Geography of Difference*. Cambridge: Cambridge University Press.

Gilman, Ernest. 1978. *The Curious Perspective: Literary and Pictorial Wit in the Seventeenth Century*. New Haven and London: Yale University Press.

——. 1980. '"All Eyes": Prospero's Inverted Masque'. *Renaissance Quarterly* 33: 214–30.

Girard, Réné. 1985. 'The Politics of Desire in Troilus and Cressida'. *Shakespeare and the Question of Theory*. Ed. Patricia Parker and Geoffrey Hartman. New York: Methuen, 188–209.

Goldberg, Jonathan. 1983. *James I and the Politics of Literature: Jonson, Shakespeare, Donne, and Their Contemporaries*. Baltimore and London: Johns Hopkins University Press.

——. 1986. 'Textual Properties'. *Shakespeare Quarterly* 37.2 (Summer): 213–17.

——. 1987. 'Speculations: *Macbeth* and Source'. *Shakespeare Reproduced: The Text as History and Ideology*. Ed. Jean E. Howard and Marion F. O'Connor. London and New York: Methuen, 247–60.

——. 1988. 'Perspectives: Dover Cliff and the Conditions of Representation'. *Shakespeare and Deconstruction*. Ed. G. Douglas Atkins and David M. Bergeron. New York: Peter Lang, 245–65.

Gosson, Stephen. 1974. *Markets of Bawdrie: The Dramatic Criticism of Stephen Gosson*. Ed. Arthur F. Kinney. Salzburg: Institut für Englische Sprache und Literatur. Vol. 4 of *Salzburg Studies in English Literature: Elizabethan Studies*. Gen. ed. James Hogg.

Grady, Hugh. 1993. 'Containment, Subversion – and Postmodernism'. *Textual Practice* 7.1 (Spring): 31–49.

Greenblatt, Stephen. 1980. *Renaissance Self-Fashioning: from More to Shakespeare*. Chicago: University of Chicago.

——. 1985. 'Invisible Bullets: Renaissance Authority and its Subversion, *Henry IV* and *Henry V*'. *Political Shakespeare*. Ed. Jonathan Dollimore and Alan Sinfield. Manchester: Manchester University Press, 18–47.

——, ed. 1988. *Representing the English Renaissance*. Berkeley: University of California Press.

——. 1990. *Learning to Curse: Essays in Early Modern Culture*. London and New York: Methuen.

Greene, Gayle. 1981. 'Language and Value in Shakespeare's *Troilus and Cressida*'. *Studies in English Literature 1500–1900* 21.2 (Spring): 271–85.

Grosz, Elizabeth. 1990. *Jacques Lacan: A Feminist Introduction*. London: Routledge.

Gurr, Andrew. 1978. *Hamlet and the Distracted Globe*. Edinburgh: Sussex University Press.

——. 1980. *The Shakespearean Stage 1574–1642*. 2nd edn. Cambridge: Cambridge University Press.

Hakluyt, Richard. 1903. *The Principal Navigations, Voyages, Traffiques and Discoveries of the English Nation*. 12 vols. London: Macmillan.

Halio, Jay L., ed. 1992. *The Tragedy of King Lear*. Cambridge: Cambridge University Press. *The New Cambridge Shakespeare*. Gen. ed. Brian Gibbons.

Hamer, Mary. 1989. 'Putting Ireland on the Map'. *Textual Practice* 3.2 (Summer): 184–201.

Harley, J. B. 1983. 'Meaning and Ambiguity in Tudor Cartography'. *English Map-Making 1500–1650*. Ed. Sarah Tyacke. London: British Library, 22–45.

——. 1988. 'Maps, Knowledge, and Power'. *The Iconography of the Landscape: Essays on the Symbolic Representation, Design and Use of Past Environments*. Ed. Denis Cosgrove and Stephen Daniels. Cambridge: Cambridge University Press, 277–312.

Harris, Anthony. 1980. *Night's Black Agents: Witchcraft and magic in Seventeenth-Century English Drama*. Manchester: Manchester University Press.

Hawkes, Terence. 1969. '"Love' in *King Lear*'. King Lear: *A Casebook*. Ed. Frank Kermode. London: MacMillan, 179–83.

——. 1973. *Shakespeare's Talking Animals*. London: Edward Arnold.

——. 1986. *That Shakespeherian Rag: Essays on a Critical Process*. London: Methuen.

——. 1992. *Meaning by Shakespeare*. London: Routledge.

Heath, Stephen. 1976. 'Narrative Space'. *Screen* 17.3 (Autumn): 68–112.

——. 1977. '*Anata Mo*'. *Screen* 17.4 (Winter): 49–66.

——. 1978. 'Difference'. *Screen* 19.3 (Autumn): 51–112.

——. 1986. 'Joan Riviere and the Masquerade'. *Formations of Fantasy*. Ed. Victor Burgin, James Donald, and Cora Kaplan. New York: Methuen, 45–61.

Hegel, G. W. F. 1977. *Phenomenology of Spirit*. Trans. A. V. Miller. Oxford: Clarendon.

Helgerson, Richard. 1992. *Forms of Nationhood: The Elizabethan Writing of England*. Chicago and London: University of Chicago Press.

Hertz, Neil. 1980. 'Freud and the Sandman'. *Textual Strategies: Perspectives in Post-Structuralist Criticism*. Ed. Josue V. Harari. London: Methuen, 296–321.

Heywood, Thomas. 1978. *'An Apology for Actors' (1612) by Thomas Heywood; 'A Refutation of The Apology for Actors' (1615) by I. G.*. Ed. Richard H. Perkinson. New York: Scholars' Facsimiles and Reprints.

Hoffmann, E. T. H. 1969. 'The Sandman'. *Selected Writings*. Ed. and trans. L. J. Keat and E. C. Knight. Chicago: University of Chicago Press, 137–67.

Holderness, Graham. 1985. *Shakespeare's History*. Dublin: Gill and Macmillan.

——, ed. 1988. *The Shakespeare Myth*. Manchester: Manchester University Press.

Hollier, Denis. 1984. 'Mimesis and Castration'. *October* 31 (Winter): 3–15.

Honigmann, A. J., ed. 1954. *King John*. London: Routledge. *The Arden Shakespeare*. Gen. eds. Harold F. Brooks and Harold Jenkins.

Howard, Skiles. 1991. 'Attendants and Others in Shakespeare's Margins: Doubling in the Two Texts of *King Lear*'. *Theatre Survey* 32: 187–213.

Huggan, Graham. 1989. 'Decolonizing the Map: Post-Colonialism, Post-Structuralism and the Cartographic Connection'. *Ariel* 20.4: 115–31.

Hulme, Peter. 1985. 'Polytropic Man: Tropes of Sexuality and Mobility in Early Colonial Discourse'. *Europe and Its Others: Proceedings of the Essex Conference on the Sociology of Literature July 1984*. Ed. Francis Barker. Vol. 2. Colchester: University of Essex, 17–32.

——. 1986. *Colonial Encounters: Europe and the Native Caribbean, 1492–1797*. London: Methuen.

Humphreys, A. R., ed. 1960. *The First Part of King Henry IV*. London: Routledge. *The Arden Shakespeare*. Gen. ed. Richard Proudfoot.

——, ed. 1966. *The Second Part of King Henry IV*. London: Routledge. *The Arden Shakespeare*. Gen. ed. Richard Proudfoot.

——, ed. 1984. *Julius Caesar*. Oxford: Clarendon. *The Oxford Shakespeare*. Gen. ed. Stanley Wells.

Hunter, G. K., ed. 1972. *King Lear*. London: Penguin. *The New Penguin Shakespeare*. Gen. ed. T. J. B. Spencer.

Irigaray, Luce. 1985a. *Speculum of the Other Woman*. Trans. Gillian C. Gill. Ithaca: Cornell University Press.

——. 1985b. *This Sex Which Is Not One*. Trans. Catherine Porter. Ithaca: Cornell University Press.

James I. 1944. *The Basilocon Doron of King James VI*. Ed. James Craigie. Edinburgh: Blackwood.

——. 1965. *The Political Works of James I*. Ed. Charles McIlwain. New York: Russell and Russell.

——. 1966. *Daemonologie; News from Scotland*. Ed. G. B. Harrison. Edinburgh: University of Edinburgh Press.

Jameson, Frederic. 1977. 'Imaginary and Symbolic in Lacan: Marxism, Psychoanalytic Criticism and the Problem of the Subject'. *Yale French Studies* 55/56: 338–95.

——. 1988. 'Cognitive Mapping'. *Marxism and the Interpretation of Culture*. Ed. Cary Nelson and Lawrence Grossberg. London: Macmillan, 347–60.

Janmohamed, Abdul R. 1985. 'The Economy of Manichean Allegory: The Function of Racial Difference in Colonialist Literature'. *Critical Inquiry* 12 (Autumn): 59–87.

Jardine, Lisa. 1983. *Still Harping on Daughters: Women and Drama in the Age of Shakespeare*. London and New York: Harvester Wheatsheaf.

Jenkins, Harold, ed. 1982. *Hamlet*. London: Routledge. *The Arden Shakespeare*. Gen. eds. Richard Proudfoot and Anne Thompson.

Johnson, Barbara. 1977. 'The Frame of Reference: Poe, Lacan, Derrida'. *Yale French Studies* 55/56: 457–505.

Jones, Eldred. 1965. *Othello's Countrymen: The African in English Renaissance Drama*. London: Oxford University Press.

Jones, Ernest. 1949. *Hamlet and Oedipus*. London: Gollancz.

Kantorowicz, Ernst H. 1957. *The King's Two Bodies: A Study in Mediaeval Political Theology*. Princeton: Princeton University Press.

Kastan, David Scott, and Peter Stallybrass, eds. 1991. *Staging the Renaissance: Reinterpretations of Elizabethan and Jacobean Drama*. New York: Routledge.

Kermode, Frank, ed. 1964. *The Tempest*. London: Routledge. *The Arden Shakespeare*. Gen. eds. Harold F. Brooks and Harold Jenkins.

Kerrigan, John, ed. 1986. *The Sonnets and A Lover's Complaint*. London: Penguin. *The New Penguin Shakespeare*. Gen. ed. T. J. B. Spencer.

Knight, G. Wilson. 1949. *The Wheel of Fire: Interpretations of Shakespearean Tragedy*. London: Methuen.

Knobel, E. B. 1916. 'The Sciences: Astronomy and Astrology'. *Shakespeare's England: An Account of the Life and Manners of His Age*. Ed. C. T. Onions and Sidney Lee. Vol. 1. Oxford: Clarendon, 444–61.

Kofman, Sarah. 1985. *The Enigma of Woman: Woman in Freud's Writings*. Trans. Catherine Porter. Ithaca: Cornell University Press.

——. 1991. *Freud and Fiction*. Trans. Sarah Wykes. Cambridge: Polity.

Kojève, Alexandre. 1969. *Introduction to the Reading of Hegel*. Trans. James H. Nichols, Jr. Ithaca and London: Cornell University Press.

Kopper, John M. 1988. 'Troilus at Pluto's Gates: Subjectivity and the Duplicity of Discourse in Shakespeare's Troilus and Cressida'. *Shakespeare and Deconstruction*. Ed. G. Douglas Atkins and David M. Bergeron. New York: Peter Lang, 149–72.

Kott, Jan. 1964. *Shakespeare Our Contemporary*. Trans. Boleslaw Taborski. London: Methuen.

Kubovy, Michael. 1986. *The Psychology of Perspective and Renaissance Art*. Cambridge: Cambridge University Press.

LaBranche, Linda. 1986. 'Visual Patterns and Linking Analogues in *Troilus and Cressida*'. *Shakespeare Quarterly* 37.4 (Winter): 440–50.

Lacan, Jacques. 1953. 'Some Reflections on the Ego'. *International Journal of Psychoanalysis* 34: 11–17.

——. 1966. 'Le stade du miroir comme formateur de la fonction du Je telle qu'elle nous est révélée dans l'expérience psychanalytique'. *Écrits*. Paris: Éditions du Seuil, 93–100.

——. 1972. 'Seminar on "The Purloined Letter"'. Trans. Jeffrey Mehlman. *Yale French Studies* 48: 38–72.

——. 1973. *Les Quartre Concepts Fondamentaux de la Psychanalyse 1964*. Paris: Éditions du Seuil. Vol. 11 of *Le Séminaire de Jacques Lacan*. Gen. ed. Jacques-Alain Miller.

——. 1977a. 'Desire and the Interpretation of Desire in *Hamlet*'. Trans. James Hulbert. *Yale French Studies* 55/56: 11–52.

——. 1977b. *Écrits: A Selection*. Trans. Alan Sheridan. London: Tavistock/Routledge.

——. 1979. *The Four Fundamental Concepts of Psychoanalysis*. Trans. Alan Sheridan. London: Penguin. Vol. 11 of *The Seminar of Jacques Lacan*. Gen. ed. Jacques-Alain Miller.

——. 1982. *Feminine Sexuality: Jacques Lacan and the École Freudienne*. Ed. and trans. Juliet Mitchell and Jacqueline Rose. London: Macmillan.

——. 1988a. *Freud's Papers on Technique 1953–4*. Trans. John Forrester. Cambridge: Cambridge University Press. Vol. 1 of *The Seminar of Jacques Lacan*. Gen. ed. Jacques-Alain Miller.

——. 1988b. *The Ego in Freud's Theory and in the Technique of Psychoanalysis*

1954–5. Trans. Sylvana Thomaselli. Cambridge: Cambridge University Press. Vol. 2 of *The Seminar of Jacques Lacan*. Gen. ed. Jacques-Alain Miller.

——. 1992. *The Ethics of Psychoanalysis 1959–60*. Trans. Dennis Porter. London and New York: Routledge. Vol. 7 of *The Seminar of Jacques Lacan*. Gen. ed. Jacques-Alain Miller.

Laplanche, Jean, and Jean-Bertrand Pontalis. 1988. *The Language of Psycho-Analysis*. Trans. Donald Nicholson-Smith. London: Hogarth and Karnac.

Lenz, Carolyn, Gayle Greene, and Carol Neely, eds. 1980. *The Woman's Part: Feminist Criticism of Shakespeare*. Urbana: University of Illinois.

Levine, Laura. 1986. 'Men in Women's Clothing: Anti-theatricality and Effeminization from 1579 to 1642'. *Criticism* 28: 121–43.

Lindberg, David C. 1976. *Theories of Vision from Al-Kindi to Kepler*. Chicago and London: University of Chicago Press.

Loomba, Ania. 1989. *Gender, Race, Renaissance Drama*. Manchester: Manchester University Press.

——, and Martin Orkin, eds. 1998. *Post-Colonial Shakespeares*. New York and London: Routledge.

Lothian, J. M., and T. W. Craik, eds. 1975. *Twelfth Night*. London: Routledge. *The Arden Shakespeare*. Gen. eds. Harold F. Brooks, Harold Jenkins, and Brian Morris.

Lukacher, Ned. 1989. 'Anamorphic Stuff: Shakespeare, Catharsis, Lacan'. *South Atlantic Quarterly* 88.4: 863–98.

——. 1994. *Daemonic Figures: Shakespeare and the Question of Conscience*. Ithaca: Cornell University Press.

Lupton, Julia Reinhard, and Kenneth Reinhard. 1993. *After Oedipus: Shakespeare in Psychoanalysis* Ithaca and London: Cornell University Press.

MacCabe, Colin. 1976. 'Theory and Film: Principles of Realism and Pleasure'. *Screen* 17.3 (Autumn): 68–112.

Mallarmé, Stéphane. 1945. *Crayonné au Théâtre: Oeuvres Completes*. Paris: Pleiade.

Mannoni, Octave. 1964. *Prospero and Caliban: the Psychology of Colonisation*. Trans. Pamela Powesland. New York: Praeger.

Manvell, Roger. 1971. *Shakespeare and the Film*. London: J. M. Dent & Sons.

Marcus, Leah. 1988. *Puzzling Shakespeare: Local Reading and Its Discontents*. Berkeley: University of California Press.

Marlowe, Christopher. 1976. *Doctor Faustus*. Ed. John D. Jump. Manchester: Manchester University Press.

——. 1981. *Tamburlaine the Great*. Ed. J. S. Cunningham. Manchester: Manchester University Press.

McLuhan, Marshall. 1962. *The Gutenberg Galaxy: the Making of Typographic Man*. London: Routledge and Kegan Paul.

Merleau-Ponty, Maurice. 1962. *Phenomenology of Perception*. Trans. Colin Smith. London: Routledge & Kegan Paul.

Metz, Christian. 1982. *Psychoanalysis and Cinema: The Imaginary Signifier*. Trans. Celia Britton, Annwyl Williams, Ben Brewster and Alfred Guzzetti. London: MacMillan.

Miller, J. Hillis. 1976. 'Ariadne's Thread: Repetition and the Narrative Line'. *Critical Inquiry* 3 (Autumn): 57–77.

Möller, Liz. 1991. *The Freudian Reading: Analytical and Fictional Constructions*. Philadelphia: University of Pennsylvania Press.

Montrose, Louis. 1991. 'The Work of Gender in the Discourse of Discovery'. *Representations* 33 (Winter): 1–41.

Muir, Kenneth, ed. 1959. *King Lear*. London: Methuen. *The Arden Shakespeare*. Gen. eds. Harold F. Brooks and Harold Jenkins.

———. 1972. *Macbeth*. London: Methuen. *The Arden Shakespeare*. Gen. eds. Harold F. Brooks, Harold Jenkins and Brian Morris.

———, ed. 1982. *Troilus and Cressida*. Oxford: Clarendon. *The Oxford Shakespeare*. Gen. ed. Stanley Wells.

Munday, Anthony. 1972. *A Second and Third Blast of Retreat from Plays and Theatres*. London and New York: Johnson Reprint Corporation.

Murray, W. A. 1978. 'Why Was Duncan's Blood Golden?'. *Macbeth: A Casebook*. Ed. John Wain. London: MacMillan, 276–91.

Nancy, Jean-Luc, and Philippe Lacoue-Labarthe. 1992. *The Title of the Letter: A Reading of Lacan*. Trans. François Raffoul and David Pettigrew. Albany: SUNY Press.

Neill, Michael. 1994. 'Broken English and Broken Irish: Nation, Language and the Optic of Power in Shakespeare's Histories'. *Shakespeare Quarterly* 45.1 (Spring): 1–32.

Newman, Karen. 1987. '"And Wash the Ethiop White": Femininity and the Monstrous in *Othello*'. *Shakespeare Reproduced: The Text as History and Ideology*. Ed. Jean E. Howard and Marion F. O'Connor. London and New York: Methuen, 141–62.

Nosworthy, J. M., ed. 1969. *Cymbeline*. London: Routledge. *The Arden Shakespeare*. Gen. ed. Richard Proudfoot.

Orgel, Stephen. 1975. *The Illusion of Power*. Berkeley: University of California Press.

———. 1985. 'Making Greatness Familiar'. *Pageantry in the Shakespearian Theatre*. Ed. David Bergeron. Athens: University of Georgia Press, 19–25.

Orgel, Stephen, and Roy Strong. 1973. *Inigo Jones: The Theatre of the Stuart Court*. 2 vols. Berkeley: University of California Press.

Orkin, Martin. 1987. '*Othello* and the "Plain Face" of Racism'. *Shakespeare Quarterly* 38: 166–88.

Palmer, D. J. 1982. '"A New Gorgon": Visual Effects in *Macbeth*'. *Focus on Macbeth*. Ed. John Russell Brown. London: Routledge & Kegan Paul, 54–69.

Palmer, Kenneth, ed. 1982. *Troilus and Cressida*. London and New York: Methuen. *The Arden Shakespeare*. Gen. eds. Richard Proudfoot and Anne Thompson.

Panofsky, Erwin. 1991. *Perspective as Symbolic Form*. Trans. Christopher S. Wood. New York: Zone.

Paul, Henry. 1978. *The Royal Play of Macbeth: When, Why, and How It Was Written By Shakespeare*. New York: Octagon.

Platter, Thomas. 1937. *Thomas Platter's Travels in England, 1599*. Trans. Clare Williams. London: Jonathan Cape.

Pliny. 1940. *Natural History*. Trans. H. Rackham. 10 vols. London: Heinemann.

Pye, Christopher. 1990. *The Regal Phantasm: Shakespeare and the Politics of Spectacle*. London and New York: Routledge.

Rabasa, José. 1985. 'Allegories of the *Atlas*'. *Europe and Its Others: Proceedings of the Essex Conference on the Sociology of Literature July 1984*. Ed. Francis Barker et al. Vol. 2. Colchester: University of Essex, 1–15.

Ravenhill, William. 1983. 'Christopher Saxton's Surveying: An Enigma'. *English*

Map-Making: 1500–1650. Ed. Sarah Tyacke. London: British Library, 112–19.

Richter, Jean Paul, ed. 1970. *The Literary Works of Leonardo Da Vinci*. Vol. 1. New York: Phaidon.

Ridley, M. R., ed. 1954. *Antony and Cleopatra*. London: Routledge. *The Arden Shakespeare*. Gen. eds. Harold F. Brooks and Harold Jenkins.

——, ed. 1958. *Othello*. London: Routledge. *The Arden Shakespeare*. Gen. ed. Richard Proudfoot.

Riviere, Joan. 1986. 'Womanliness as a Masquerade'. *Formations of Fantasy*. Ed. Victor Burgin, James Donald, and Cora Kaplan. London and New York: Methuen, 34–44.

Rogers, J. D. 1916. 'Voyages and Exploration: Geography: Maps'. *Shakespeare's England: An Account of the Life and Manners of his Age*. Ed. C. T. Onions and Sidney Lee. Vol. 1. Oxford: Clarendon, 170–97.

Rorty, Richard. 1980. *Philosophy and the Mirror of Nature*. Oxford: Basil Blackwell.

Rose, Jacqueline. 1986. *Sexuality in the Field of Vision*. London and New York: Verso.

Roudinesco, Elisabeth. 1990. *Jacques Lacan & Co.: A History of Psychoanalysis in France, 1925–85*. Trans. Jeffrey Mehlman. Chicago: University of Chicago Press.

Sartre, Jean-Paul. 1969. *Being and Nothingness: An Essay on Phenomenological Ontology*. Trans. Hazel E. Barnes. London: Methuen.

Scot, Reginald. 1930. *The Discoverie of Witchcraft*. Ed. Montague Summers. Great Britain: John Rodker.

Scott, William O. 1988. 'Self-Difference in Troilus and Cressida'. *Shakespeare and Deconstruction*. Ed. G. Douglas Atkins and David M. Bergeron. New York: Peter Lang, 129–48.

Seaton, Ethel. 1964. 'Marlowe's Map'. *Marlowe: A Collection of Critical Essays*. Ed. Clifford Leech. Englewood Cliffs, N. J.: Prentice-Hall, 36–56.

Sedgewick, Eve Kosofsky. 1985. *Between Men: English Literature and Male Homosocial Desire*. New York: Columbia University Press.

Seltzer, Daniel, ed. 1963. *The History of Troilus and Cressida*. New York: New American Library. *The Signet Classic*. Gen. ed. Sylvan Barnet.

Shickman, Allan R. 1991. 'The Fool's Mirror in King Lear'. *English Literary Renaissance* 21.1 (Winter): 75–86.

Sibony, Daniel. 1977. '*Hamlet*: A Writing-Effect'. Trans. James Hulbert and Joshua Wilner. *Yale French Studies* 55/56: 53–93.

Sinfield, Alan. 1985. 'Give an account of Shakespeare and Education, showing why you think they are effective and what you have appreciated about them. Support your comments with precise references'. *Political Shakespeare*. Ed. Jonathan Dollimore and Alan Sinfield. Manchester: Manchester University Press, 134–57.

——. 1992. *Faultlines: Cultural Materialism and the Politics of Dissident Reading*. Oxford: Clarendon.

Singh, Jyotsna. 1989. 'Different Shakespeares: The Bard in Colonial/Postcolonial India'. *Theatre Journal* 44.4: 445–58.

Skelton, R. A. 1971. 'Maps of a Tudor Statesman'. *A Description of Maps and Architectural Drawings in the Collection Made by William Cecil, First Baron Burghley, Now At Hatfield House*. Ed. R. A. Skelton and John Summerson. Oxford: Printed for Presentation to Members of the Roxburghe Club, 3–35.

Sophocles. 1984. *The Three Theban Plays: Antigone, Oedipus the King, Oedipus at Colonus*. Trans. Robert Eagles. London: Penguin.

Soyinka, Wole. 1988. *Art, Dialogue and Outrage: Essays on Literature and Culture*. Ibadan: New Horn Press.

Spivak, Gayatri Chakravorty. 1985. 'Three Women's Texts and a Critique of Imperialism'. *Critical Inquiry* 12.1 (Autumn): 262–80.

——. 1990. *The Post-Colonial Critic: Interviews, Strategies, Dialogues*. Ed. Sarah Harasym. New York: Routledge.

Stubbes, Phillip. 1877. *Phillip Stubbes's Anatomy of the Abuses in England in Shakspere's Youth, AD 1583*. Ed. Frederick J. Furnivall. 2 vols. London: New Shakspere Society.

Taylor, Gary, ed. 1982a. *Henry V*. Oxford: Clarendon. *The Oxford Shakespeare*. Gen. ed. Stanley Wells.

——. 1982b. '*Troilus and Cressida*: Bibliography, Performance, and Interpretation'. *Shakespeare Studies* 15: 99–136.

——. 1991. *Reinventing Shakespeare: A Cultural History from the Restoration to the Present*. London: Vintage.

Tennenhouse, Leonard. 1986. *Power on Display: The Politics of Shakespeare's Genres*. New York: Methuen.

Thomas, Keith. 1971. *Religion and the Decline of Magic: Studies in Popular Beliefs in Sixteenth- and Seventeenth-Century England*. London: Penguin.

Thomson, Peter. 1992. *Shakespeare's Theatre*. 2nd edn. London: Routledge.

Tokson, Elliot H. 1982. *The Popular Image of the Black Man in English Drama, 1550–1688*. Boston: G. K. Hall and Co.

Tourneur, Cyril. 1966. *The Revenger's Tragedy*. Ed. R. A. Foakes. London: Methuen.

Turner, G. L'E. 1983. 'Mathematical Instrument-Making in London in the Sixteenth Century'. *English Map-Making: 1500–1650*. Ed. Sarah Tyacke. London: British Library, 93–106.

Ure, Peter, ed. 1956. *Richard II*. London: Routledge. *The Arden Shakespeare*. Gen. ed. Richard Proudfoot.

Urkowitz, Steven. 1980. *Shakespeare's Revision of King Lear*. Princeton: Princeton University Press.

Walter, J. H., ed. 1954. *Henry V*. London: Routledge. *The Arden Shakespeare*. Gen. ed. Richard Proudfoot.

Weber, Samuel. 1973. 'The Sideshow, or: Remarks on a Canny Moment'. *Modern Language Notes* 88: 1102–33.

——. 1991. *Return to Freud: Jacques Lacan's Dislocation of Psychoanalysis*. Trans. Michael Levine. Cambridge: Cambridge University Press.

Weimann, Robert. 1978. *Shakespeare and the Popular Tradition in the Theatre: Studies in the Social Dimension of Dramatic Form and Function*. Baltimore: Johns Hopkins.

Wells, Stanley, and Gary Taylor, eds. 1988. *The Complete Works*. Oxford: Clarendon. *The Oxford Shakespeare*. Gen. eds. Stanley Wells and Gary Taylor.

West, Cornel. 1982. *Prophesy Deliverance! An Afro-American Revolutionary Christianity*. Philadelphia: Westminster Press.

Willbern, David. 1986. 'Phantasmagoric *Macbeth*'. *English Literary Renaissance* 16.3 (Autumn): 520–49.

Wimsatt, W. K., ed. 1969. *Doctor Johnson on Shakespeare*. Harmondsworth: Penguin.

Yates, Frances. 1966. *The Art of Memory*. London: Routledge and Kegan Paul.
——. 1969. *Theatre of the World*. London: Routledge and Kegan Paul.
——. 1979. *The Occult Philosophy in the Elizabethan Age*. London: Routledge.
Young, Robert, ed. 1981. *Untying the Text: A Post-Structuralist Reader*. Boston: Routledge.
Zimmerman, Susan, ed. 1992. *Erotic Politics: Desire on the Renaissance Stage*. New York and London: Routledge.
Zizek, Slavoj. 1989. *The Sublime Object of Ideology*. London: Verso.
——. 1991a. *Looking Awry: An Introduction to Jacques Lacan through Popular Culture*. Massachusetts: October.
——. 1991b. 'Grimaces of the Real, or When the Phallus Appears'. *October* 58 (Fall): 44–68.

Index